AUTO AUDIO

Other books by Andrew Yoder

Pirate Radio Stations: Tuning in to Underground Broadcasts
Build Your Own Shortwave Antennas--2nd Edition
Shortwave Listening on the Road: The World Traveler's Guide
Pirate Radio: The Incredible Saga of America's Underground,
Illegal Broadcasters
Pirate Radio Operations
The TAB Electronics Yellow Pages
The Complete Shortwave Listener's Handbook--5th Edition
Home Audio: Choosing, Maintaining, and Repairing Your Audio
System
Home Video: Choosing, Maintaining, and Repairing Your Video
System

AUTO AUDIO

CHOOSING, INSTALLING, AND MAINTAINING CAR STEREO SYSTEMS

Andrew Yoder

Second Edition

McGraw-Hill

New York San Francisco Washington, D.C. Auckland Bogotá
Caracas Lisbon London Madrid Mexico City Milan
Montreal New Dehli San Juan Singapore
Sydney Tokyo Toronto

McGraw-Hill

A Division of The McGraw-Hill Companies

Copyright © 2000, 1995 by The McGraw-Hill Companies, Inc. All rights reserved.
Printed in the United States of America. Except as permitted under the United States
Copyright Act of 1976, no part of this publication may be reproduced or distributed in any
form or by any means, or stored in a data base or retrieval system, without the prior written
permission of the publisher.

1 2 3 4 5 6 7 8 9 0   FGR/FGR   0 6 5 4 3 2 1 0

ISBN 0-07-134689-9

The sponsoring editor for this book was Scott Grillo, the editing supervisor was
Peggy Lamb, and the production supervisor was Sherri Souffrance. It was set in
Windsor Light through the services of Cabinet Communications (Editing, Design,
and Production).

Printed and bound by R.R. Donnelley & Sons, Inc.

 This book is printed on recycled, acid-free paper containing a minimum of 50% recycled, de-inked fiber.

McGraw-Hill books are available at special quantity discounts to use as premiums and sales
promotions, or for use in corporate training programs. For more information, please write
to the Director of Special Sales, McGraw-Hill, 2 Penn Plaza, New York, NY 10121. Or
contact your local bookstore.

CONTENTS

Contents

6 SPEAKERS 147

7 SPEAKER ENCLOSURES 189

CONTENTS

ACKNOWLEDGMENTS

Because of the scope of this book, it could not have been written without help from many people and organizations. Thanks to Richard and Judy Yoder, Ed and Angie Piwonka, Corbin and Bryn Yoder, and Keith Haffling.

Thanks to Ryan Veety, Steve Hunter, Sarah Galloway, Jani Ahola, Steve Bilawchuk, Alasdair Patrick of Audioquest; Sam Fontaine of AudioControl; Ryne C. Allen of ESD Systems; Eric C. Kreis of Kenwood USA; Rich Hering of Brookside Veneers; Ralph Nichols of Polydax; David Berkus of Sanyo Fisher; Justin Yamada of Morel Acoustics; Anita Bose from I2Go, Steve Singleton from Coustic, Martha Whiteley from Panasonic, Gordon Sell and John Whitacre of Blaupunkt, Andy Marken of Matsushita, Jamie Robeson from Gateway.

Thanks also to Joey Lee from Alpine, Alex Algard of SoundDomain, Melvin Clapman for Audiovox, Lucette Nicoll for JL Audio and Xtant, Amelia Edgar for Clarion, IASCA, Soundstream, Cadence, Parts Express, Eric Stevens of Image Dynamics, Stan Harrison of Harrison Labs, Keith Carter of Bostwick, Don Zamora of Altec Lansing, A.V. Mannino of M & M Electronics, Allen Baron of Polk, Roger Alves and Scott Erickson of Scosche, Ken D'Amato of Audison USA, Velodyne Acoustics, and Madisound.

Thanks to April Nolan for giving the first book in this series a

Acknowledgments

chance. Also to Scott Grillo for acquiring this book; Peggy Lamb for the editing and supervisory work; Sherri Souffrance for helping to complete this project; and to Frank Kotowski, Jr. for final editing. Thanks to the rest of McGraw-Hill for getting this book out of the warehouse and into libraries and peoples' bookshelves.

Very special thanks to Yvonne for improving my writing quality and for always pushing me to do better.

POTENTIAL FOR HEARING LOSS

Warning! The sound equipment described in this book is capable of causing permanent damage to your hearing.

It has been proven that if someone is subjected to 90 dBA (decibels average) of sound for 8 hours per day, he or she will eventually experience a permanent hearing loss of varying intensity. Some sound systems have even reached 150 dBA. Imagine the potential for hearing damage!

The car stereo sound-off competitions, magazines, and manufacturers often glorify high-volume systems; in fact, the sound-off competitions revolve around volume, clarity, and quality of the installation. The manufacturers can sell many more of their products if buyers intend to use higher power, so manufacturers obviously push for higher power and attempt to glorify it.

The fact is that hearing damage is common, and it has been on the increase in the past 30 years. Industrial and manufacturing jobs, rock concerts, and high-powered stereo systems are to blame for most of these problems, which are compounded by the fact that human hearing degrades extensively with age. Natural hearing loss does discriminate by sex; by the age of 65, the average woman will lose from 7 dB of hearing at 500 Hz to 15 dB at 4 kHz; the average man will lose from 7 dB of hearing at 500 Hz to 37 dB at 4 kHz (Fig. 1-1).

The natural decline in hearing begins its steady downward slope from age 30 onward. When this decline is assisted by loud music, the hearing loss can easily be accelerated to the point where you could be hard of hearing by the time you are in your thirties or forties (assuming, of course, that you are presently in your teens or twenties). By the time you reach retirement age, you could be totally deaf.

POTENTIAL FOR HEARING LOSS

If you think that this section is intended to scare you, you're right. Hearing loss is tragic, and it's permanent. If you are so serious about audio that you can spend hundreds of dollars on an audio system for your car, then you should certainly be serious enough to take care of your ears so that you can continue to enjoy the hot sounds on the wide-open road.

INTRODUCTION

For years, music has inspired and driven me to do more, faster and more passionately. To me, music isn't just something to end silence: it's blood coursing through my veins or a breath of fresh air rushing into my lungs. Music isn't just background Muzak; it's the soundtrack to my life.

Ultimately, this book isn't about auto audio; it's about music. To narrow it down, it's about music in your car. Unfortunately, you just can't have guitar heroes Paully Sanders and Michael (Olga) Algar dueling in your car any time you want to take a drive, so you must find a way to reproduce their harsh sounds. That requires a sound system built specifically to tolerate the harsh environment of the car and to operate from the car's 12-V electrical system.

These factors alone make for many different possibilities; however, auto audio has been quickly evolving over the past few years, so what is available today is more advanced (by light-years) than equipment from the mid-80s. Also, all cars vary in style, complexity, and acoustics. In some cases, an installation might be simple in one particular car, but that same installation might require days worth of work to install in another car. In other cases, an installation might sound great in one car, but it might not sound so good in another. Availability of equipment, car stereo dealerships, and buying information are other potential problems. And, last of all, the money that you plan to unload on a car stereo system is one of the key factors behind the components in the system you finally purchase.

As it is, auto audio is a very complex subject—all to achieve one simple purpose, to have good-sounding music in your car. Because of the complexity of the audio issues, many people seem to forget the bottom line (good-sounding music) because they get caught up in various side tracks.

One of the largest sidetracks to auto audio is competitions. All across the country, people participate in sound-offs. At these events, car audio systems are judged on how loud the system can go (e.g., the sound pressure level), the imaging, the layout of the installation, the looks of the installation, tricky designs (such as hiding amplifiers under fake floors and motorized head unit doors), and the like. These events are interesting and they have greatly advanced the technology of auto audio; however, these competitions sometimes cause condescending attitudes toward people with "lesser" systems.

Because these systems are based, in part, on cosmetics, cosmetics play a large role in the overall system. In fact, the cosmetics of the system are sometimes emphasized to the point where the audio system is installed in such a way that it is difficult to find any practical use for either it or the car. Some competition cars cannot even be driven on the street legally. Others, such as one trophy winner that has gold-plated amplifiers and speakers, is so absurdly overdone that you could never drive it in public without one or more bodyguards.

The quest of this book is simply to help you put good-sounding music in your car: no hype, no egos, no glitter. I have tried to include methods of obtaining a system as cheaply as possible because many of us don't have the money to buy a high-end system for the car, but it is often possible to find a fair- or good-sounding system that will fit your budget.

Another difference in this book is that I have directed it toward the novice with no car audio or electrical experience. I am not an engineer or a mechanic. Instead of glossing over some of the problems that I had with installing systems, I have described them so that you can better understand what you will be encountering and some of the routes that you can take to overcome difficulties.

I have spent a considerable amount of time writing this book and making the information contained within as useful as possible. I certainly hope that you will find that it is useful as well.

SECOND EDITION UPDATE

When *Auto Audio* debuted in 1994, it was the only real car stereo book for hobbyists (there were some undergound booklets and spiral-bound books, but nothing else). Soon afterward, *Auto Audio* became one of TAB/ McGraw-Hill's best-selling do-it-yourself electronics books. Since then, other authors and publishers have produced their own books on the subject, but this is the original.

This edition of *Auto Audio* has been revised considerably from the first edition. Although speakers have changed very little since 1994 (aside from the increased use of metal speaker cones), some elements of technology have changed dramatically—especially those areas that could benefit from computer enhancement. For example, DVD and video in the car, MP3 file playback, and audio DVDs are significant improvements in car audio systems since the mid 1990s. Additionally, a new chapter on building enclosures and working with building materials has been included, and the installations chapter now includes many more systems.

COMMENTS

I don't do equipment recommendations and I don't have the resources to respond to all of the questions about system designs and installations (read and write to *Car Audio & Electronics, Carsound, Auto Sound & Security,* and *Car Stereo Review,* instead); however, if you would like to drop me a line concerning this book or your personal experiences with auto audio, feel free to contact me.

Andrew Yoder
P.O. Box 642
Mont Alto, PA 17237
ayoder@cvn.net

1

CHOOSING A SYSTEM

Possibly the toughest aspect of owning a custom car audio system is just searching through piles of magazines, catalogs, and sale fliers to pick out the components that you want. There's a mind-boggling array of car stereo equipment on the market and it can be rather difficult to research all of it. After a while, you might be ready to pull out your hair and continue listening to the radio in your 1987 Yugo.

Of course, the audio on the speakers cuts in and out and the tape deck eats cassettes, so you're stuck, right? After having a few more tapes eaten and hearing the vocal tracks cut in and out of your favorite Doors song, you might break down and ask the local car stereo installation center to "pick something that sounds good for X amount of dollars." Taking that route will most likely pull in a good system, but one that's not worth the stack of bills that you will have to pull from your wallet. Otherwise, you might read through the car stereo magazines and find a few highly rated components. Once again, this is a great way to pay for much more than you are getting. The next option is to get nervous over all of the prices that you have seen in the car stereo magazines and from the local installation shop and settle on something that is inexpensive from a discount department store. This route is somewhat different from the other two; you will get exactly what you pay for. Taking the third route will probably land you a cheaply manufactured system that sounds bad. The last option is to search through stereo magazines and on company Web pages, and check out the prices from the mail-order companies. With a little work and luck, you will wind up with a good system at a low price.

ADVICE AND INFORMATION

Ultimately, you need to absorb as much information as possible to make good decisions, both in terms of choosing equipment and installing every-thing. When you start assembling a system, you want to finish it immedi-ately and get music cranking through your car again. Some commutes or cruises around town with your system down, and your patience is wearing thin and you're ready to have everything working again...even if the system isn't "quite ready."

The fact is that it's tough to let your working car be a "project car" for any length of time. If you take the short-term "gotta get this done so I can get my tunes back" approach, setting up a car stereo system can be incredibly annoying. But, if you take the long-term approach, it can be a really fun and interesting hobby. And the information that you absorb is the key to it being a real hobby and not just a task (like changing your oil).

But whether you want to make auto sound into a hobby or if you simply want to get a better system into your car, it's always best to read and absorb as much information as possible. Obviously, if you are making a hobby of building and installing auto stereo systems, you really must know as much about cars, audio, and specific audio components as you can. If you are putting together a system as quickly and efficiently as possible, it's still good to research these elements to give you the best system possible for your time and money.

FOLLOWING THE MAGAZINES

The mobile audio magazines on the market are excellent sources of infor-mation for purchasing a system for your car (Fig. 1-1). You can find infor-mation and specifications on most of the pieces of equipment that are currently on the market. Both *Audio* and *Car Audio and Electronics* feature massive guides to car stereo prices and specifications in one of their Spring issues. These listings are excellent if you are planning to become an active car audio consumer. Aside from the listings, these magazines also feature plenty of product reviews, new equipment glimpses, glossy manufacturer advertisements, and helpful tips.

On the downside of following the magazines is their inherent commercial nature. At this writing, none of the popular newstand car audio magazines feature distributor advertisements. As a result, it is very difficult to deter-mine what is a good price for any given component. Nearly all of the maga-zines that pertain to other hobbies are loaded with "Crazy Bob's Discount House of ..." style advertisements. For some reason, the car stereo hobby is devoid of these ads and it certainly hurts the hobbyists! The only prices that

Fig. 1-1 *A small pile of car audio-related magazines from the past five years. AUTOtronics is now history.*

are listed in these magazines are the manufacturer's suggested list price, which often is as much as several hundred dollars over the distributor's selling price on the higher-end components. Just by reading the magazines, the average consumer is left in haze—not knowing the average price for any given piece of equipment.

Although the advice that is given by the various car stereo experts is very good, you also have to remember who pays the bills at the magazine office. Your subscription or newsstand price money is only part of the cashflow received by these magazines. The major source of revenue is generated by all of those beautiful, full-color, full-page advertisements throughout the magazine. As a result, the magazines are quick to push the expensive components and maxi-systems, whether they are necessary or not. Instead of finding test reports and reviews of average components or good deals, you will find test reports and reviews of the very best that the industry has to offer or you'll read about new, innovative technology that *everyone else* will be talking about in five years.

More disconcerting to me is the general bias of the magazines toward expensive cars and expensive, high-end audio. Very few of them feature articles on how-to installation, troubleshooting, maintenance, or repair. You are more likely to find a bright, glossy, photo review of a classic car with 23 coats of paint, a chrome engine, $10,000 worth of stereo equipment inside, and a bikini-clad girl draped across the hood. Maybe this is fine drooling material for some folks, but it won't show you how you can improve the sound system in your car.

The tone of some of the magazines is also reflected in some of the how-to articles that appear. Instead of taking a hands-on approach, the emphasis is generally on picking out a system, taking the magazine to an installer and saying "I want something like this." In fact, one recent step-by-step photo article showed how the upholstery was removed from a new car and how custom upholstery was made in the factory with an embroidered logo. It *was* nicer than the original, but it was a far from do-it-yourself as casting and machining your own engine block out of molten steel.

Another article from one of the car stereo magazines flat-out told the consumer *never* to install their own equipment or to buy used components. Both of these claims are bogus; if you are careful, patient, and understand your limitations, you can buy used equipment and (barring physical problems) successfully install at least some of your own setup.

I suppose that a sociologist could relate the car stereo industry to the change in consumer ideals over the past several decades. In the 1980s and 1990s, electronics have become disposable; whenever something breaks, the first impulse isn't to fix it, but to throw it away and buy a new one. To most people today, if something breaks down once, it is considered to be "junky and unreliable." This is a shame because the high-quality car stereo equipment is built to last. It has to be, otherwise it couldn't survive the heat, cold, and constant vibrations. At least some of this equipment could be repaired and put back into service without much trouble.

As I've described thus far, my favorite car stereo angle is the do-it-yourself approach. Currently, I give *Car Stereo Review* the highest marks for do-it-yourself (DIY) help. *Car Audio and Electronics* and *Autotronics* used to be the DIY leaders, but the two magazines merged and now *CA & E* takes more of a glossy, show-car approach. All of the current car stereo magazines at least have occasional how-to articles, so even if you don't subscribe to all of them, it is worth checking the newsstand every month to see if any other magazines are carrying a good article that is worth buying the issue for. It might be a comparison of different amplifiers (for example), a good DIY article, or even an ingenius idea used in one of the show cars. One must-have issue is the directory of equipment that is annually provided every April in *Car Audio and Electronics*. This massive guide shows the list prices and some specifications for literally thousands of pieces of equipment from hundreds of manufacturers. If you're a hobbyist, back issues of the April *CA & E*s are really valuable when checking up on used equipment.

In the long run, the car stereo magazines are excellent resources. If you are serious about setting up a good system, it is a must to subscribe to several of these. As stated earlier, remember the general bias of some of the magazines against used equipment, and that they do not focus on do-it-yourself installations or repairing broken equipment.

INTERNET AUDIO SURFING

When I wrote the last edition of this book in the Spring and Summer of 1994, the Internet was an emerging technology and the World Wide Web was in its infancy. Very few car stereo companies or hobbyist pages were yet established. At that time, I was only using a DOS-based system to access e-mail and Usenet groups, such as **rec.audio.car**. And I wasn't alone; the Web was thought of as being an experimental luxury by some people. This isn't surprising, considering that many areas did not yet have local Internet-access telephone numbers. In my case, and for many other non-city dwellers, checking e-mail and reading Usenet meant calling long distance...so Web surfing was an unnecessary excess. Now, it seems as if almost every telephone exchange has an Internet access number.

Of course, the methods of informational access have been revolutionized in the past five years. At that time, hunting for information meant reading the magazines (looking at the advertisements) and writing letters to the companies for their sales brochures.

Now, the Web contains some mighty vast repositories of information about car stereo equipment, cars, and more. The following URLs are excellent sources of information:

USENET

rec.audio.car
Rec.audio.car is the "old-time" Usenet site for car stereo information. Although it was once the premier place to reach the mobile audio community, it's now just one in a sea of sites. For the most part, I now avoid it because I've seen much better information and responses to questions on SoundDomain's SoundForum.

WEB PAGES

Auto Sound & Security
http://www.autosoundsecurityweb.com
The Web page for *Auto Sound & Security* magazine. Not a whole lot here.

The site mostly includes the feature and table of contents from their most-recent issue, an events calendar, plus information on obtaining subscriptions and back issues.

Car Audio and Electronics
http://www.caraudioelectronicsweb.com
The Web page for *Car Audio and Electronics* magazine. Not a whole lot of information here. In addition to some general information about the contents of the most-recent issue are a few columns.

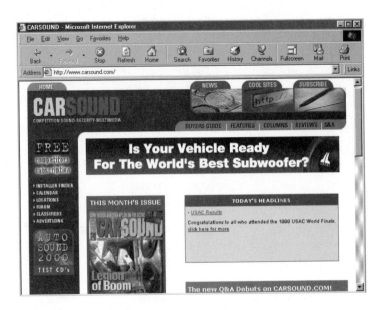

Fig. 1-2 *The Web page for* Carsound *magazine at* **http://www.carsound.com**.

Carsound
http://www.carsound.com
The Web page for *Carsound* magazine. This site features the most information of the Web pages for any of the car stereo magazines. In addition to the typical calendars and subscription information, this site includes features, columns, news about car audio, and an on-line buyer's guide for car stereo products. This guide is searchable, but is fairly jumbled and hard to read. Personally, I much prefer looking through the equipment with the compare feature on the Crutchfield site and looking at equipment on the Soundpros site. Seeing that much of this site is still under construction, perhaps the Buyer's Guide section will be improved.

Crutchfield
http://www.crutchfield.com

This is much more than just an electronics sales site. One awesome feature of this page is *compare*. You can go through the site and identify the make, model, and year of the car that you will be installing the audio system into and the page will automatically sift out equipment that is not compatible with your car. Then, you can go through this list of equipment, pick the units that you would like to see the specifications for, hit a button, and compare the features and specifications. For example, from this comparison, I can see that the $119.95 Denon DCR-670RD has a better signal-to-noise ratio (60 to 52 dB) and a slightly better wow-and-flutter percentage (0.11 to 0.13%) than the $129.95 Pioneer KEH-P2800 (among plenty of other specifications and features). It's an excellent, easy service: certainly easier than paging through dozens of brochures, checking specs. Crutchfield also has a lot of information about systems and a set of FAQs for choosing equipment.

dB Drag Racing
http://www.termpro.com/dbdrag/index.html

The official dB Drag Racing homepage includes a schedule of upcoming events, and lists of statistics and winners in dB Drag Racing-sanctioned competitions. A must-see for anyone who sees car stereo as a competitive sport.

IASCA
http://www.iasca.com

The official IASCA homepage includes a schedule of upcoming events, and lists of statistics and winners in IASCA-sanctioned competitions. A must-see for anyone who sees car stereo as a competitive sport.

SoundForum
http://www.sounddomain.com/forum

In my opinion, this is the best of the discussion boards for car audio. Better than **rec.audio.car**, this board is free of much of the spamming and pointless flaming that exists on the Usenet. Of course, as with anything on the Internet, you still need to be careful and not naively believe everything you read. However, the quality of information on this discussion board is higher, in part because posts can be canceled by the board owners, you must register before posting any messages, and you can't block send messages to it (as is the case with the Usenet). Additionally, this board is broken into eight categories to make it easier to sort through messages.

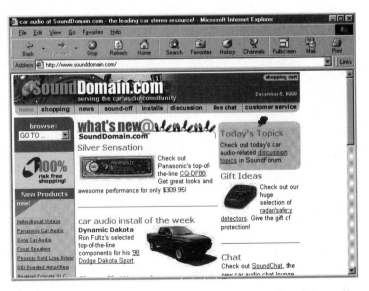

Fig. 1-3 *Installations, forums, and much more await at **http://www.sounddomain.com**.*

SoundInstalls
http://www.sounddomain.com/installation/installation.cgi

This is a great idea. SoundDomain created a pictorial database of audio systems on their Web page. Not only is it interesting and helpful, it's also free and available to anyone who wants to include photos of and information concerning their system. Another great feature is that the information is searchable by make of car and make of equipment, so you can quickly see if the database has a VW Beetle with Alpine equipment, for example. If so, you can see some photos and information about their installation.

Sound-Off
http://www.sounddomain.com/sound-off

Yup, this is another SoundDomain page. This page features a state-by-state listing calendar for most every car stereo event imaginable in the United States. Included is competition information for IASCA, USAC, dB Drag Racing, and other events. These events might not be a big deal for someone who just wants to get a better-sounding stereo in their car, but they're something special for hobbyists. And they're a great way to see first-hand how a system was put together.

Soundpros
http://www.soundpros.com

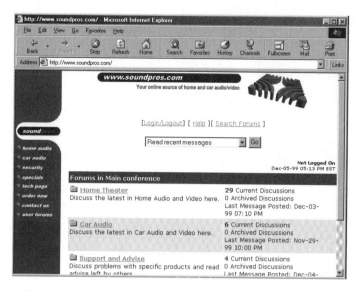

Fig. 1-4 *The Web page for Sound Pros at **http://www.soundpros.com**.*

Don't confuse this one with **www.soundpro.com** (a provider of mixing boards and other equipment for professional music and broadcasting applications). This audio dealer has a car audio forum on their site. At this writing, it's still very new and a far cry from SoundDomain's SoundFoums.

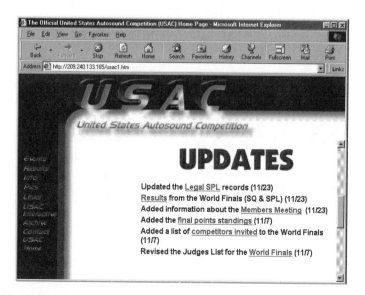

Fig. 1-5 *The Web page for the USAC at **http://www.soundoff.org**.*

Streetdreams
http://www.streetdreams.com
Unlike the other sites included in this section, this site is not dealer, magazine, or sound-off organization operated. Despite the lack of "big-money" backing, there's some helpful information here, including some example installations and a listing of the standard wiring colors for different vehicles. At the pace it's growing, this site could include plenty of interesting information in the years to come.

USAC
http://www.soundoff.org
The official USAC homepage includes a schedule of upcoming events, and lists of statistics and winners in USAC-sanctioned competitions. A must-see for anyone who sees car stereo as a competitive sport. Don't automatically type "**www.usac.com**" or you'll wind up at the homepage for a travel/adventure company.

EVALUATING YOUR NEEDS

In order to find the equipment that you want, you must first evaluate your needs and requirements so that you don't wind up with a bad-sounding system, a system that isn't useful to you, or a system that is overpriced. This section is a very light look at the different elements of a car stereo system. You can use each of these sections as a springboard for the chapters where they are covered in much greater depth.

AN EXAMPLE OF CHOOSING A SYSTEM

Different people have different tastes in sound and different needs. My personal audio needs seem to vary a bit from the norm. For example, CD head units are one of the most popular choices for equipment to be replaced, but, to date, I've been unwilling to take the digital leap. My reasons aren't because I'm antitechnology or even because I think that digital recordings are second-rate compared to analog (which is irrelevant because cassettes audio is actually inferior to just about anything on the market). It's simply convenience, flexibility, and protection.

For convenience, I already have plenty of music recorded onto cassettes from records and CDs, and I still buy records and cassettes, so the cassette format is the natural choice. Also, I am tempted by the better fidelity of CDs, but I'm afraid that I'll wind up dropping CDs on the floor and scratching them badly, rendering them useless. Finally, I could record backup CD-Rs of the CDs that I do have in my collection and I could record some of my records to CD-R, but it just seems like a big waste of time and money. Automatically, a cassette head unit is a must. To upgrade system fidelity, I could go with a CD changer to be controlled from the cassette head unit, but with my current CD collection, I can't really justify the hassle and extra money. Maybe in a few years, however.

Most of the music that I listen to is rock that is recorded with average or worse-than-average fidelity recorded onto a lower-fidelity medium (cassettes). I simply don't need to spend $1000 for speakers that would accurately reproduce every high. On the other side, I don't particularly like most low-end music (rap, hip-hop, etc.), so I don't need a brigade of subwoofers to blast the neighborhood with drum-'n-bass music. Although I do listen to music louder in the car than I do elsewhere, the in-car volume probably doesn't go over about 80 to 100 dB.

The next most popular replacement is the speakers. The standard factory speakers are standard midranges, as opposed to the aftermarket three-ways or midrange/tweeter combinations. Except for the emerging higher-quality systems, factory speakers are one of the first components to be replaced. I replaced the factory speakers in my car, but left them in our minivan, which contains a decent-sounding Infinity system.

Subwoofers are a matter of musical preference. In general, it's best to have at least one sub to give the music a bit more "ooomph." If you like the rap or hip-hop-related styles of music, you'll want to go heavy on the subs. For me, a lighter-duty approach fits the bill quite nicely, and having two kids, I need all of the available working space in the vehicles. Subwoofers require plenty of power, so you can plan to buy at least one amplifier if using them; more are required for the heavy bass systems.

Your system could require more or less revising than mine did. For example, if your factory-installed car stereo system sounds fairly good and the cassette deck was standard, you might just want to replace the factory speakers with solid, aftermarket two-way or three-way speakers. Another good upgrade is to add one or two woofers or subwoofers. The small, cheap speakers that are generally sold with all but the most expensive cars just can't reproduce the bass frequencies. That's because to accurately reproduce the bass frequencies and withstand the greater movement, the speakers and magnets must be larger and the cone must be heavier. This costs much more money and uses more space; space that some people would much rather devote to hauling things in the trunk. If you are working on a tight budget and want to slowly convert your system over, you should start with the speakers; they generally make the greatest difference in sound quality.

HEAD UNITS

The first aspect of your car's sound system is the head unit. The type of playback is almost always upgraded. For example, a radio-only unit might be upgraded to cassette player or a cassette deck might be removed in favor of a CD unit. I suppose that you could upgrade the quality of an AM/FM radio, but the unit that you would have to get would be one that was made by the car manufacturer for your particular car; no new aftermarket AM/FM car radios are sold in the United States. Currently, you will need to consider whether you want an AM/FM receiver cassette deck, compact disc player, or MiniDisc player. But, you can bet that at least one DVD head unit is in the works, and with DVD video entering the multigenerational phase and gaining market acceptance, DVD head units will be out soon if the format can pass over all of the legal hurdles in its path.

You should never get a system that uses a different format than you have at home. For example, don't buy a car CD player unless you also have a CD player at home or at work (with most people owning CD players, this example is unlikely). Because of this rule, the MiniDisc players should be avoided in most cases. MiniDiscs have a small, devoted following—especially among those who work with professional audio (such as broadcasting), but only a few head units and home stereo decks are sold. With the low prices of CD-R and CD-RW computer drives (which can record music) and discs, MiniDiscs are much less appealing than they were five years ago.

Presently, the lowest-priced units are cassette decks, which are typically sold in the $50 to $200 range. The problem with the cassette format is quality, and the manufacturers are constantly attempting to improve the audio quality of both the tape and the playback devices. CD head units have really dropped in price, usually in the $150 to $400 range at this writing. Whether or not DVD head units hit the marketplace, the CD format appears to be set for years to come. The format is well established and provides the best quality per dollar. For more information on head units, see Chapter 3, which covers the equipment in much more detail.

POWER

Power is one of the main factors in deciding the cost, size, and amount of work that is required for a system. My most recent systems have been relatively easy to install and relatively inexpensive to buy. The 20-W-per channel head unit was enough to supply my need for power. But most people who want a high-end or bass-heavy car audio system want to play it LOUD. To do so, an average basic system would consist of at least 30 W per channel for the midrange/treble speakers (whether via "high-power" head unit or through an amplifier) and another 100 W per channel amplifier for the subwoofers. The cars and pickups that compete in the sound-offs usually have four or more amplifiers.

Power has its price. Not only do the amplifiers cost money, but you have to figure out where to mount that many blocks of steel. Under the seat is one possibility (but it could get in the way and the space might be too limited in some cars) and putting that many amplifiers in the trunk will eliminate a lot of space. Do you really want that much power? In addition to the space problems, you will have to run all of the wires that are required to interconnect all of the amplifiers.

The next problem is that if you install high-powered amplifiers, the energy to power the system must be created by your car. Most car power-generating and saving systems (the alternator and battery, respectively) generate and save enough power to operate the car and a few optional accessories, such as an air conditioner; the parking, backup, and head lights; the heater; the cigarette lighter; and the stock radio. With a high-powered amplifier or several amplifiers, you will likely overtax your alternator, which will drain your battery. With the added current flow, you will likely need to replace some of the wiring with heavier gauges of wire to prevent overheating. Is having a massively loud system worth having to replace your alternator and some of the wiring? For me, no, but many people would disagree.

One of the toughest questions in the car stereo field is "How much power is enough?" A number of variables complicate the procedure. A standard arrangement in a compact car, a pickup, and a sedan would need somewhere from 25 to 50 W per channel. A station wagon, van, or minivan would probably need about 50 to 100 W per channel, possibly via two amplifiers because of the extra space that needs to be filled with sound. Multiple amplifiers are not necessary at first; you can always test out a system first with one amplifier, then, if you decide that you need more power, you can add another one later. This procedure could save you hundreds of dollars if you originally planned to buy two amplifiers but decided that just one sounded fine.

The other complication with amplifiers is that the manufacturers often use deceptive tactics to boost the power rating of their equipment. Power can be rated in a number of ways. A few of the common measurement techniques are in *input power*, *output power*, *peak power*, and *average power*. To make a measurement look higher, they could measure the peak input power. To actually determine how much power an amplifier is outputting, average output power would be used. Most amplifiers don't list the measurement style on the box or amplifier that was used to determine their figure. Chances are that the manufacturer used a measurement that will pad their figures. More information about amplifier power is covered in Chapter 5.

SOUND-PROCESSING EQUIPMENT

Very little (if any) sound-processing equipment is necessary for the basic car stereo system. However, any higher-level or more-complex system (such as the bass-heavy subwoofer-laden systems) will require some types of sound-processing equipment.

A very basic piece of equipment is the *crossover*. Over the years, a number of people have been confused about what crossovers are and what they do. Crossovers are just a combination of a lowpass filter and a highpass filter. The lowpass filter allows only low-frequency audio signals to pass through and the highpass filter allows only high-frequency audio signals to pass through. With both filters working together, all of the high-frequency audio signals can be passed to the two-, three-, or four-way speakers and the low-frequency audio signals can be passed to the woofers or subwoofers. Crossovers are especially useful in systems that use multiple speakers, not just the multiple-driver speakers. Without the crossovers, the sound systems will sound mushy or distorted, especially if it has a few woofers or subwoofers. Also, without crossovers, the separate-speaker systems will have all the audio frequencies being played by all of the speakers. If much volume is used, it won't be long before the heavy bass movement blows out the tweeters. In these cases, crossovers are necessary as a safety precaution, as well as an improvement in sound quality. Crossovers are covered separately in Chapter 8 and speakers are covered in Chapter 6.

Another of the favorite pieces of sound-processing equipment, the *equalizer*, actually changes the audio signal; crossovers only direct the signals to the speakers. An equalizer is useful because with it you can boost or reduce the audio at a number of different frequency ranges. If an audio source is particularly muffled, you can raise the controls of some of the higher-frequency bands to "brighten" the sound. Or, if you want to perk up the bass on a certain track or album, you can boost the controls of the lower-frequency bands. With an equalizer, you can shape the audio of whatever you listen to suit your tastes. They are especially useful if you have a cassette head unit in your car and if you listen to many different home-recorded tapes that need to have the audio altered.

Equalizers are real components, just like head units and amplifiers; they aren't necessarily just a panel full of slider potentiometers. As a result, you can expect to pay anywhere from $40 to over $1000, depending on what extra features the unit has and how well the unit is manufactured. You can get more than just an equalizer in even the typical equalizer package. Many equalizers also have amplifiers built in to the cabinet; these amplifiers can either be used without amplification to power to speakers or they can be used as preamplifiers to feed an external amplifier. Another option is that some units have built-in crossovers, which reduces the headaches of arranging and installing a system. Equalizers are covered further in Chapter 4.

The last common component that you could add to a system is a *digital sound processor (DSP)*, which is sometimes known as a *sound processor*. These systems can shape audio (music or talk) to sound as though it is a live performance in any number of different locations. Some of the different common sound-enhancement settings include "Jazz club," "Concert hall," etc. These settings allow you to adjust the sound. Audiophile equipment reviewers have raved about their versatility, but are they worth the price to you? The units presently cost well into the hundreds of dollars, which could be quite a bit of money to you for an added bit of audio flexibility. Also, most purists, such as the people who engineered and produced the album that you are listening to, would say that the audio has been recorded in the way that it was intended to sound. Sound processors are covered further in Chapter 4.

SECURITY

With the increase in the technical level, expense, diversity, and sound quality of car audio systems, the levels of auto break-ins and stereo theft have also greatly increased. These days, especially if you live in an urban area, you must consider security when buying your sound system. Otherwise, chances are that you will invest a great deal of time and money in a stereo system, only to have it stolen. If that isn't bad enough, your car will probably be damaged by thieves.

This section has nothing to do with car security systems or ways to prevent robbery, but rather how to choose equipment that won't attract the wrong kind of attention. A low-profile look can be very difficult to accomplish if you are serious about sound and audio gadgetry; there are just so many components and so much size to a competition-quality sound system that it's hard to hide it all. As a result of the extra difficulty in installing a loud, great-sounding low-profile sound system, the judges at car audio sound-offs also rate cars on how well hidden the equipment is.

You don't need to own a massive and expensive system to shop around for products that will minimize your chances of being robbed. Many head units are being built for extra security. Three of the common head-unit security methods are:

Detachable faceplate The entire face of the head unit can be unsnapped and carried in your pocket. Without the faceplate, which contains all of the control electronics, the head unit is virtually useless. Virtually all new head units have detachable faceplates (Fig. 1-6).

Fig. 1-6 *The removable faceplate on a head unit.*

Removable head unit If the owner wants to be sure to avoid having the head unit stolen when the car is in dangerous locations, the entire head unit can be easily pulled out of the car and carried away. This feature, popular in the early to mid-1990s, is becoming less popular in head units (Fig. 1-7).

Security codes For head units with security codes, if the head unit is disconnected from the power, it will not function. It will only work whenever it is reconnected to power and the security code is reentered in to the head unit. This method is also becoming less common.

The safest and most convenient security method is the detachable faceplate.

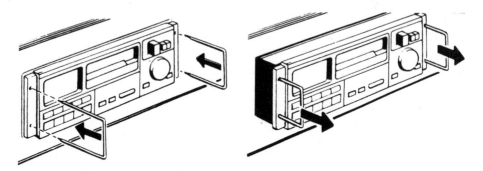

Fig. 1-7 *Pulling a removable head unit out from its mounting location.* Philips

It is easy to remove, most head units without faceplates don't really look like car stereos, and most thieves are smart enough not to steal a head unit that is missing the faceplate. On the downside, head units with detachable faceplates are more expensive than other styles. Also, if you are as absent-minded as I am, you could lose the face plate, which would be catastrophic.

Removable head units are handy if you live in a safe area and if you are sure that you remove the head unit any time that you are in a dangerous location. That way you can be certain that no thief will steal your head unit. On the other hand, if you live in an unsafe area or one with occasional car robberies, you will need to remove the head unit every night, which would be very inconvenient. With the removable head unit type of security system, you are helping out the criminal if you leave the deck in the car. All that person needs to do is pull the unit out and run!

The security code system of protecting against robbery seems to have the worst track record of the three methods. It is effective; once the head unit is stolen, it will not work until the thief punches in the security code, which isn't going to happen. So, the thief is stuck with a dead head unit. The problem is that the security code warnings on these units don't seem to stop them from being stolen. The average thief doesn't stop to read the service information about the radio before he or she steals it. It's probably dark outside and it just looks like a good, high-tech head unit. Whether or not the radio works, it gets stolen from the owner. I have a friend who has had two head units with this type of security system stolen in the past three or four years. If you opt for a head unit of this type, don't count on it deterring anyone from stealing it; it might help, but chances are that it won't.

Also, if you enter the security code and power is removed from the car (in replacing a battery, for example), you will need to reenter the security code to get it working again. If you lose the card with the code, you're in trouble. A few years ago, I had a head unit with security code. To be "safe," I never entered the code and I taped the security code card to the top of the head unit. Living in a relatively safe area, I never had trouble with being robbed and I never lost the code (which was important when I finally sold the unit).

If compact discs are your forte, you can easily hide that expensive deck by purchasing a disc changer, as opposed to a head unit. The CD changer differs from the traditional CD dash-mounted head unit in that it isn't restricted to an in-dash mounting position and it can play many discs back to back. From a security standpoint, the CD changer is an ultimate stealth audio component because its standard mounting position is in the trunk.

Do I need to buy:
❑ Head unit
❑ Front speakers
❑ Rear speakers
❑ Subwoofer
❑ Amplifier(s)
❑ Equalizer
❑ CD changer
❑ Sound-deadening material
❑ Wires and cables

There, no one can see if anything of value is inside. Also, most people might think that it is normal to see someone breaking into a car; they might merely assume that the person has locked their keys inside. However, virtually no owner breaks into his or her own trunk. Thus, the trunk-mounted CD changer is a great theft deterrent.

Aside from a protected head unit, speakers are another target that can be concealed. The best locations to mount the speakers would be within the car's factory-installed speaker mounting locations. You might not be able to get quite the speaker size that you desired into the factory space, but any visible custom audio work will only draw unwanted attention. The most difficult speakers to conceal are the woofers and subwoofers, which are often 10 to 18 inches (20.54 cm to 45.72 cm) in diameter. These speakers are most effectively hidden in the trunk, where they are not attention grabbers and where the bass sounds can still be powerful through the backseat.

Although safety was never an issue in car audio up until a few years ago, it could make a large impact in the types of equipment that you buy and the ways in which you install that equipment.

SIMPLIFIED EQUIPMENT SELECTION LISTING

The following list was constructed so that you could review it quickly and decide what general type of system would be appropriate for your needs and your car. It is not intended to be a complete guide to comparing all of the many features that are available in car stereo components. If each different feature, such as paper speaker cones versus titanium speaker cones versus polypropolene speaker cones versus carbon speaker cones versus resin speaker cones versus neodymium speaker cones, etc., was covered, the list would be so long that it could not be of value to anyone but the audio expert, who already knows what he or she wants out of an audio system.

Remember that it is generally better to upgrade in size and power than in quality. Upgrading the size and power of a system means *adding* more speakers, more amplifiers, more sound-processing equipment, and/or a trunk-mounted disc changer. Upgrading the quality of a system, on the other hand, means *replacing* speakers, the head unit, amplifiers, etc. If you start small and buy quality components slowly, you will save money in the long run.

The advantages and disadvantages listed are subjective and their importance can vary from person to person. For example, the large cost difference between the cassette head units and all other types of head units will often be a more important advantage than all of the other cassette disadvantages combined. Also, it is easy to list advantages and disadvantages for head units because several different types are currently marketed. For most other components, the major disadvantages are extra cost and space; or, when only two opposing types of a component are listed (such as multiple-driver speakers versus raw speakers), the advantages of the one type are the disadvantages of the other.

HEAD UNITS

CASSETTE DECKS

Advantages

❖ auto cassette decks are the least expensive form of head units

❖ cassettes are the least expensive recording medium

❖ cassettes are the most common recorded medium available

❖ can be easily and inexpensively adapted to play compact discs through a portable CD player via an adapter or through a jack on the head unit

❖ you can easily record your own custom cassettes at home

Disadvantages

❖ auto cassette decks have more moving parts than other head units and are more likely to develop maintenance problems over the years

❖ the sound quality is not nearly as high as the other mediums

❖ cassettes will slowly wear out, drop out, tangle, and generally degrade in sound quality as they are used

COMPACT DISC PLAYERS

Advantages

❖ the audio is the best that is currently available

❖ used compact discs are becoming available at affordable prices

❖ with care, compact discs will not degrade in quality

❖ no parts wear against the discs, so neither the CD nor the head unit are as likely to wear out as a cassette deck

❖ compact disc players are presently the least expensive digital head units on the market

Disadvantages

❖ compact disc head units are prone to skipping on rough roads and especially before they are warmed up

❖ compact disc head units are still much more expensive (on average) than auto cassette decks

❖ compact discs must be handled very carefully; otherwise, they could become inoperative from scratches, warpage, etc.

❖ CD recording equipment is less common and is more expensive than cassette recorders, so custom-recorded CDs are not an option for many people

❖ unlike auto cassette decks, you cannot input a portable player to the head unit for increased flexibility in listening mediums

❖ commercially recorded compact discs currently sell for nearly twice as much as commercially recorded cassettes

MiniDisc PLAYERS

Advantages
❖ MiniDiscs are much smaller than the other mediums

❖ cases protect MiniDiscs, so they are more durable than compact discs

❖ with care, MiniDiscs will not degrade in quality

❖ no parts wear against the discs, so neither the MiniDisc nor the head unit are as likely to wear out as a cassette deck

❖ you can easily record your own custom MiniDiscs at home

❖ the sound quality is better than that of cassettes

❖ it is easy to rerecord and reformat the recordable MiniDiscs

Disadvantages
❖ to make custom recordings at home, you would also need to purchase a MiniDisc recording deck, which is presently neither common nor inexpensive

❖ the future of the MiniDisc format is uncertain at best, and beginning to look rather dismal with the acceptance of DVD and the emergence of MP3

❖ the fidelity is not quite on par with that of compact discs

❖ the price of a high-quality MiniDisc head unit is presently 2 to 10 times more costly than a comparable auto cassette deck

❖ the price of MiniDiscs are presently 2 to 10 times more costly than cassettes

FULL-RANGE SPEAKERS

MULTIPLE-DRIVER SPEAKERS

Advantages
❖ less expensive because they use fewer parts than separate raw speakers

❖ can be installed in a smaller space

Disadvantages
❖ the system is cannot be tailored to spread out the sound with different sizes of speakers mounted throughout the vehicle

❖ you cannot choose each speaker separately; when you buy one, you've bought them all

❖ because all of the speakers are held within the cone of the largest speaker (the midrange), the sound will not be quite as clean as if the individual speakers were mounted apart from each other

RAW SPEAKERS

Advantages
❖ the system is can be tailored to spread out the sound with different sizes of speakers mounted throughout the vehicle

❖ you can choose each speaker separately to fit within your tastes for sound

❖ the sound is cleaner

Disadvantages
❖ more expensive because each speaker must be purchased individually

❖ much more space is required for installation

WOOFERS AND SUBWOOFERS

FREE-AIR WOOFERS AND SUBWOOFERS

Advantages
❖ can be mounted in rear decks or other areas without the need for sealed enclosures

❖ less space is required for installation

❖ less money and work is required for installation

Disadvantages
❖ usually cost slightly more than comparable standard woofers and subwoofers

❖ will usually attract attention that a quality stereo system is in the car

❖ require a sealed enclosure for optimum performance

STANDARD-MOUNT "RAW" WOOFERS AND SUBWOOFERS

Advantages
❖ are the least-expensive type of woofers and subwoofers

❖ can be mounted in locations that require less space than commercially enclosed woofers and subwoofers

❖ can be mounted in locations that are more convenient for the owner

Disadvantages
❖ require, by far, the most custom installation work

❖ if the speakers are being professionally installed, the cost will be much higher

❖ require that you follow specific equations or predesigned box plans for the size(s) of your particular speaker(s)

ENCLOSED WOOFERS AND SUBWOOFERS

Advantages

❖ the enclosures have been engineered to match the speakers perfectly

❖ provide a very professional look in a durable box or tube

❖ are easy to remove if your car is in an unsafe location or if you need the extra car space

Disadvantages

❖ are much more expensive (per speaker) than just buying "raw" speakers

❖ can require a great amount of space in the back seat, trunk, or hatchback of a car

❖ can easily be stolen once a thief breaks into the vehicle

❖ must be mounted in a location where they won't become a dangerous projectile in the event of a car accident

AMPLIFICATION

DEDICATED EXTERNAL AMPLIFIERS

Advantages

❖ the loudness of the audio can be customized to suit your needs

❖ are built to handle much more continuous power and heat than the other types of amplifiers

❖ one or more dedicated external amplifiers are necessary to provide large amounts of power, such as for heavy-bass and competition systems

❖ many have built-in tunable crossovers

Disadvantages

❖ are much more expensive than purchasing a high-power head unit instead

❖ depending on the power consumption of the amplifier(s), the load of the other accessories on the power system, and the total power output of your alternator, you might be forced to upgrade your alternator

EQUALIZER/AMPLIFIERS

Advantages

❖ are very convenient if you plan to purchase an equalizer

❖ can be mounted in the dash
❖ are relatively inexpensive

Disadvantages

❖ are not designed to withstand large amounts of heat and power for extended periods of time

❖ cannot reproduce audio as accurately as nearly any dedicated external amplifier

HIGH-POWER HEAD UNITS

Advantages

❖ requires much less space than a separate amplifier
❖ costs only slightly more that a low-power head unit
❖ requires less installation work than a separate amplifier
❖ requires less space than a separate amplifier

Disadvantages

❖ only the highest powered units will provide more than 25 W (each) into four different channels (speakers)

❖ if the amplifier is damaged, the entire, costly head unit/amplifier will need to be repaired

CONCLUSION

Hundreds of different car stereo component models are available, and without keeping abreast of the recent information, you can easily get lost in the sheer numbers. The special 1998 directory edition of *Car Audio and Electronics* listed 1187 different models of dedicated amplifiers! Those are merely the models that were being sold by the manufacturers in 1998; hundreds of other models have been sold and discontinued in years past and hundreds more will be available in future years.

If you are interested in car audio and plan to upgrade your system in the years to come, be sure to subscribe to one or more of the magazines on the topic and save all of the copies. If you are considering purchasing used equipment, check at the library for back issues of *Car Audio and Electronics, Car Stereo Review*, etc. In particular, look for review comparisons of equipment, such as the "10 Amplifiers Reviewed" types of articles.

Remember, the keys to success in purchasing most anything are good information, level-headedness, and discernment. Don't be blinded by either amazing, superficial technologies, or by dirt cheap prices. Buy the best-quality equipment that you can for the money that you are willing to spend.

EQUIPMENT BUYING

Just about everywhere you look, someone is selling new car stereo equipment. In a world inundated with auto audio equipment, getting a great system for a great price can be difficult. But with the technological improvements over the years as the prices continue, it's getting a little easier. This chapter is intended to provide some background shopping information for the novice car stereo buyer. If you're at a higher level or if you've already purchased equipment, feel free to skip this chapter...or just skim it for kicks.

BUYING NEW EQUIPMENT

BUYING FROM A LOCAL INSTALLER

One good way to assemble a good-quality system is to research equipment through the magazines and the Internet. After making a list of highly rated equipment, you could go to a local car stereo installer and have them put together the system for you. The system will most likely be solid, but the prices could be high.

The people who operate these businesses are professionals who have installed many systems and who have had plenty of experience installing various pieces of equipment throughout different locations of the car interior. They have seen which amplifiers run into problems with clipping and distortion and which pieces return to the shop for repair. One problem is that the installers have ultimate authority when suggesting new equipment to the novice car stereo owner-to-be. Thus, the novice might have no idea what any given piece of equipment typically sells for. You could even be charged for more than the suggested retail price.

Fig. 2-1 *A local car stereo shop--in this case, it also doubles as the local Radio Shack outlet.*

Another problem is competition. Most people just pick out the closest car stereo shop, pick out the equipment, and get everything installed. You won't find all that many advertisements for these shops. As a result of the lack of competition, you won't find gas station-style price wars with car stereo equipment from the installation shops.

The last problem with blindly picking all of your equipment from a local installer is sheer numbers. Chances are that the car stereo shop of your choice is a rather small business that sells equipment and installs it for people in the community. The bottom line is that they probably sell a relatively small amount of car stereo equipment. Although the previous two paragraphs hint at the possibility that your local car stereo shop might be intentionally turning your ignorance into large profits, there's another condition to consider. Dealers must purchase specific quantities of equipment to sell to their customers. If they don't have the clientele to reach a certain quota of sales, they can't afford to buy a larger quantity of a certain product. Buying in smaller quantity means that the manufacturer won't give the shop as good of a price per unit. As a result, the price at the local shop might appear to be high, but, in reality, might be as cheap as they can possibly sell it at.

One real plus to using the local installers is that they will often do custom installation work. They aren't cheap (one local shop charges $25/hour for custom installations), but many people prefer to spend hundreds of dollars on a professional installation, rather than risk damaging the interior of their car.

This information is not necessarily intended to keep you from purchasing products from the local car stereo shops. Buying locally is a good way to support the people in your community and also to support quality car audio

Fig. 2-2 *Who really has the best prices? Sale fliers from Best Buy and Circuit City.*

in your hometown. Supporting the local shops could mean helping your friends, helping the local economy, and (possibly) enabling the shops to sponsor car audio events in your area. On the other hand, you probably will not find as good of a price at the small, local shops. How much money do you want to spend and who do you want to have your money? If you would rather spend a few extra dollars to help out your local shop, then by all means do it. You can bet that a long-distance mail-order shop or a chain store probably won't ever help out in your community.

BUYING FROM CHAIN AUDIO STORES

Since the first edition of this book, the popularity and growth of specialty chain stores have exploded. Now, it seems amazing that I had never been in a Borders or Barnes & Noble superstore when I wrote the first edition. These stores are everywhere now. The same thing has happened with electronics and computer stores. The big national stores are Circuit City and Best Buy, where you can buy most anything electronic at one huge supermarket-type store (Fig. 2-2). I've also seen some Media Play stores, which are huge electronics/computers/videos/music stores, but they seem to be much less common than Circuit City.

Other stereo and electronics stores are regional, often with a number of stores across several states. For example, in Pennsylvania, we have a number of outlets from Sun Electronics, Wee Bee Audio, and Bryn Mawr Stereo. The regional stores are typically smaller than the giant national outlets and their operations often vary in style between the flashy major stores and the hometown style of the local stereo shops.

Superficially speaking, the chain stores are like a best of everything: typically excellent prices and some stores have free installation. For example, one of the regional chains always had among the best prices that I could find anywhere (in a store or via mail order), but their staff was clueless and as unhelpful as possible. Other stores that I've seen have both higher prices and more knowledgable (and helpful) sales staff.

Before you buy anything from one of the chain stores, you should be sure of their policies (how they handle returns, whether they have special credit plans, if they perform custom installation work, etc.), then compare their offerings to those from other dealers.

BUYING FROM THE DISCOUNT DEPARTMENT STORES

If you get tired of running around, looking at ads, and doing research, you might check out the car stereo equipment at the local discount department store. After all, your "significant other" wants to check out some clothes and you want to look at the tennis racquets. There, you see equipment at unbelievable prices: cassette head units for only $25 to $75, amplifiers for only $30 to $50, and entire speaker systems for only $20 to $50. You even see some of the "bass cannons" that the locals have mounted in the trunk or back seat.

Here, you can pick up your entire system for under $100 *and* you still have the features that you wanted: an autoreverse cassette head unit, a separate amplifier, and a set of two-way 6"-x-9" (15.24 cm x 22.86 cm) speakers.

Music in your car, pure and simple. If you have listened to the television advertisements from the discount department stores, you will know that the reason why their products are so inexpensive is because they have the "buying power" of thousands of stores: they don't just buy by the crate or even by the truckload!

All of these claims are correct; these stores buy in volume and they *do* pass the savings on to you. However, they only have enough room for a small quantity of car stereo components, which are probably stuck in with the automotive aisle. In general, the discount department stores attempt to give the consumer every feature possible for the least amount of money. This attitude is what sells products. As a result, you will see is that the autoreverse cassette head unit is much less expensive than the autoreverse cassette head unit that you find in the car stereo magazine advertisements. What you won't see is that the company that made the less-expensive deck probably skimped on the parts inside. Perhaps they saved a few cents per deck by using a less-sturdy PC board that will crack after a few years of use. Or maybe they used cheaper switches and knobs on the front panel that are much more likely to break. They almost certainly used cheaper heads, which means that the sound won't be as good and the heads will wear out quicker. The quality of the parts that go into a unit are much more important than the extra features and conveniences that you see on a deck. Nowhere is this more apparent than when comparing the equipment in discount department stores to that of higher-quality consumer-grade equipment.

Of course, there is a time and a place for everything. If you are on an extremely tight budget and you aren't serious about sound systems, you might want to try this route. One of my friends bought a new head unit for $25 while he was in high school. The system went into distortion before it even got loud and the sound, even at low volumes, was poor to fair (at best). When he was at college, some stupid thief stole the virtually worthless head unit. In my friend's case, the stereo was worthwhile. It was cheap and he could play tapes in the car. That sure beat listening to the AM radio. Better yet, the head unit was stolen before it completely died. If he had a good head unit, he would have lost much more. In situations such as this, where cheap music is needed for only a short while, the el cheapo systems are worthwhile.

On the other hand, do not substitute cheap equipment for units that are built well if you plan to use the system for any length of time. Whereas the discount specials will reliably operate for maybe a few years, you can easily expect 5 or 10 years of good service from the better models. In the long run, researching the market and spending a few extra dollars on a solid system will be less expensive than buying inadequate systems that frequently break down.

THE RADIO SHACK EXCEPTION

One exception to the "cheap equipment-at-national chainstores" rule is Radio Shack. Although Radio Shack isn't a discount department store, it is basically a discount *electronics* department store. Because of the national-bargain nature of the store, Radio Shack doesn't dig into the audiophile scene. They do, however, carry everything from low-grade to mid-grade consumer equipment. It can be rather tough to find comparison information on Radio Shack equipment in the car stereo magazines. Evidently, Radio Shack has enough business from their own stores throughout the country and from the distribution of their sale fliers that they don't need to advertise in these magazines. In turn, the name *Radio Shack* is almost never mentioned in any of them. If you want to compare systems, you will have to check out the car stereo section at the local Radio Shack store yourself.

MAIL-ORDER AND INTERNET COMPANIES

If you have done your background work, you will find your best price on any given piece of car stereo equipment from one of the mail-order companies.

Fig. 2-3 *So, what if Santa shops at Crutchfield? Should you buy there, too?*

Because these companies employ telemarketers, have computerized inventories, and sell thousands of units, they can afford to buy in huge quantities and, in turn, sell their equipment at a lower price than anyone else. Of course, this is just a generalization and some mail-order companies aren't inexpensive sources of equipment. Still, if you play the part of a smart consumer and shop around, you will probably be satisfied with the price.

Only a few of the very largest mail-order distributors advertise in the national car stereo magazines, and these ads are only for catalogs; no current equipment prices are listed. If you are interested in the mail-order route, try looking through pages on the Internet. If you are among the meager few without regular Internet Web service, you're in trouble. You'll have to scrounge around for hardcopy catalogs from some of the large dealers, such as Crutchfield (Fig. 2-3), J&R Music World, and Damark. Compare the prices and go for the best deal.

In my opinion, it is best to make a list with a number of different components that would be satisfactory for your needs. Then, pick up their catalog or, if they don't have a catalog, ask the customer service representative for some of the recent sales. That way, if some mail-order company has a magnificent sale or closeout on a system that might be a little better than you thought you could afford, you can still be flexible enough to pick it up.

A peculiar, somewhat-related price discrepancy occurred whenever I was buying a head unit for my car a few years ago. I only had one in mind because I wanted shortwave reception. After some searching, I found that one dealer had it for less than half of the list price. I called back a few days later and found that the price had gone up by nearly $100! The salesman said that the manufacturer had them on sale to the dealerships. He also said that at that point, they couldn't even buy those head units for the price that they had been selling them for. He might have been feeding me a line about the unit, but it was a European import and I never saw them anywhere for less than $50 over that original sale price after that time (even as they were being discontinued and closed out). The bottom line is: Be cautious and thorough when searching for cheap prices. A higher price might not be the fault of the installation shop, the salesman, or the installer, so please don't verbally abuse them!

Unfortunately, many mail-order companies don't have customer service representatives that are abreast of the current catalogs, like traditional showroom salesmen and saleswomen are. To make matters worse, it can sometimes be difficult to talk to the customer service representatives for more than a few minutes. You're usually lucky if you can get out more than: name, address, credit card number, price, and catalog order number. To get a feel for what mail-order companies you can and can't talk to, call around, work with the companies that you like best, and write them a supportive letter to let them know that you liked their customer service policy.

Of course, to order from one of the mail-order companies, you will either need to have a credit card out and ready or you will have to send a check or money order to the company's address. Either way, the concept of sending hundreds or even thousands of dollars off to some address that you saw in a magazine isn't terribly appealing. What if that "one million square foot warehouse" that is "packed with stereo equipment on the waterfront" is actually just an empty apartment in Brooklyn with two telephones? You really have no way of knowing, unless you have visited the store's showroom or unless you know someone who has ordered from that company before. Although you can't be certain of the integrity of the company that you are ordering from, one good method to help you evaluate a company's performance is to check magazines from previous months for advertisements. If you can find that a company has been in business awhile, it's a good sign. It's an even better sign if you can find advertisements from that particular company from at least several years ago...and the ads in question have gotten larger in size. That probably means that the mail-order company has performed well over the years and has, in turn, consistently built up a larger customer base. Other good signs are if their Web page features the Better Business Bureau seal or if they are highly regarded in the Internet forums.

And that brings me to another part of the buying experience: buying from online companies, which is essentially the same as ordering via mail order. I just love researching and buying things online; you can discover so much more information about companies and their products from their Web pages. For example, both Crutchfield and SoundDomain have awesome pages, with plenty of extra useful information for hobbyists and beginning installers. Thus, it's no surprise that these companies both have excellent reputations. In addition to being able to check for companies that appear to be reliable, you can very easily compare prices between different companies.

Still, even after researching the mail-order company, you might have reservations about sending that much money. That's a natural reaction and it is always better to be cautious than to risk your money. So, if you have found a company that you would like to order from, only order part of what you want—maybe only a relatively inexpensive set of speakers. That way, if the company sends everything quickly and you are satisfied with their service, you can order the more expensive components (such as head units, CD changers, etc.) later. If you are not satisfied with the service, write a letter to the company and to the Better Business Bureau, if necessary. Chances are that you will be very happy with the service that you receive from one of the mail-order companies. Personally, I don't know of anyone who has had any problems ordering from them.

Another dilemma is placing your credit card information on other Web pages. For the most part, I don't have a problem with online payments. Most have secure, encrypted pages that have been checked by e-commerce companies. However, if they don't, be wary. Just to be safe, I often look on the Web page for a toll-free phone number and order via the phone instead.

BUYING USED EQUIPMENT

If you are daring and like to live life on the edge, then you might be game for car stereo Russian roulette. Except, in this game, you win if you hit a working component and get reamed monetarily if you pull a dud. Or, you might be handy with a soldering iron and some test equipment and be perfectly capable of repairing your own car stereo equipment and save a fortune. Either way, buying used equipment is not for the faint of heart.

As you might expect (especially if you frequent yard sales, auctions, or flea markets), you can find nearly any type of equipment in any condition for virtually any price. It's only a matter of looking to find what you want or need. Unfortunately, you probably will have to sift through hundreds of pieces of equipment until you find the right piece(s). Still, with patience and determination, buying used can be both rewarding and fulfilling.

Fig. 2-4 *You've found a dream system in a classified ad. Does it all work? Are the prices well below new cost? If the system is so great, why is he selling it?*

WHERE TO BUY USED EQUIPMENT

As stated in the previous paragraph, looking for used equipment requires patience and determination. If you are a "slave to convenience," you will quickly tire of the used equipment game and pickup your car stereo components at premium prices elsewhere. This route is fine if you have at least $1,500 ready for a car audio system; at least you won't have to take any risks or have any hassles this way.

CLASSIFIED ADS

One easy way to find the type of equipment that you want is to check out the classified advertisements in the local newspapers, in the shopper-type free classified papers, or on computer bulletin boards (Fig. 2-4). It's much easier to sift through classified ads than it is to search through thousands of pieces of equipment at a flea market, electronics show, or auction.

The classified ads are excellent because they're a clearinghouse for audiophiles, technoids, and "sonic destroyers," who constantly buy new equipment and sell off their old components. The prices in the classified ads are often very good, usually about one-third to three quarters of the price that they paid for the equipment. However, they are not quite as inexpensive as those at flea markets. Most people who will take the time and money to put a classified ad in a daily newspaper will expect to receive a price that is closer to what they originally paid for the components.

One necessity, when scouring the classified ads for good prices, is to keep abreast of the discount prices from the stereo distributors. What sounds like a great deal might be rather sour. The audiophiles and technoids commonly buy equipment with new features as soon as it hits the market. As a result, they pay the premium prices to be the first person around to have whatever it is that they have. When something new rolls around, they will buy it and sell off the old equipment. Even if they are selling the particular piece of equipment for 66% of what they paid for it,

Buying used: A checklist
☐ When did you buy it?
☐ Where did you buy it?
☐ Did you buy it new or used?
☐ Why are you selling it?
☐ Have you ever had any problems with it?
☐ Do you smoke?
☐ Do you have the manuals and the manufacturer information?

you might be able to find a stereo discount store that has a closeout on the same model, but is selling it for less than half of the original list price. For that matter, I picked up one amplifier for approximately 25% of the manufacturer's list price from a mail-order company that sells factory-serviced, discount, and closeout products. Chances are that I couldn't have found the same model in a classified ad for a price this low.

Another trap to beware of is people who purchase new equipment, raise the price, and resell it in the classified ads as new or almost new discounted equipment. This practice isn't common, but occasionally someone will try to make a few bucks off of an unknowledgeable person in this manner.

When you find a component that you are interested in buying, make a list of questions to ask the owner. In addition to the type-specific questions that you need to write down, ask the questions shown in the checklist.

Of course, not everyone will be honest with you, but some people will be. A few signs to beware of are physically damaged or dirty equipment. Physical perfection is not a must, but heavy wear can cause problems in some equipment. For example, an amplifier can usually get stepped on and scratched, yet still work perfectly. But a worn cassette deck might have more problems: Heads can wear out; fragile buttons can wear out or become intermittent as a result of dust, smoke, or grease; and motors and gears can break down and strip. If the owner says that he or she doesn't smoke and that the unit was purchased new, but the front panel (in the case of a head unit or an equalizer) is yellowed from nicotine, then you know that the owner's answers are unreliable. If you know the years of different equipment releases, you can figure out whether or not the owner is telling the truth about buying the unit new. Also, when checking the physical condition of the equipment, be sure to check the serial numbers and equipment part numbers. As mentioned in the previous section, beware of equipment that has the identification stickers ripped off, and *do not buy* any components that have the numbers scratched or etched out. This stuff is almost certainly stolen. Buying stolen equipment not only encourages thieves, but it could get you in trouble. And if the seller is willing to steal equipment, they would surely lie to you about whether or not it is working properly.

The best way to find out whether or not a component works is to test it out in a car stereo system. Few people will bother to sell an nonworking system if it is still in the car; it's easy see if it works and how well. If the component that you are checking out is anything but a speaker, check to see if the power indicator (usually an LED) lights. Then, be sure that the wires are all connected. Otherwise, in the case of speakers or amplifiers, the owner might let you listen to the system, including the part that you want to buy. Check to be sure that the particular amp or speaker system is actually connected to the system that you're listening to.

If you're checking out a head unit, be sure to press all of the buttons and make sure that they work. Either a particular control system in the unit could be knocked out or a button could be broken or intermittent. You won't know if you don't check them. Don't just let the owner press a few buttons, say "see, it works great, are you going to buy it?" Hastiness and high-pressure sales are a warning sign that the system doesn't work as well as it should, that the price is too high, or that the owner is an impatient jerk. Beware in any case because if the owner is a jerk, he or she won't be reliable and won't help out if you run into any problems.

After all of these negative signs to avoid and potential reasons to distrust the owner, there is one very positive sign to be on the look out for. It is an excellent sign if the owner has the original box, manuals, installation information, and/or receipts. For one thing, it rules out the possibility that the unit was stolen. Also, the component is less likely to have been bought second-hand by the original owner. One of the most important positive signs about having all of this information is that if the owner was so careful with the information that pertained to the component, he or she was probably just as careful (maybe more so) with the component itself.

If you listen to the system (or if everything looks good with a component

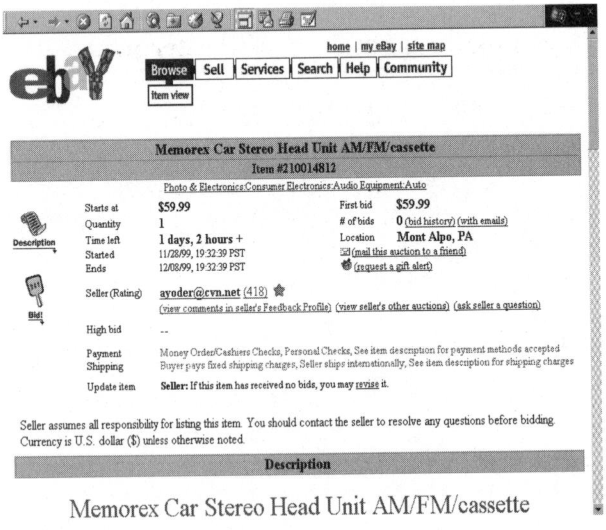

Fig. 2-5 *Although this seller might have 418 positive comments, do they really know anything about car stereos? Could this particular unit be from a bad lot that somehow made it out of the factory?*

that has been pulled from a system), and the component sounds good in that system and the price is in your range, get ready to pull out your wallet or checkbook. If not, or if you aren't sure, use that night to reevaluate your needs. Then, if you still want the component, call the owner the next day, be sure that it is still for sale, and buy it. In the worst case of waiting, the component could sell overnight. In the worst case of buying when you're unsure, you could buy something that doesn't work properly, something that doesn't have a great price, or something that you really don't want.

BUYING USED EQUIPMENT ONLINE

Another possibility and possible dilemma is buying used equipment via one of the online auctions. I won't completely go into the details of buying via online auctions; chances are that you are either already familiar with them or would rather not waste too much book space on a tangental topic. I have not purchased any car stereo equipment at an auction, although I have bought and sold plenty of items via eBay. eBay is currently the big one, although I've heard that Yahoo's auctions are beginning to pick up, so I'll just stick to eBay. You can find good buys on eBay (Fig. 2-5), but some things sell for more than they're worth on the auctions. From what I've seen, most used car stereo equipment sells on eBay for more than it would cost from other used outlets. Why would I want to buy a two-year-old cassette head unit, missing the wiring harness, for $10 to $20 less than the price of a new comparable unit from Crutchfield?

Again, there are some good deals to be had, but figure up the real value of the unit before bidding. Now's the time to pull out those back issues of the *Car Audio & Electronics* April directories. Remember, these issues list the list prices, not the average actual selling price of the equipment. In most cases, you can expect that a typical dealer price would be about 75% of the list. Unless the equipment is new or almost new, still under warranty, and in the box, with all of the cables and booklets, don't pay more than about 40 or 50% of the list price. Pictures are especially helpful for head units (to see what all is there), but they won't do much good for speakers or amplifiers, which can be blown without causing any visible physical damage (at least not in a little 72 dpi .JPG).

A final warning is to check the user's feedback section. This section allows other users to comment on their dealings with the seller. The possible feedback selections are positive, negative, or neutral. The person leaving the feedback can also leave a message that's as long as 80 characters. Overall, it's a pretty good system of checks and balances. Personally, I don't have a problem buying something from someone with 150 (or more) positive comments and no negatives, but I wouldn't bid on something from someone with three positives and three negatives.

The online auctions can be good places to buy car stereo equipment, so long as you are both cautious and prepared. Unfortunately, the risks are fairly large and chances are slim that you'll find a real deal, such as from a hamfest.

INSTALLATION SHOPS AND MAILORDER COMPANIES

If consumer safety is a top concern, yet you are still interested in picking up used equipment at better-than-full price, the best locations to scour are car stereo installation shops. These shops were also covered in the buying new equipment section. Although the installation shops are not always a prime outlet for purchasing new gear because of the often-pricey dollar amounts, they can be an excellent source for used equipment. The mail-order companies were touted as being the least expensive location for purchasing new equipment—if you know what you want. Both are lumped together in this section for used equipment for two reasons: company sales and warranty/money-back guarantees.

Of the ways to buy used car stereo equipment, the only two ways that you can buy serviced equipment are from installation shops or from mail-order stereo companies. The second-hand stores and pawn shops are also companies, but these are more of an as-is, all-risk adventure.

The advantage of having a company sell you a used product is that they have more of a responsibility to their customers than an individual with some old equipment has. Not only do the companies need to worry about spreading a bad reputation, but they also have to worry about being blacklisted by the Better Business Bureau. Besides all of that, many people who take up car stereo installation and repair take pride in their work and they wouldn't want to knowingly sell equipment that didn't work.

Considering the amount of equipment, variety of cars brought in, and expertise that are present in the typical installation shop, you should feel free to ask about used equipment. Talk to the sales representative or owner (depending on the size of the shop) and find out if they have any standard way to show used equipment in operation to customers. If so, you will be able to listen and compare the different units. If not, maybe the sales representative will be able to suggest someone to you who has the same piece of equipment in their car. Or, perhaps they can at least give you some good advice on the type of sound that that particular component will provide.

The company aspect of sales fits in with the warranties and money-back guarantees. After all, it would tough to sell any equipment at a high enough price to make a profit without some consumer insurance. As a result, the average installation shop or mail-order company that sells used equipment has anywhere from a one-week to a 30-day money-back guarantee. With this standard guarantee, you are usually able to return the stereo component for any reason and get all of your money back, less shipping costs (if applicable).

The average warranty on used equipment will last anywhere from 30 to 90 days. Generally, if the stereo component fails within the time of the warranty period, you can get your money back or have the unit repaired free of charge. These warranties are usually voided if you have opened the unit, physically damaged it, or if the unit was damaged because you connected it to a voltage or to an audio signal incorrectly. For any warranty or money-back guarantee, be sure that you have a hardcopy of the signed agreement and be sure to read the specific terms. Some companies will void warranty agreements for reasons that might seem trivial to you. If you void a warranty and can't get your money back, it's your fault.

On the whole, buying used equipment from installation shops and mail-order companies is a good move. Some shops don't like to bother with hiring a repairperson, so you might have a few problems finding what you want, unless you live in a major city. Check in the yellow pages for installation shops in your area and be sure to call first to make sure that they sell used equipment. Look through the stereo magazines for advertisements from the mailorder companies. You shouldn't have any problems with buying used and repaired equipment from these companies.

PAWN SHOPS AND SECOND-HAND STORES

On the flip side of buying equipment from installation shops or mail-order companies is scouring the pawn shops and second-hand stores. With pawn shops and second-hand stores, you trade a few extra dollars for the security of having a guaranteed unit. With pawn shops and second-hand stores, you don't need to shell out much money, but you are completely at risk.

EQUIPMENT BUYING

The second-hand "thrift" stores are generally lousy places to look for car stereo equipment. You might find something in one out of every five stores that you look through, but it will usually be an 8-track player from 1976 or something equally undesireable (although some people are beginning to collect 8-track players, believe it or not). Few people donate car stereo systems to the Salvation Army.

Pawn shops, on the other hand, are great stores to look through for used car stereo equipment or any other interesting electronics devices. When financial hardships strike, it seems as though the first things to be liquidated are the items of high technology. Likewise, it seems as though the people who need to quickly liquidate their possessions are those who dabble in high technology. If you are taxing your budget to buy your upcoming car stereo system, beware of this warning sign! Don't overburden your budget or your beloved system could find a temporary home in a pawn shop!

The two big warnings about buying from a pawn shop are that you won't get a warranty or a money-back guarantee on your equipment and you could easily run across stolen equipment. You are totally at risk in pawn shops, so be sure to check the physical condition of the piece that you are interested in: check all the buttons, switches, and knobs to make sure that they all seem to function properly. Also look for worn jacks, scratches, dents, oil or grease, burns, and melted areas. If one (or more) of these conditions exist, the price is 10% (or less) of the original sale price, and you are good with repairing audio equipment, it is probably worth your time and money to buy the component. Otherwise, *avoid it!* You will only lose money on it.

As stated in the section on buying from classified advertisements, avoid stolen equipment. You can't be sure that anything is or isn't stolen, but if

Fig. 2-6 *Time to pack it in. The vendors in the flea market area at the Fort Wayne hamfest and computer show start packing it away, which is a great time to get some bargains.*

the component's serial number has been scratched or etched out, it has almost certainly been stolen. It is also best to avoid a piece of equipment if the serial number sticker or tag has been removed, painted over, or covered. Buying stolen equipment not only supports the thieves (who make having even a fair stereo system in your car risky), it is illegal. If you find any equipment that has been altered in this way, complain to the store management, and if you have a chance, complain to the proper state or local government bureaus. I have heard that some states have been working to organize and clean up the pawn shops within their boundaries and thus remove the stigma of pawn shops as being a clearinghouse for stolen goods. In these areas, you should have fewer problems with purchasing equipment.

Unfortunately, Pennsylvania seems to be almost devoid of pawn shops. The closest ones to my present location are about 45 minutes away, in different states. But if you live in a city, you should have no problem finding several. One friend of mine regularly scopes out the bargains in three different pawn shops in his locale. If this is your situation, good luck!

HAMFESTS, COMPUTERFESTS, FLEA MARKETS, AND CONSUMER ELECTRONICS SHOWS

The flea market section at hamfests, computerfests, and consumer electronics shows are the best place to go for absolute minimum prices, with the trade-off of absolute maximum risk. Unfortunately, most people know nothing about these shows, and are missing out on some great buys and interesting technology.

About half of the time when I mention to someone that I am going to a hamfest, the response is a joke, such as "So, are you gonna eat a lot of pork? Ha ha." Yeah, real funny. A hamfest is an amateur radio gathering, where some large, open area (such as a county fairground) is filled with commercial amateur radio venders and another section (usually a section of the parking lot) is filled with a flea market. The flea market is filled with old shortwave and amateur radio parts that range anywhere from brand new to dating back to the turn of the century.

Just a few decades ago, nearly anyone with an interest or expertise in electronics was also an amateur radio operator. Of course, that was before the spread of personal computers and other electronic gadgetry. In many cases, the computer hobby overlaps the amateur radio hobby. Thus, most hamfests are also computerfests. Because of the overlap between computers and amateur and shortwave radio, you can also find other consumer electronics at these events. Some of the larger events are even advertised as "consumer electronics shows" and all sorts of electronic equipment is present (Fig. 2-6), although the core is still amateur and shortwave radio and computers. The smaller hamfests usually have little more than just shortwave and amateur radio equipment. However, the larger events are really interesting; you have no idea what you might find! (Fig. 2-7)

Most of the fests that I have been at recently have been either radio or computer dominated. However, one large fest that I went to a few months ago had a fair amount of car stereo equipment in the flea market. One table had a load of head units (mostly cassette decks) in fair to good condition. Unlike some of the other "buyer-beware" kind of hamfests, this guy offered to help put it in the car, so it had a temporary warranty, of sorts. Most of the equipment that he was selling was from the early to mid 1990s and the prices were pretty good. Too bad, I didn't have my van nearby or I might've bought a new head unit!

The main disadvantage to these fests and shows are that people pull junk out from everywhere and sell it off. With the exception of the guy in the last paragraph, after you buy a unit and take it home, it's yours. There is no store or home address to take it back to—just an empty fairgrounds. Hence, the low prices.

Fig. 2-7 *Part of the huge Parts Express tent, set up at the Dayton (Ohio) Hamvention, the largest hamfest in the world.*

But the equipment and the sellers vary widely. I have had everything from very honest and friendly sellers, who were not afraid to tell me anything that was wrong with a unit, to those who flat-out lied about their equipment. Once I bought a home cassette deck for $3. When the guy said that it worked fine, I thought "Yeah, right," but the price was excellent and the condition was good. I brought it home and it worked fine! In another case, I bought a beautiful, formerly expensive Denon home CD player for $35...and it still works fine.

Strangely enough, out of all of the equipment that I have looked over during my past decade of hunting at hamfests, I have not seen any visible signs of stolen equipment. It seems as though the flea market section at these type of events would be a great location to sell hot equipment, but they aren't. If anything, they are a great location to unload basement ballast.

Standard flea markets are not as good for finding car stereo equipment. The prices and dealer honesty is about as variable as what you would find at a traditional hamfest. However, the dealers at hamfests are all interested in electronics, so there is a much better chance that you will find midgrade consumer car audio equipment. At the traditional flea market spot, you will only find low or very low grade equipment: a $30 (list price) cassette deck in fair condition for $25, a 8-track player that would match the one that you saw in the Salvation Army last week, and a pullout AM radio from a 1985 Citation.

CONCLUSION

By choosing a reputable dealer, you can easily buy car stereo equipment, possibly even for a good price. Or if you are prepared and search around long enough, you can find some good equipment at fantastic prices. Of course, there's an element of risk to all of this.

Now that the elements of researching and buying equipment are out of the way, it's time to start into some chapters on equipment. Chapter 3 is dedicated to head units.

HEAD UNITS & MORE

The heart of any sound system is the head unit, the source of audio for any auto audio installation. The head unit is a source of audio for the entire system (a receiver, cassette deck, compact disc player, or MiniDisc player) that also controls the audio with various settings (such as faders, noise-suppression circuits, etc.).

CHECKING THE EQUIPMENT

Before you buy anything, you need to look over your car to see what types of head units will fit properly. Some cars, such as the Chevy Cavalier, include some air-conditioning controls in the front plate of the head unit. These cars require special head units that are built specifically for particular cars, so your choice of replacement head units will be limited.

The standard size for aftermarket head units is DIN, although a few 1 1/2 DIN and double-DIN units are out there. Many cars use either stock DIN- or 1 1/2-DIN-sized units. If, for example, your car uses a 1 1/2-DIN unit and you buy a DIN-sized head unit, you will also need an adapter to mount the head unit. Real problems occur if you try to mount a taller head unit into a smaller hole. This often requires professional custom interior work to properly install and match the interior. Fortunately, about the only double-DIN head units out there are expensive combination cassette/CD players, loaded with extra features.

Mounting depth of the head unit could also be a problem when installing a head unit. The *mounting depth* is essentially the length of the head unit (front to back). Most vehicles use plenty of space for standard head units, but a few (such as the 1980s General Motors double-DIN units) have a really short mounting depth that will not allow for standard-sized units without some modification of the car.

Another concern is the wiring harness. The *wiring harness* is a plastic connector that has several multicolored wires sticking out of it. The problem with wiring harnesses is that the connectors from the car won't match those from the head unit. So, you'll need to buy a special wiring harness and splice the wires together. Any head unit that you purchase from Crutchfield comes with a free wiring harness to match the harness in your car, so that's one of the benefits of buying there. Otherwise, you'll have to buy an appropriate wiring harness from another dealer. With these adapters, you'll still need to splice wires, but it's much easier and better than cutting off the wiring harness and winging it. The Plymouth Voyager, for example, contains a wiring harness with unmarked wires. Essentially the only way to install a new head unit is to either get a wiring harness with the wires marked or to check with the manufacturer for a wiring diagram or schematic to determine which wires carry what voltage or signal.

Next, you'll need to connect the wires from the head unit's harness to the vehicle's harness. Some companies recommend using solder to make the connections, but I think that solder in the car is sloppy and inconvenient, and the connections are higher maintenance. The best choice is terminal blocks, which are available for only about $1.50 from Radio Shack. With terminal blocks, the wires can just be screwed in tight with a miniature electronics or computer screwdriver.

At this point, you should be about ready, so let's take a look at some head units. For more information on wiring and specific installations, see the end of this chapter, Chapter 8 (Wiring and Cabling) and Chapter 12 (Installation Techniques).

HEAD UNITS

The head unit is the standard source of music (and the buttons and knobs that control the music) in the car. Normally, the head unit is mounted in the dash board, although it can be mounted in other locations with lesser degrees of convenience and usefulness.

RECEIVERS

In the not-too-distant past, nearly every car had a receiver in it. No confusing buttons. No multifunction knobs to contend with. Just one knob for tuning and an on/off volume control. If you were a real fancy two-stepper, you had the boys in Michigan install a radio that could receive both AM *and* FM (Fig. 3-1).

Fig. 3-1 *No, it's not your dream head unit. It's an AM-only Crosley car radio from the 1930s or 1940s.*

Times have changed; these days, I don't know of any companies that sell aftermarket car receivers. For that matter, there wasn't much in the way of aftermarket car stereo sound systems before about 1975. A few cassette and 8-track players were available and that was about it (Fig. 3-2). So, over the years, although cassette players are very common in factory and after-market applications, all radio-only units are factory installed. There's got to be an exception to this rule somewhere, but I don't know of it. If anyone has an aftermarket car radio (only), I'd like to see it or pictures of it!

Fig. 3-2 *Maybe you've been inspired by "That '70s Show" or "Freaks and Geeks" to pick up an 8-track player, such as this Westminster deck. Some things are better left in the 1970s.*

RADIO AND AUDIO TECHNOLOGY

Although many people don't understand all of the basic theories behind AM (MW) and FM (VHF) broadcast radio, that's ok for these purposes. Under-standing the differences in modulation techniques between these two mediums won't do you a bit of good when tuning in a station on your car's head unit. As a result, the basic information about the standard broadcast bands is not included in this book. I suppose the same case could be made about CD, DVD audio, and MiniDisc technical information. However,

Head Unit Specifications
- ❏ *Power*
- ❏ *Sensitivity*
- ❏ *CD or cassette playback*
- ❏ *CD changer controls*
- ❏ *Security systems*
- ❏ *RCA preamp outputs*
- ❏ *Remote control*
- ❏ *DSP or equalizer effects*

almost no one these days buys a head unit for the quality of the radio, but these other mediums are instru-mental in making a purchasing decision. Also, technical broad-casting information is contained in dozens of books going back 40 years, but DVD audio and digital broadcast-ing are cutting-edge technologies and I currently know of no books that cover these subjects.

Although the broadcast basics are not covered within this book, some of the other, newer technologies and options are included. A million and one different head-unit features are currently available, in part because a few of the high-end components overlap their features into other types of audio components, such as signal processors, equalizers, and amplifiers. Most of these functions are not listed here because they are not common in head units and because they are covered in other areas of this book.

The most important specifications for the head unit are power, RCA outputs (if you plan to use amplifiers with the head unit), and CD changer controls. The only important receiver specification is FM mono sensitivity.

POWER

One very important feature of every head unit is the power that it is capable of putting out to the speakers. Some of this information is covered further in Chapter 5, which features dedicated power amplifiers. Head units vary greatly in the amount of power that they can deliver to a set of speakers.

Because power amplifiers can be built into smaller areas as high technology continues to miniaturize components, modern head units are capable of putting out far more power than was possible just a few years ago. If you listen to music at lower levels, you should have no problem finding a head unit that will satisfy your volume requirements, and you won't even need to buy an amplifier.

On the other hand, some head units are capable of only producing a line-level output, and others are rated at only about 4 W output (or less) for each of the four channels. To be very useful, these low-power units require a dedicated power amplifier. These decks are built around the theory that better equipment can be built if the unit is only focused on play back and that all power amplification circuitry is contained in a separate, shielded unit. Indeed, the preamp-out low-power units are all high-end models (Fig. 3-3)

Fig. 3-3 *Although it only offers preamp-level outputs, this Clarion DRX-9575Rz contains more features than you can shake a stick at, including TV tuner control, full-color display (with screensaver!), motorized faceplate, RDS, DSP, and much more.*

RCA OUTPUTS

Most head units have a set of RCA jacks on the back that output a low-level signal. These jacks are used so that the signal can be fed from the head unit to an external amplifier. A high-level signal (such as the wires that run from the head unit) will overload an amplifier and probably cause equipment damage. If you are going to run an amplifier, a set of RCA outputs is required (Fig. 3-4). Some head units even contain several pairs of RCA jacks.

FM MONO SENSITIVITY

Sensitivity is the capability of a head unit to pull in weak radio signals. If it has poor sensitivity, weaker stations will not be audible on this radio (strong signals will still be audible on a set with poor sensitivity). If it's important

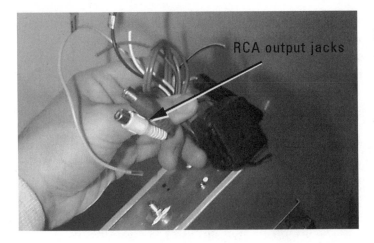

RCA output jacks

Fig. 3-4 *Most head units offer RCA line-level outputs, but in most cases via RCA jacks. This head unit has RCA output cables instead.*

for you to hear distant stations, then you want a head unit with good sensitivity. Sensitivity isn't usually included with the features in a car stereo catalog, but most manufacturers do list it in the in-depth equipment specifications. The values for sensitivity are in dBf, which might seem a bit complicated. The easy way to check sensitivity is: the lower the number, the better. You can expect a good receiver to have an FM mono sensitivity of about 8 or 9 dBf, although the figures often go as high as 13 dBf.

RDS

RDS (Radio Display System) is a system where radio data can be received on a standard radio (Fig. 3-5). Instead of merely transmitting music and talk, some FM radio stations broadcast data as well. Even though this signal

Fig. 3-5 *The RDS display at work in the Blaupunkt Reno.* Blaupunkt

is being transmitted along with the broadcast material, you can't hear it. Instead, this data can be received by your radio and the computer technology inside is capable of deciphering and displaying this information. The RDS function has some useful properties, but it's currently underutilized by most stations. The dozen or so stations using RDS that I've received have only transmitted their callsign continuously. Maybe it's because few head units have RDS. The various RDS modes, as configured by Denon, are as follows. The usefulness of these functions are based on whether or not the station actually transmits all of these different codes.

Program Service Name (PS) The callsign or slogan of the station that the radio is currently receiving is displayed.

Program Type (PT) The different radio formats are broken down into 31 different categories. The broadcasting station will broadcast its format, which is then displayed on the RDS head unit. This is useful because you can pick a format and the head unit will automatically tune a station that is broadcasting that particular format.

Alternative Frequencies (AF) If the station that you are listening becomes weak and the head unit is set in the AF mode, it will automatically tune the radio to another station with the same format that has a stronger signal.

Program Identification (PI) Members of various radio networks will have a PI code, which will identify them as being a part of that particular network. If you store several radio stations in the memories, you can use the PI mode to automatically tune to another station from the same network, if the one that you are listening to becomes weak and fades out.

Traffic Program Identification (TP) If the TP symbol appears on the head unit display, then that particular radio station also provides RDS traffic data.

Traffic Announcement Identification (TA) With the head unit set to the TA mode, the radio will automatically tune to a station that is about to broadcast traffic information. If you are listening to a cassette or a compact disc, the head unit will automatically preempt it to play the traffic update.

Clock Time (CT) Rather than set your own clock, the clock can be controlled by the time that is transmitted by the radio stations, for more precision.

RDS has continued as a feature on some higher-end head units and receivers, but it's not an especially widespread feature. All of the functions of RDS were highly touted by the companies pushing the systems about five years ago. And I liked what I saw of RDS. Although it is kind of nice to see the station callsigns come up when tuning in a broadcast, it was much handier to see other information, such as the song title and artist, scroll across the screen (as is the case with MiniDisc players).

LOUD FUNCTION

The loud function is fairly typical on home and mobile audio systems. The loud button functions as a bass and midrange booster; press it and the music punches through with a much thicker sound. Human hearing has a much higher threshold for audibility at the lower frequencies. As a result, if you normally listen to music at low volumes, it will sound "thinner" than if you rocked the car. To compensate, manufacturers added this circuit so that music could be faithfully reproduced, whether or not the volume was high or low. Because of its purpose, the loud function should not be used if the volume is already cranked up.

AUTOMATIC RADIO MUTING AND CONTROL CIRCUITS

Some companies have added various automatic radio muting and control circuits to alter the reception quality of broadcast stations. With some radios, if you tune off of a station or if two stations are overlapping each other, the radio will play static or interference. In other cases, head units have extra circuitry so that if a weak signal or no signal is detected, this circuitry will automatically reduce the volume of the radio so that you aren't blasted with static. A more basic feature is the automatic stereo/mono switch, which nearly all head units have. When a stereo signal is received that is above a certain level, it is put out in stereo; if it is below that predetermined level, it will be heard in mono so that the extra noise will not be heard. In another system, the higher frequencies are gradually rolled off as the radio signal strength decreases so that the interference will be less noticeable.

MUTE

Mute is a very handy do-nothing function. Press it and it automatically eliminates the audio from the head unit. Press it again and the everything returns immediately. Mute is convenient because you don't have to turn the volume down or turn off the power when you want to say something important to a passenger, need to stop at the bank drive-up window, or receive a cellular phone call.

DISPLAY

Although it isn't a function in and of itself, the *LCD (liquid crystal display)* was necessary for all of the high-end head units. The LCD can be built to display much more specific and complicated graphics than *LED (light-emitting diodes)*

displays could (although the newer LED displays have been developed to display fairly complex graphics). But still, for head units with more complex features, such as those with RDS capabilities, LCD or active-matrix (see the next paragraph) displays are often necessary. The problem with LCD displays is that anything to be displayed must be physically created to show up on the LCD. Also, the LCD displays are black on a yellowish backlighted background. A few years ago, the trends seemed to be running toward LCD displays, but now they've become much less popular among electronics manufacturers.

But even this is technology changing. Some of the computerized units are using miniature active-matrix displays, similar to those that are used in

laptop computers. Instead of the unchanging, monochrome screen of LCDs, the active-matrix displays can show assorted graphics in color. Some of the more-complex models even offer large (e.g., 5" x 8") video panels that can be used for playing back video or other computerized data (such as CD-ROMs, e-mail, etc.)

COMPACT DISC CHANGER CONTROLS

With compact disc changer controls, a cassette or CD head unit can control a compact disc changer that is mounted in the trunk. These can vary from manufacturer to manufacturer. So, before you buy a system of this type, be sure that the head unit and compact disc changer are compatible.

PRESET MEMORIES

One of the most convenient applications of computer technology that has been applied to radio is *preset memories*. In the analog era, car radios had several pushbuttons and, with some work, you could program each one to move the dial to a certain point whenever you pushed the button. Now, you can quickly program a number of different buttons quickly and each will immediately put you on the exact frequency (the old mechanical pushbuttons often varied in frequency each time you pressed the button).

SCANNING

With the *scanning* function, the head unit will tune through the radio band that you have selected and it will allow you to hear the different strong radio stations. Like many of the features here, the scanning function varies a bit among different manufacturers. In some cases, it finds a strong station, stops for a brief time to allow you to hear what's on, and then it moves on. When it hits the end of that particular broadcast band, it stops. In other cases, the scanning function will stop every time that it finds a strong station. It will only be reactivated if you press the button again.

REMOTE CONTROL

Some deluxe head units have their own remote control so that you can just press a button to change anything. Remote controls are most useful when a compact disc player is mounted in the trunk and you need to control it while driving. I used to be skeptical about remote controls until the steering-wheel-mounted remote controls were introduced (Fig. 3-6). These would make driving much safer while controlling the head unit. I guess that the only drawback is you might inadvertently change the instructions for the head unit while driving. Can you do hand-over-hand turning without switching from CD to radio and skipping tracks?

Fig. 3-6 *A thumb remote-control switch that can be mounted on the steering wheel for added convenience and safety.* Blaupunkt

PULLOUT HEAD UNITS AND DETACHABLE FRONT PANELS

As was described in Chapter 1, pullout head units and detachable front panels (also known as *faceplates*) are of great value if you live in an area that is high in crime. Pullout head units allow you to pull the head unit out by a handle and quickly disconnect it whenever you stop somewhere that you think it might be at risk (such as at work, a motel, an airport, etc.). This feature has been essentially dropped in favor of the more-convenient detachable front panel.

With the detachable front panel, all of the control circuitry is located in a single panel of the head unit. Just pop it off and you can stick it in your pocket and walk away. In the meantime, only a useless black box remains until you snap the front panel back on.

Recently, some head units have been developed with security codes that are inserted via a keycard, which operates much like a motel or apartment security card. These have the same disadvantages of the security code models that were mentioned in Chapter 1.

The most visually dramatic of security system is that which uses a rotatable front panel. When the car is off, just a blank panel is visible. Upon starting the car, the front panel of the head unit will automatically rotate and become visible. Who knows if this system actually deters thieves from stealing these head units, but they sure look cool!

FADER

The *fader* is an infinitely useful control that determines the amount of volume that is put out from the front or rear speakers. By pressing the button or turning the knob, you can focus more of the power to the front or rear. This is great if you want to play with the sound stage and fill the entire car with audio or if you have a sleeping child in the back seat and want to keep from waking him or her.

LOCAL/DX CONTROL

The *local/DX control* can attenuate the signals that are received by your head unit. If you want to hear local stations without the problem of overloading the front end of the radio and having some radio stations splatter across the band, then you should set the control to the local position for attenuation. If the signal is weak, then switch it to the DX position and the signals will no longer be attenuated. This control is particularly useful if you travel and are frequently in both cities and minor-market radio territories.

CASSETTE DECKS

Cassette players have been around for so long that most everyone seems to take them for granted, but they are still vastly popular. With the advent of the MiniDisc, CD-R, and DVD-R, they are increasingly becoming the forgotten workhorse. Also, few new developments in cassette technology have been occurring. Most of the technological advances in cassette technology over the past 20 years have been in areas that aren't always noticeable. Clear plastic cassette shells are the most noticeable advancement of the lot. Most of the breakthroughs have involved adding more and denser ferromagnetic coatings, using coatings that are more permanent on the tape, developing tape that is more resistant to stretching, and creating plastics that do not shrink, warp, or melt in the presence of extreme heat, as would be found in a car's environment.

This section starts with a few basics about cassettes, how they are manufactured, and how they differ in quality. The cassette function of head units vary in quality more than probably any other aspect of car stereo equipment, so it's interesting and helpful to learn a little about the medium.

When choosing a cassette deck, the most important specifications are signal-to-noise (S/N) ratio, frequency range, and wow and flutter.

BASICS

The cassette is a miniature reel-to-reel tape that has been encased in a plastic shell to reduce the messiness and the potential for damage to the

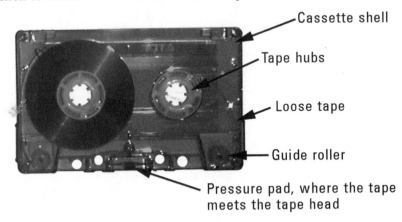

Fig. 3-7 *A standard cassette that has been opened to show its internal components.*

recording's sound quality (Fig. 3-7). This case contains two hubs, which are used as either takeup or supply reels, depending on which side the cassette is turned to. The cassette also contains a pressure pad where the tape contacts the heads of the player, and two guide rollers, which allow the tape to smoothly roll through the shell without wearing excessively. All of these parts are necessary for a cassette. However, one major record company produced cassettes for a while that were so cheaply made that no guide rollers were included. Instead of having the tape roll around the guide rollers, it rubbed its way around two plastic posts. Because of the poor design, the cassette squeaked as it played and started to wear out quickly. Upon discovering this, I cracked the cassette open and placed the reels in a much more solid, better-quality cassette shell.

Cassettes are reels of plastic film that have been coated with ferromagnetic material. Technically, this material isn't all ferromagnetic (i.e., made with any compound or mixture of iron); some is made with chromium dioxide, other types are coated with a mixture of iron oxide and chromium dioxide, and still others use other elemental compounds, such as cobalt. This material can be magnetized or demagnetized with ease. The particles of the recording material are assembled in a parti[...] on a blank tape. However, when you record something, these [...] magnetized so that they face in different directions, according t[...] sounds that are being [...]rded. When this cassette recording is played back, the tape passes over the magnetic heads of the deck. The particular formation of the tape induces a small signal voltage in the heads, according to the patterns of the magnetized tape particles. These signals are then amplified and later turned back into audio by the speakers.

Important Cassette Specifications
- ❏ *Signal-to-noise ratio*
- ❏ *Frequency response*
- ❏ *Wow and flutter*

Features
- ❏ *Autoreverse*
- ❏ *Noise reduction*
- ❏ *Power load/eject*
- ❏ *CrO_2/metal bias selection*

Cassettes were a real challenge for the manufacturers because the tape was reduced to about half of the width that was used for reel-to-reel tape. As a result, they had to design much more efficient recording coatings. I even saw a cassette prototype from the 1960s that was huge—approximately the size of a videotape! For some time, the cassette was snubbed by audio experimenters because the medium simply could not compete with the record and reel-to-reel formats. By the late 1970s and early 1980s, high-

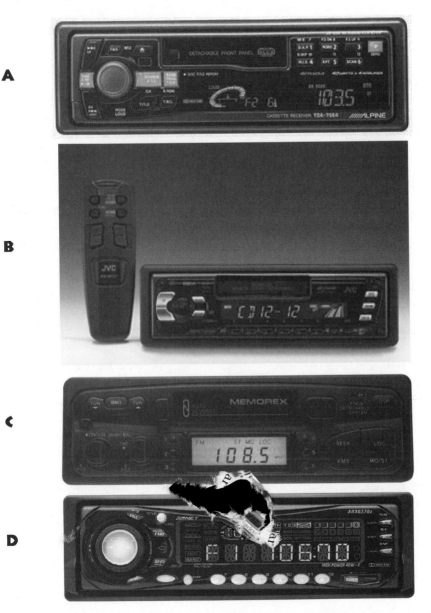

Fig. 3-8 *Several different cassette head units, with a wide variety of different features and styles.* 3-8A Alpine, 3-8B JVC, 3-8C Memorex, 3-8D Clarion.

quality cassette technology was openly available, and that helped trigger the boom in car stereo systems (Fig. 3-8).

SIGNAL-TO-NOISE RATIO

Signal-to-noise ratio is the ratio of the sound of the cassette recording to the volume of hiss that is present upon playback. A high level of hiss is very distracting when listening to an audio system, so signal-to-noise ratio is one of the very most important figures when choosing a cassette head unit. The ratio is listed in dB and it should be as high as possible. Most head units have S/N ratios between 50 and 70 dB, but 60 dB is a typical minimum if you're serious about listening to cassettes. The less-expensive head units from companies with good reputations typically have S/N ratios less than 60 dB, so it's very important to look through the specifica-tions to be sure that you're not getting a unit that you'll be unsatisfied with.

COMPARISON: RELATIONSHIP OF S/N RATIO TO COST	
S/N ratio (in dB)	Price range
Above 65	$140-400
60-65	$120-400
55-59	$90-150
0-54	$30-140

The table shows an informal survey of the relationship between price and S/N ratio. It only covers approximately 50 of the more-common models at "typical" sales price, so it's not scientific, but it should give you a good idea of how S/N affects cost. The prices overlap considerably because some lesser-quality head units are loaded with fancy extra features and other units take a more Spartan approach, by focusing all of the expense on quality and forgetting about features.

FREQUENCY RESPONSE

In this case, the *frequency response* refers to the audio frequencies of the cassette's playback (it could also refer to the frequency response of the FM radio portion of the head unit). The maximum human hearing range is approximately 30 to 20,000 Hz (20 kHz). As described in the hearing-loss section in the front matter, the high-frequency range of most people's hearing (especially for men) degrades significantly by middle age. So, the highest one or two thousand Hz of response aren't nearly as important when choosing a head unit. The bottom range of the response (30 kHz) is fairly easy to reach, so most head units go down to 30 kHz (although a few start as high as 50 kHz). Most important is the high-frequency response. A minimum high-frequency response for regular listeners would be about 16 kHz maximum. The best decks go as high as 20 kHz, and head units in the $50 to $120 range often have a response peak between 14 and 16 kHz. As with S/N ratio, it's important to look through the specifications for this rating.

WOW AND FLUTTER

Wow and flutter sound more like cartoon characters than audio specifications. These two adjectives are used together to describe any variations in tape speed that can distort the audio. Although wow and flutter is very important to the overall sound quality of a cassette head unit, it's not a primary specification to research because most any head unit with good S/N ratio and frequency response will also have a very low wow and flutter figure. A good figure to shoot for is about 0.1%. Some head units go down to about 0.06% and others are as high as about 0.15%.

FEATURES

Like any audio component, the cassette head unit can contain a number of different helpful functions that will influence what you will purchase.

Noise suppression The most common noise-suppression techniques for recording are Dolby B and C, both of which were developed by Dolby Laboratories. The two Dolby systems are intended to remove the tape hiss that is evident when playing tapes, especially during quiet passages when high-frequency instruments are dominant. This tape hiss is picked up form various sources, but it primarily emanates from the tape head. Whenever Dolby noise reduction is used on a particular recording, the system suppresses some of the frequencies. When the correct Dolby setting is pressed during playback, the frequencies that were suppressed during the recording are now boosted by the same amount as they were suppressed. By using this method, hiss can effectively be reduced. I've never really liked using noise reduction, but then again, I seem to be alone on this issue.

Dolby C is an improved version of Dolby B, but Dolby B is more common than Dolby C. Both are frequently used on the same units, however. If an album was recorded in Dolby B, it will sound better (or at least be more accurately represented) if it is played back in Dolby B, even if Dolby C is a feature of the head unit you're listening with.

Autoreverse One of the first extra features to add to a cassette deck is autoreverse. *Autoreverse* is the function by which a cassette player will automatically move the heads over and begin playing the other side of a tape once it has hit the end. With this feature, a tape can play continuously for as long as you can stand it.

Blank skip With this function set, the tape player will automatically fast forward (or at a speed that is slower than fast forward, but faster than play) the tape when no audio is sensed. When audio is sensed on the tape, the player will stop at that point and resume playing. This feature is particularly useful if you have a narcoleptic friend who sends you audio letters.

Music sensor With this function set, you can press fast forward and the player will fast forward the tape until the song ends. Then, it will detect that the tape is blank and it will stop and resume playing. Likewise, the music sensor can also be used when rewinding. It will rewind until it detects the blank space at the beginning of the song. Then, it will stop and resume playing.

Tuner call With tuner call, the radio will automatically begin playing on the radio frequency that you were last tuned to . This feature is handy if you enjoy listening to cassettes and flipping back to hear what is on the radio. However, the one time that I had a ground-loop problem on the radio, the tuner call was terribly annoying. Anytime I popped the tape out, I was tormented with a loud whoomp-whoomp sound.

Automatic bias selector The setting of the playback mode, which is determined by the type of coating on the tape, on the head unit can negatively affect the sound of a cassette if the it doesn't match the bias of the tape. The automatic bias control on a head unit senses what bias is being used on a given cassette and it automatically sets the proper playback mode.

Power load/power eject *Power load* and *power eject* both refer to the mechanism that installs or ejects a cassette into or from a head unit. In a unit with power load/power eject, you can enter the tape to a certain point, then the power mechanism will take over and slowly pull the tape into position. When you press eject, the motor will gradually push the cassette back out. With a standard unit, you must push the tape until it physically loads into place. When you want to remove the tape, you must press the eject button to physically eject the cassette from the inside.

COMPACT DISC PLAYERS

Now that compact discs have been in common use for about a decade or so, the novelty is beginning to wear off and they are finally becoming a standard audio medium. No longer do you hear stories about how people have spent a few months of wages to gradually purchase 100 compact discs, only to lose them all to a collection agency after the frivolous spending spree. Now that I've seen new discs commonly available for $4 apiece and cutouts for $1, I know that the compact disc is truly the music medium for the 1990s, although it will be interesting to see how long it will hold its spot in the Twenty-first century.

As you have probably expected, it's now time to cover some information about how compact disc players operate.

BASICS

The compact disc is simply a thin disc of aluminum that is encased in a plastic laminate to protect the recording. The music that is to be recorded onto compact discs must be in a digital medium; that is, it must be converted into a massive amount of 0s and 1s. When the disc is recorded, a multitude of error-correcting data and system information (track information, markers, etc.) are also added to the disc along with the music. All of this data must be downloaded, so the aluminum disc is etched with minuscule pits. The pits and the unpitted areas translate as data that represents the 1s and 0s.

One of the key components in a compact disc player is the laser optical assembly. When a compact disc is running inside of the head unit or changer, a low-powered laser is firing straight up through the player and at the tracks of the disc. The unpitted areas of the disc reflect the light back, but the pitted areas reflect almost nothing back. The end result is a tremendously fast flickering of light—coded messages sent in the same manner, but *much* faster than the boys could on "Hogan's Heroes." These coded reflections are received by a photodetector, which changes the light flickers into electrical impulses. These binary electrical impulses are then converted into analog impulses. Then, they are amplified and converted from electrical analog impulses into sound by the speakers.

This information about how a compact disc player operates is tremendously simplified. The analog-to-digital and digital-to-analog processes are extremely complicated, especially when you consider that such things as coding and sampling must also be configured into the system. *Sampling* is the process by which the compact disc player plays an analog sound, then checks the digital source, then plays another sound. This cycling occurs 44,100 times per second (44.1 kHz), although many players now sample several times more than that per second to ensure that the information being received/played is accurate and not error-ridden. Sampling at harmonic frequencies (as just described) is known as *oversampling*. Many of the high-cost compact disc players sample up to 8x the standard sample frequency. At this point, oversampling starts to become overkill and the law of diminishing returns kicks in.

Another factor, *relative volume*, also needs to be considered. Every audio waveform has a length (the frequency of the sound), which determines the pitch of the sound and a height (the amplitude of the sound), which determines the volume of the sound. In order for the compact disc player to accurately reproduce music and not wind up with all of the frequencies reproduced at the same volume, the samples are quantized to a 16-bit number between 0 and 65,535. The end result is that every tiny piece of audio that is reproduced by the compact disc can be reproduced at any one of 65,536 different volume levels!

These codes that determine various aspects of the compact disc's sound and technical operations all require a vast amount of information. A full compact disc (approximately 74 minutes) requires in the neighborhood of 34,000,000 bits of information to produce. If this information was all held on a standard computer floppy disk, the selection would have to be placed on 48 5.25-in. (13.34 cm) discs! The alternative to this is to determine some sort of compression code, which is how DVDs and MiniDiscs can be digital and hold as much music as they do.

COMPACT DISC CHANGERS VERSUS HEAD UNITS

Compact disc changers a re strange units that have no real parallels to the home audio market, unlike most other aspects of auto audio (Fig. 3-9). For the most part, the compact disc changer is a black box that plays a number of discs from remote locations within the car. The changers have no real extras other than the number of discs that can be contained within, whether the changer can be controlled via remote control (Fig. 3-10), and if it has an FM transmitter so that you can listen to the discs on your head unit without any hardwired connections.

On the other hand, the compact disc unit is an actual head unit; it fits in the dash (probably in a DIN-sized hole), chances are that it has a broadcast band radio built in, the outputs are amplified well above line levels, and it includes many other audio controls (such as faders, repeat tracks, play, pause, stop, etc.). In all, the compact disc head unit is a completely working unit and the changer is a drone that requires a head unit to feed into.

Technology has a way of blurring the lines between different products. A few years ago, for example, there were fax machines and copiers. Now, most

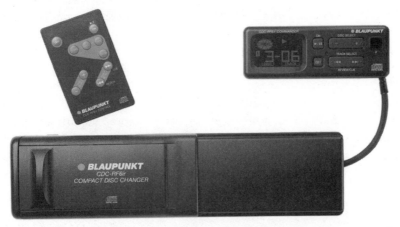

Fig. 3-9 *A compact disc changer, with hardwired and wireless controls.* Blaupunkt

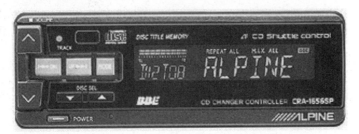

Fig. 3-10 *A closer view of a controller for a CD changer.* Alpine

Fig. 3-11 *Who says that all compact disc changers must be plain boxes that get stuck in the trunk? An in-dash changer/head unit.* Alpine

fax machines can make copies and the big choice is plain paper or thermal rolls. The same types of lines have been blurred between CD head units and changers. Alpine now offers the MDA-W890 in-dash CD changer (Fig. 3-

11), which is a standard double-DIN head unit that offers multi-disc playback. The convenience advantage of having an in-dash CD changer is obvious. However, you might rather plug a plainer head unit into the dash and keep the CD changer in the trunk.

In choosing between a compact disc changer and a head unit, the decision will be based in part on how much money you plan to spend and on whether or not you want to be able to play both cassettes and discs. If you have the money, then you should go with a cassette head unit that sports CD changer controls and a compact disc changer. If not, the best choice

Fig. 3-12 *A compact disc changer, with hardwired and wireless controls.* 3-12A Kenwood, 3-12B Blaupunkt, 3-12C Clarion.

would be a cassette head unit and a portable compact disc player (which functions through the cassette unit via a cassette-shaped adapter). The cost of a compact disc head unit is presently at least $100 higher (the present approximate cost of a portable disc player) than a cassette head unit of comparable quality (Fig. 3-12).

SPECIFICATIONS

Unlike cassette player performance, CD deck performance is a little harder to quantify. Instead of document able performance statistics, CD performance is often based more on such things as shock absorption and the use of multiple D/A converters to reduce decoding errors. These are difficult to quantify because the equipment might perform very well under idea conditions, but vary, depending on the environment (vibration, etc.). The only measurement used to convey CD playback performance is signal-to-noise ratio, and nearly all CD players are in the excellent range of 80 to 100 dB.

Here's an example of how misleading the S/N ratio is with CD players. Currently, one model is selling for approximately $120 and another is selling for about $600, but both have a signal-to-noise ratio of 100 dB, and plenty of other units that range in price between these two have the same or lower S/N ratios. For the most part, the S/N ratio, although very important for cassette head units, will probably make very little impact on your decision to choose a CD head unit.

FEATURES

Because of the more accurate music reproduction from compact discs, fewer extra features are necessary in order for them to play well. Most of the features are computerized and relate to the manner in which the discs are sorted and searched.

Number of discs The parallel to the cassette players' autoreverse function for CD players in car and home audio, including compact disc changers, is the number of discs that can be stored in a unit. Some changers can handle as many as 18 discs at the same time. Even in-dash compact disc head units are now able to handle up to three discs at a time. The prime consideration here is the length of time that you can listen to the music without having to pop out the discs. With the three-disc changers, you could potentially listen to continuous music for 2.5 hours.

Disc access time Disc access time refers to the amount of time between a disc being inserted or changed and when it begins to play. This figure seems to vary quite a bit in meaning from manufacturer to manufacturer. Even so, the times would only vary by a few seconds. If you have brag to your friends about how your changer can access discs 1.26 seconds faster than theirs, then you really need to get out more often.

Random access When you pile a boatload of discs into a changer, it is interesting to hit the random access function. This feature will pick out tracks at random from any of the discs. Random access isn't quite as exciting when used on a one-disc head unit, but perhaps it will spice up an old favorite a bit.

Intro scan The intro scan executes similarly to the radio scanning features. Press the button and it plays the first few seconds of each song. After it moves through the entire disc, you can choose what songs you want to listen to. Or you might just choose another disc.

Repeat The repeat function allows you to repeat the track or the compact disc that you just listened to.

Changer remote control Some compact disc changers have their own remote controls so that it is possible to have some of the useful programmable features that are otherwise only found on head units. Most of the features that are on the remote controls relate to the playback of the discs, but this is still a handy feature.

MiniDisc PLAYERS

MiniDiscs are the DATs of the 1990s. Just like the DAT tape format, MiniDiscs are a digital format that has survived for years in obscurity, used only by music/radio professionals and audio hobbyists. In the mid-1990s, it appeared that the MiniDiscs might be the recording format of the future, replacing cassettes once and for all, after more than 30 years of dominance. But, the high cost, lack of compatibility, lack of publicity, and unavailability seems to have driven the MiniDisc format away from the people and into relative obscurity.

The MiniDisc is somewhat like a quarter-scale CD locked inside of a floppy disc case. In this sense, the relationship between the compact disc and the MiniDisc is the same as that between open reel tape player and the cassette tape player. The protective cartridge is an important advancement. This means that an entire commercial recording from an artist will fit onto a 2.7- x 2.7-in. (6.86- x 6.86-cm) disc. Unlike the CD (or the record, which the CD replaced), the disc doesn't need to be pulled out of its case and placed into the playing device; just pop the whole package into the player and that's it .

But the smaller size and the computer disc-style case are only the positive physical differences between the MiniDisc and the compact disc. The major difference is that the MiniDiscs can be recorded upon, over and over again. Sony's laboratories say that a MiniDisc can be recorded on over one million times and not show any degradation in quality. This reliability is based on the fact that the disc is digitally encoded and optically read by a laser. No parts or heads wear against the recorded material and eventually ruin the surface. In fact, MiniDiscs are claimed to be virtually indestructible. The manufacturer says that only a combination of laser and an electromagnetic signals can erase the tracks, so you won't have to worry about the discs being erased while sitting in the sun or on top of a set of speakers. However, you should not test the limits of the MiniDiscs and feed them to your dog, just because the manufacturer says they are virtually indestructible. For that matter, you might want to be as careful with MiniDiscs in the car as you would cassettes; although the material won't erase, the disc's cartridge could curl up in a back window sauna.

For years, some audio manufacturers worked toward developing recordable compact discs. However, the technology just wasn't available at a reasonable price for consumers. The result would have been something like cutting your own master record for any songs that you wanted to record off of the radio. MiniDiscs fill that technological void.

MiniDiscs are available with two different types of disc materials. Commercially produced albums are recorded on what look like miniature CDs inside of a standard MiniDisc plastic case. Prerecorded commercial albums, which use this laser disc material, cannot be recorded on. If you want to record on a MiniDisc, you will need to purchase blank discs. I am curious as to why the manufacturers are using two different disc materials. If the recordable MiniDiscs are virtually unerasable, then why are commercial releases recorded on compact disc material? It shouldn't have anything to do with controlling potential album bootleggers because a compact disc is easy to copy. It does raise questions, at least in my mind, about the reliability and the potential of accidental erasure of MiniDiscs. In a few years, the buying public will find out just how well the recordable MiniDiscs retain their imprinting over time.

One problem with the MiniDisc format is the flipside of the question "how do they fit all of that music onto such a small space?" In order to fit the recording time on, they were forced to compress all of that digital information into a 2 1/2-in. (6.35-cm) diameter disc. Using a special digital compression technique, the system purges the audio frequencies that are above and below the human hearing range. By reducing the overall width of the audio, less space is required to copy that information, and more music can be recorded in the same amount of space. In the case of the MiniDisc, more information can be recorded in much *less* space.

There is a problem, though, with removing those frequencies when the disc is recorded. Considering that the frequencies are out of the human hearing range, theoretically, there should be no decline in audio quality. But this is the real world, and what might appear to work on paper sometimes doesn't in real life. The general consensus has been that MiniDiscs don't sound quite as good as compact discs, but sound much better than the average cassette. That being the case, an audiophile would be bothered by this slight difference in audio quality, but you might not even notice.

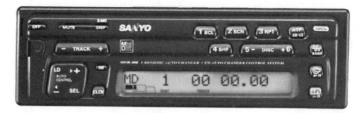

Fig. 3-13 *One of the early generations of MiniDisc head units.* Sanyo

One of the positive aspects of the digital technology is that the MiniDisc player will mark the different tracks that you have recorded. Then, you can immediately listen to any track on the disc, just as you would with a compact disc player (Fig. 3-13).

This same technology produces some amazing results when coupled with the flexibility of digital disc recording. Tracks from any part of the MiniDisc can be erased; then any tracks that follow the one that was deleted move up in order. For example, maybe you recorded 32 songs on a MiniDisc and you decide that you don't like the nose flute song that was recorded on track 8. You can delete track 8 and track 9 becomes track 8, track 10 becomes track 9, etc. If the nose flute song (formerly track 8) lasted 2:33, then you have an extra 2:33 of space left of the disc. Maybe you then want to round off the disc with a wacky song by The Dickies, just to scare your friends. You have 2:33, plus whatever space was left over on the disc from before. This new song becomes track 32. This feature would be very handy for someone who records cassettes or records, then decides to eliminate different songs from the disc recording .

Along with these wonders of digital recording come other little touches that add to the convenience of MiniDiscs. For example, the fixed-position (car and home decks) feature an electronic display that shows the song title and track number of the song that is being played. This information is all stored in a disc table of contents, along with the title of the disc. The recording MiniDisc decks have a keyboard so that you can enter pertinent disc and song information onto the disc that you are recording. With this system, you could record your copy of the latest album by One:21 onto a MiniDisc, type all of the song titles, and they will appear on the readout of the deck every time that you listen to the album. This information can be changed, so if you misspelled a song title or decide to eliminate a song, all of the information will update correctly.

Obviously, the MiniDisc has some real advantages, especially when used for mobile or portable applications. For people with large collections of compact discs or even records, it would be much less risky to record these albums onto MiniDiscs and keep these copies in the car. That way, even if your car was robbed or if it fell into some other disastrous situation, your masters of the music would still be safe at home. Also, the MiniDiscs are smaller and much more convenient to pop in and out of a deck than a compact disc.

Despite the generally glowing reports of MiniDisc performance, the price and compatibility problems are severe. If you already have a home MiniDisc player and a decent-sized MiniDisc collection, then you would probably be quite happy with a MiniDisc head unit. However, if you don't, a CD head unit would be a much better choice. The performance would be better and the money that you could save on a CD head unit could be spent on a CD-R drive so that you could record your own CDs and use copies (instead of the original CDs) in your car. Increasing pressure from DVD audio should also have a negative impact on MiniDisc sales. Overall, it seems unlikely that the MiniDisc will last in the car stereo market for too many more years.

MP3 Audio

MP3 is a contracted form of the term *MPEG-3*, which, further, is an abbreviation for *Motion Pictures Expert Group Audio Layer 3*. MP3 audio is important because it uses compression algorithms to condense audio into a much smaller stored area. For example, a CD can hold approximately 640 megabytes of data, which translates to approximately 74 minutes of "CD-quality" audio (i.e., 44.1 MHz sampling, stereo, 16 bits). However, hours of songs stored in the MP3 format can be stored on a single CD, and the quality is generally considered to be "near CD."

In other words, although most audiophiles probably won't like it, the majority of people will appreciate its convenience.

Specifically, several companies are bridging the gap between computers and portable audio with small, handheld MP3 players. These little pager-sized boxes are intended only to download and playback MP3 files. It's interesting that a genre of hardware would be developed specifically for a type of software (instead of vice versa), but that's exactly what happened.

The first generation of MP3 players are long in innovation, but a bit shorter in practical applications. The benefits of MP3 are obvious; the format compresses audio to fit into a much smaller data space. Because MP3 files are so much smaller than the WAV files of the past, the MP3 files are being offered for free downloading on different Webpages. These free songs, in turn, make downloading and playing back MP3s desirable. So, after you download a few hours of files, you might want a dedicated MP3 player, rather than being limited to only listening to the songs at your computer or than wasting the time and effort recording all of the files to cassette.

With a portable MP3 player, you can feed audio to your car system in much the same way that you pass audio from a portable CD player: either by passing the audio through cables to the inputs of the head unit or by rebroadcasting it from an FM transmitter to the receiver in your head unit.

The problem is that the downloadable data is all stored in RAM flash cards, which are currently still fairly expensive. So, most MP3 players only have 32 or 64 megs of flash memory, which means about 30 to 60

Fig. 3-14 *One of the new generations of MP3 players, the i2go player. Like most of the portable MP3 players, the i2go is about the size of a pager.* i2go

minutes of available audio. This isn't bad for going on a jog ("Hey, no skipping CDs!"), but such a limited space for music won't do much to pep up your morning commutes. You can bet that it won't be too long until 128- and 256-meg units will be available sometime in the semi-near future for a reasonable price (Fig. 3-14), but for the time being, there are handier ways to record and playback your own music for the car.

COMPUTERIZED AND NAVIGATIONAL HEAD UNITS

It's funny how predictions for the future turn out. The February 1967 issue of *True* magazine featured what the year 2000 would be like. Among other things, it stated that only the richest people will be able to afford to eat anything but algae derivatives and that many business people will commute to work to their distant suburban homes in helicopters. Utterly bizarre predictions. But, despite their lofty ideals, few in 1967 would have predicted that, by the beginning of the Twenty-first century, millions of Americans would own computers more sophisticated than the supercomputers of their time. And who would have guessed that many of these computers would fit into a small bag or briefcase?

By now, most of the head units are computerized to some extent. For

Fig. 3-15 *One of the first truly computerized head units, the AutoPC (top). Shown below is its accompanying CD changer.* Clarion

example, all units use digital PLL tuning, most have scan radio functions, all CD players have D/A converters, and many actually process data via RDS controls. But these are computer-type chip functions, not the main functions of true computers.

Enter the Clarion AutoPC (Fig. 3-15), a full-out computer and cellular communications system integrated into a CD head unit. Considering that particular functions are generally developed and gradually added to electronics components, it's amazing that so many new features were integrated into one head unit. The AutoPC is currently an anomaly in the car stereo world, but you can bet that many of its features will be gradually incorporated into "standard" head units, the same way that digital clocks are integrated into current head units. Although I wouldn't normally list all of the features on a particular head unit, in this case, I think that it represents (to some extent) head units of the future. It will be interesting to see which of these features are well accepted into the car stereo marketplace and which ones fail and quickly face extinction.

COMMUNICATIONS VOICE ACTIVATION

Ever wanted to talk to your car stereo? At times, I've said some nasty things to mine, but it never did anything. The AutoPC voice-recognition circuitry that enables it to "understand" and react to 200 different word commands.

cell-phone integration If you have a cell phone, it can be plugged into the cell-phone interface of the AutoPC. Then you can tell it to call a particular number and you can talk on the telephone hands-free. I hope that loads of people buy this head unit so that they'll stop swerving around in front of me while trying to drive and hold a phone!

Fig. 3-16 *Receive e-mail in your car with the AutoPC and the Cue wireless receiver.* Clarion

e-mail access Another amazing feature, possible only by signing up with CUE wireless services and purchasing one of their receivers, allows you to give voice commands for the AutoPC to check your e-mail. And it will. It can also receive pager alerts (Fig. 3-16)

address book Through this feature, you can store important e-mail addresses and telephone numbers in the AutoPC.

NAVIGATION

GPS (Global Positioning System) An optional GPS plug-in module allows complete GPS capabilities. The GPS information will show you your exact location. Also, the GPS information can be input to the navigational section of the AutoPC. Finally, the GPS data is also used by the optional ASSIST system so that your position can be located in case of an emergency.

Points of Interest Just tell the AutoPC where you want to go and, if the place is listed in the POI database, it will list the address of the place on the front-panel display.

Extended Data CDs An optional CD-ROM is compatible with the AutoPC, supplying map information of most urban roads and highway systems.

INFORMATION DATA INPUT

The AutoPC has yet another option, a 16-MB flash card so that you can transfer address or other information from your laptop computer.

Vehicle diagnostics The AutoPC is compatible with Vetronix CarPort modules. One of these modules connects the AutoPC to the vehicle's on-board computers (assuming that the car is new enough to be computer controlled) to monitor and control different elements, such as speed, engine RPM, and diagnostics. Informational updates If you subscribe to CUE Informational Services for e-mail and pager alerts, the AutoPC will also be capable of supplying traffic reports, news, sports, and stock market briefs.

MUSIC

* CD/CD-ROM player
* 35 W per channel
* Four line-level outputs
* AM/FM receiver
* Optional CD changer module

OTHER COMPUTERIZED HEAD UNITS

As you might expect, the AutoPC is not the only computerized head unit in the sea. In general, the other systems are a little more underground in nature, in the sense that they are produced by smaller companies and probably won't show up at your local car stereo shop or Circuit City store.

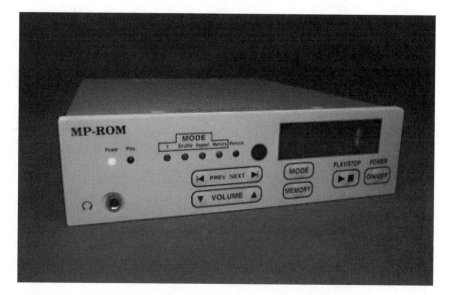

Fig. 3-17 *The future of car audio? The disc-based MP-ROM player, which can play back CDs, DVDs, and more.* MP-ROM

It's interesting that some diehard experimenters have been building their own car MP3 systems. The main problem with the handheld MP3 systems is that they use flash RAM to record the data. Either much more RAM is necessary or the unit needs a traditional storage device. Some experimenters have built their own MP3 systems using either hard drives or CD-ROM drives for storage and playback (Fig. 3-17). In one system, to add new music, the owner opens the case, pulls out the hard drive, takes it inside, plugs it into another computer, and copies over new MP3 files. Considering the size of hard drives these days, you could load literally days' worth of music onto a hard drive. These systems are often essentially just a computer in the trunk, rather than being a little audio player. (Fig. 3-18). Some of these audio hackers even go so far as to write their own software and operate the systems from the dash with either a touch screen or a simple button menu pad.

Fig. 3-18
The rough look: A hacked-together in-car computerized MP3 audio system in its early stages. Ryan Veety

The CD-ROM systems might just seem like a standard head unit, only hacked together to make an ugly, inconvenient CD player, but they, too, have some huge advantages. The biggest advantage is that, with the proper software, they will play back MP3 files. A CD can hold ten times as much information as one of those 64-meg flash RAM cards. Again, assuming that 64 megs equals about an hour, a CD could hold approximately 10 hours of MP3 files, which would be terrific for even long trips in the car.

One of the worst problems for these systems is that most experimenters are using power inverters to operate the drives and computer equipment. Few power inverters (only the most expensive) produce true sinosuodial DC waveforms, and the resulting audio has a hum. Some people experiment with noise filters, but it would be better to run use a DC-fed system and take clean power signals from the start. An easy way to do this is by using components from a laptop computer, which use DC power. The power would still have to be converted from approximately 12 volts to whatever voltage the laptop requires, but at least the noise would be eliminated.

These systems are often quite crude, but I think that they might just be the future of head units. Even if the MP3 format gives away to a system that's more convenient or has a higher compression rate, these systems will still have made a great impact on auto audio world.

DVD HEAD UNITS

Computerized head units might seem like a product dropped off by a futuristic race of people, but DVD head units are the next real wave of car audio. Most people already know DVD and only perceive it as a video-only format. DVD video players have been on the market for a few years now and are now in well past the first generation. Many video stores are even offering DVD rentals, a true sign that the format is becoming accepted by the masses.

The DVD medium is so popular because loads of information (4.7 GB) can be stored on a single disc of the same size as a CD (which can hold only 640 MB). As the DVD video format was being developed, a DVD audio format was created as well. DVD audio discs could have been sold concurrently with DVD videos and players, except for one glitch: the big problem with implementing DVD audio discs was legal, not technological. The major record labels were unsure of the effect that DVD would have on music sales. For example, if the DVDs would be recorded with the same bit/sampling rates as CDs, a DVD could store 7.34 times (approximately nine hours worth!) more audio than a standard CD. Thus, if the typical album contains 40 minutes of material, more than 13 standard albums could fit onto a single DVD. And if the entire collection of Led Zeppelin albums can fit onto one DVD, what would that do to their total cost? Undoubtedly, it would drop considerably because few people would be willing to pay more than $100 for a single DVD, even if total output would cost even more in CD form. And if this is bad news for the recording industry, then recordable DVDs could have a tremendously negative impact.

COMPATIBILITY

The beauty of DVD is that it uses the same hardware as the CD. It uses the pulse-code modulation method of pits and lands that are reflected back by a laser. As a result, DVD video players are already compatible with audio CDs. This alone has undoubtedly added to their popularity. Why not buy a $299 home DVD player or a $190 DVD computer disk drive if it is capable of playing back DVDs and CDs (and other formats, in the case of the disk drive). So, even if DVDs totally replace CDs, you'll still be able to play back your old CDs in a DVD player.

DATA DENSITY

Many audiophiles have complained that CDs sound harsh or sterile, compared to good-quality records. Whether it's my ears or my home system, I can't perceive the diminished quality of CDs. Regardless, the main advantage of DVD is its data density. When audio DVDs hit the market, they should please the audiophiles because the DVD audio standards are generally much denser than those offered from CDs. For example, a CD is recorded with 16-bit audio at a sampling rate of 44.1 kHz. The maximum DVD setting is 24-bit audio at a whopping sampling rate of 192 kHz. At these settings, literally many more times information is used to produce the same length of music, so the sound reproduction should be much more lifelike from DVDs at this setting than CDs.

Another difference is that the frequency range of audio DVDs is greatly expanded. The frequency range of CDs is 5 to 20 kHz, but the range of DVDs is from DC to 96 kHz. These extra frequencies are outside of the range of human hearing, but although they are inaudible, many people believe that they affect the sound of other audible frequencies. This aspect of DVD audio sound should also impress the audiophiles.

EXTRA FEATURES

Because DVDs can hold much more data than CDs, that data can be used for other features, such as adding video, including text, or using the home theater six-channel standard. Together with the better quality and compatibility of DVDs, the extra features of DVDs make them the ultimate format.

Video Of course, DVD is best known for video, so it's no surprise that DVD audio is capable of video playback or additions. So, an album could include a video track for some songs or even still-frame images.

Text In addition to video, The DVD audio discs can display text, such as track listings, band information, lyrics, liner notes, and even links to Web sites.

Multiple channels Stereo was the hot stuff in the 1950s and 1960s. In the early 1970s, quad sound systems were experimented with and were regularly available for a few years. As the name suggests, the quad system featured four independent music channels (two front and two back). I don't really know why quad failed; it seemed like a useful format and old quad 8-tracks and records are still in demand. For about

25 years now, the music has remained stuck in the old stereo mode, despite the popularity and innovations of such quad albums as Pink Floyd's "Dark Side of the Moon" and Mike Oldfield's "Tubular Bells," which exploited the directional aspects of quad (sounds traveling from front to back, side to side, and diagonally).

Some of the DVD audio specifications allow for six channels, rather than just two. This follows the so-called 5 + 1 home theater channel specification (quad audio channels, plus a front center channel and one subwoofer channel.

AVAILABLE HEAD UNITS

At the present, the only available DVD head unit is the Panasonic CX-DV1500, which is a DVD-ROM unit, specified for navigation. This system is intended only to read in navigational information from an informational DVD, not to play back DVDs.

DVD audio is so new, in fact, that Panasonic released the exact specifications for the medium only as this chapter was being written. So, at this writing, exactly zero DVD audio players are available. However, Panasonic announced that their first generation of DVD audio players would be available in October 1999. They made no formal announcements about car audio DVD head units, but the company has stated that this equipment would be manufactured. This equipment will probably be available in either late 2000 or early 2001, although it will surely be longer before it gains widespread acceptance (if it does).

Because of all of the benefits of DVD audio, coupled with its compatibility with the DVD video format, I believe that this format will succeed. Just because of the improved audio and extra channels, this format should be a favorite of audiophiles and car stereo fans.

The big question will be the final format of most of the DVDs on the market. For example, they could be have the same audio specifications as CDs, plus a video track. Or they could be a super-high-fidelity version, recorded in 24-bit mode at 192-kHz sampling, with two channels (right and left) of audio. Older collections of music that were mastered with 16-bit audio at 44.1 kHz (standard CD audio) could be compiled with hours of music on a single DVD.

When the DVD audio discs become available, it will be important to read the contents of the package before purchasing it. Unlike previous music recording mediums, DVD audio is more of an entertainment package than just a music recording. If you are considering a good CD head unit, first check the availability and cost of a DVD audio head unit. The initial list prices of the home DVD audio decks are expected to be between $1000 and $1400, so expect the first generation of DVD head units to be in the same price range. But, as was the case with CD head units, expect the price to quickly drop as more manufacturers test the DVD waters. Once the manufacturers get the bugs worked out of the first-generation systems and the prices drop, DVD head units should be well worth the money.

SATELLITE AND TERRESTRIAL DIGITAL RADIO

The DVD system started out with a video standard, followed by an audio standard. Digital satellite broadcasting is following the same trend. For much of the 1990s, television programming has been available via the *Direct Broadcast Satellite (DBS) system*, which includes hundreds of digitally encoded "smart" channels.

Since that time, companies have worked on a comparable *Digital Audio Broadcasting (DAB) system*, which would essentially consist of many different national radio stations that could be heard across most of North America.

The benefits of DAB are that you could hop in your car and drive from coast to coast, listening to the same radio station in CD-quality audio, with no fadeouts or interference of any kind. In addition, the stations would provide some niche programming (jazz, blues, reggae, etc.) not currently available in some radio markets. And if you couldn't find some programming to interest you, you can always program the radio to receive pay-per-listen music, such as concerts or other special events. Unlike the DBS television system, the DAB system uses higher-power transmitters so that only a flat 2-in. disk is required as an antenna.

Detractors of the DAB note that it could economically wreck the current terrestrial broadcast system (i.e., all of the radio stations in the AM and FM bands) by drawing away listeners and potential advertisers, that the system would probably only be available for a monthly subscription fee, that the broadcasting system would require too much radio-frequency spectrum that could be available for other services, that special DAB receivers would be necessary for the home and the car, and that fewer people would have access to the airwaves.

DAB is already in service in Europe, where the concept was originally conceived in 1981. Because many of the terrestrial European broadcasting outlets were already government controlled, it was easier to implement a satellite broadcasting service. Car audio enthusiasts in Europe can pick up such DAB equipment as the JVC SX-KD1500R DAB receiver/CD player head unit (Fig. 3-19). In the United States, where broadcasting is almost entirely controlled by private organizations, the DAB system has been fought by the National Association of Broadcasters (NAB).

Fig. 3-19 *A digital audio receiver for Europe: the JVC SX-KD1500R DAB receiver/CD player head unit.* JVC

Europe's DAB broadcast system uses Band III (around 221 MHz) and the L Band (1452 to 1492 MHz). In the United States, it was expected that a functional system would be set in place in the S Band (2310 to 2360 MHz) by 1997, but this has not yet happened (and might not ever). It's also technologically possible to set up the DAB system on the current FM band (88 to 108 MHz), but the legal ramifications of attempting to move off thousands of FM broadcast stations makes this system an impossibility.

Despite the reluctance of the United States to enter into DAB, Canada is making strides in this direction. Already, the CBC is broadcasting on the band and a total of 53 Canadian stations are already transmitting DAB on the L Band or are scheduled to do so in 1999.

Instead of the satellite-based DAB system, the NAB is pushing for *In-Band On-Channel Broadcasting (IBOC)*. If this system is passed by the FCC, all of the stations would be broadcasting their signals digitally within the standard FM band. The problem is that broadcasters will need to purchase new transmitting equipment and listeners will need to buy new receivers and head units to tune in this system. The claimed benefits of IBOC are interference-free listening, CD-quality audio, and the ability to transmit data (such as ads, weather, stocks, sports, etc.)

that can play back on the front-panel display of the receiver or head unit.

The disadvantages of IBOC are cost and restriction of broadcasting. The cost of converting to digital could sink some of the stations that are financially faltering (rural and niche radio, especially). And the NAB is using the IBOC in an attempt to eliminate low-power FM (LPFM) broadcasting proposals. Depending on the type of LPFM service (several different proposals are before the FCC), the LPFM could enable thousands of new community and niche broadcasters to begin operating. Because all of the LPFM are proposed for the current analog system, IBOC will eliminate the potential for these stations.

According to CBC Radio, the IBOC test at the 1995 NAB convention showed many Canadian delegates that "IBOC has still not proven itself in three key areas: functioning well under real-market conditions, delivering CD-quality sound, and providing sufficient auxiliary data capacity to allow for new, revenue-generating services."

In another report, the CBC also stated "...it [IBOC] is unlikely to out-perform in any markedly superior manner conventional analog FM signals, particularly in cars."

By the Canadian timetable, all AM and FM stations are to be switched to L Band broadcasts sometime around the year 2010. Considering the amount of time required to switch the system over to digital broadcast-ing, the number of receivers that would be rendered obsolete, and the number of new receivers that would have to be manufactured, it will be years before an IBOC system is adopted, if it is.

The bottom line is that Canadians should start looking for DAB head units because, before long, the AM and FM bands will be empty, except for American stations. In the United States, the system proposals are still up in the air, so it's best to stick with standard AM/FM head units, unless you live near the Northern border and can tune in the Canadian broadcasts.

HEAD UNIT INSTALLATIONS

Normally, a head unit replacement is one of the easier car audio installa-tions to perform, which is fortunate, considering that it's also one of the most important. But as with all auto manufacturers, the designs and construction techniques vary greatly among different models, and often even just between different years of the same car model. For examples of some of the problems that you might encounter, see Chapter 12, which covers the installations of several specific systems. The rest of this section covers some of the generic points (that are common in most cases) of installing a head unit.

The first point of installing a head unit begins before you physically begin to install it. Before all of this process begins, be sure to survey the car and everything that might hinder you. Look over the dashboard. Some dashes have a single plate that can easily be removed after un-screwing a few hex nuts or screws (Fig. 3-20). Others have very compli-cated assemblies that will make you want to strangle the incompetent car engineer who designed it. For example, my sister's old 1990 Chevrolet Beretta has a single faceplate that covers both the cassette head unit and the air conditioning controls. The only way that you could install an aftermarket head unit in this car would be to cut that plate. The stereo in that car was certainly designed to be the *only* system you would ever have!

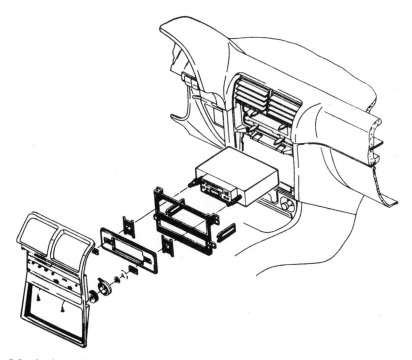

Fig. 3-20 *A view that shows how the dashplate and radio of the Suzuki Swift (1992 and 1993) can be removed.* Scosche

Different cars use a variety of sizes for the head units (Figs. 3-21 and 3-22). For example, General Motors cars sometimes use double-DIN holes and a shorter-than-normal mounting depth. Be sure that your head unit

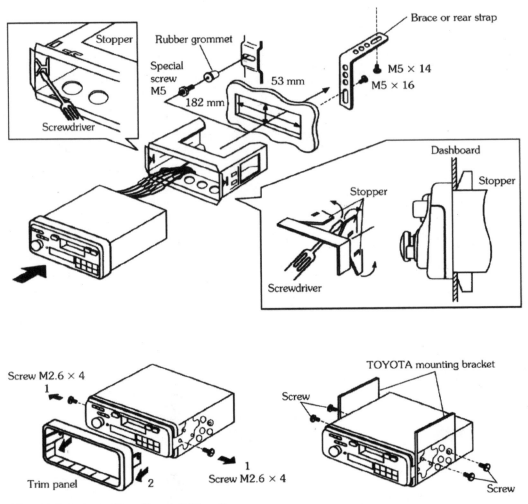

Fig. 3-21 *Installing fixed DIN units.* Sanyo

will mount in the dash properly—or purchase a mounting kit so that it will fit perfectly (Fig. 3-23). If you have any question about the mounting, call some of the mail-order companies for information.

Crutchfield's Website features an excellent database, whereby you can check to see if particular head units will fit into your car. After typing in the make/year/style of your car, the site will automatically filter out any head units that won't easily fit into its intended place in the dash.

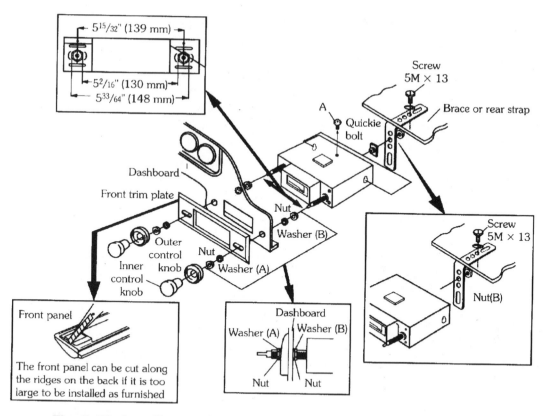

Fig. 3-22 *Installing shaft head units.* Sanyo

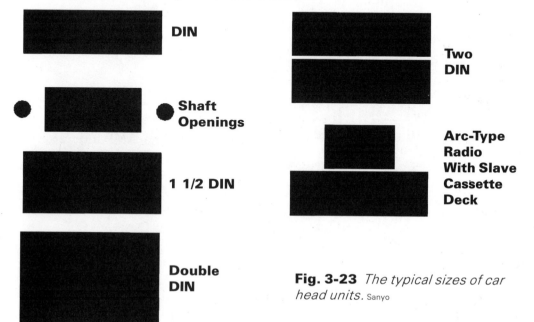

Fig. 3-23 *The typical sizes of car head units.* Sanyo

After you have spent some time surveying the situation and when you feel confident about the installation, be sure that you have all of the proper tools so that you can perform the task. Before you dig into the installation, remove the cable from the negative battery terminal as a safety precaution. Then, if necessary, remove the dashboard or the front panel around the head unit. This might take some work, so be sure that you have plenty of time and work slowly. If you run into difficulties with removing the dash or the dash plates, try not to get frustrated or angry. If you can't go any further, swallow your pride and take the car to a mechanic to have the section removed professionally. You might not have the tools to remove some of the specialty screws and nuts, the removal cost is low, and it is better than damaging your car's dashboard.

Once the panel is out, you can remove the radio and prepare to install the head unit. In many cases, the radio will mounted directly to the dashboard frame and you can just remove the screws, pull the unit out, and disconnect the antenna and the wiring harnesses. In other cases, you might need to use DIN-removal tools to pull out the head unit from the hole. These tools are U-shaped handles that plug into two small holes along the edges. As the tools lock in place, they disengage prongs that

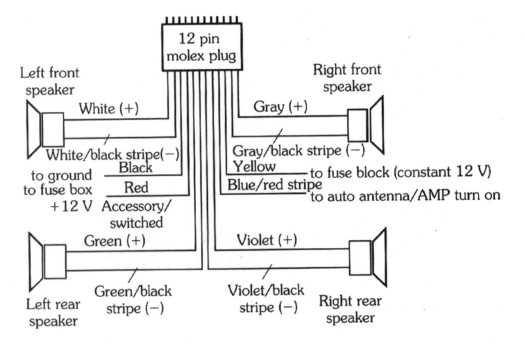

Fig. 3-24 *The Sanyo wiring color code, which is an example of one of the many different codes that are available.* Sanyo

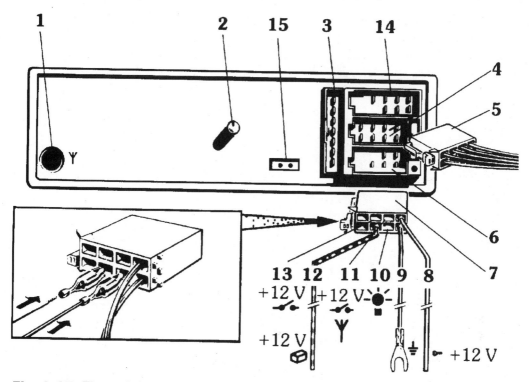

Fig. 3-25 *The various rear connections of the Philips DC-777 head unit.* Philips

1. Antenna socket
2. Threaded stud for rear support
3. Line-out multisocket
4. Loudspeaker multisocket
5. Loudspeaker multiplug
6. Power supply multisocket
7. Power supply multiplug
8. 12-V supply lead
9. Ground lead
10. Connection for night illumination
11. Switched 12 V for electronic antenna or the relay of auto-matic-motor lead
12. Permanent 12-V supply lead
13. Switched 12 V for remote supply of a booster/amplifier or an active loudspeaker
14. Multisocket for optional remote-control unit
15. Connection for batteries of optional retractable unit

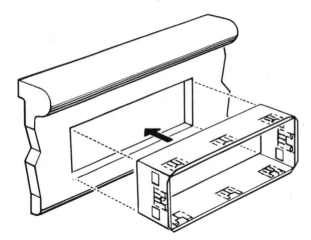

Fig. 3-26 *Slide the outer sleeve into the hole in the dashboard.* Philips

lock the head unit into the opening, and you can then pull the head unit straight out.

Depending on the style of the hole in the dash, your radio might fit perfectly, you might need a mounting adapter, or you might need to cut a hole in the dash plate. If so, the method described in the first VW Rabbit installation in Chapter 11 is simple and relatively easy. First, remove the head unit that is in this location and determine the functions of as many of the wires as you can (Fig. 3-25). Some head units have a pictorial diagram of the wires' functions stamped onto the outside of the radio's metal sides.

In this hole, you will probably need to fit a head unit sleeve. Slide the sleeve into place (Fig. 3-26). If it won't fit, you might need to file out the corners of the mounting hole (Fig. 3-27). Then, slide the sleeve into

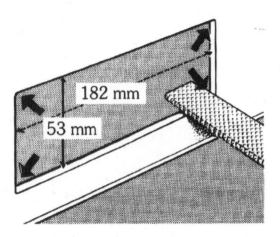

182 mm

53 mm

Fig. 3-27 *If necessary, file the edges of the hole to make the outer sleeve fit.* Philips

place and pop the tabs out (Fig. 3-28). The popped tabs lock the sleeve in place.

Fig. 3-28 *Pop out the tabs in the outer sleeve to lock it into place.* Philips

The speaker and power connectors from the car won't mate with those on the head unit. Clip in the wiring harness(es). Then screw the wires into the terminal blocks, pair by pair. Check over the connections to be sure that all of them are properly matched. Also, it's a good idea to keep the power wires all in a row and separated from the speaker wires. This makes the wires easier to track and to troubleshoot, in case of later problems.

Once you have correctly connected all of the wires together, reconnect the car's battery ground and test the head unit. Listen closely for crackles that result from short circuits or intermittent open circuits, hums, and speakers that are connected to the wrong channels. If you have any of these problems, troubleshoot your connections and try it again.

Once you have the system working properly, slide the head unit into place until it locks into the mounting sleeve (Fig. 3-29). It's important to give the head unit some back support because if it is wobbly, the increased vibrations will increase wow and flutter in cassette decks, cause more skips in CD players, and possibly make components fail prematurely (and it's suddenly time to buy a new head unit). Most head units come with a backstrap, a long, thin piece of metal with lots of holes. There is no particular correct way to mount the backstrap; it should be screwed on to both the back of the head unit and one of the supports inside of the dashboard.

Finally, replace the dashboard or any other parts of the car that you might have stripped off to reach the head unit's position. Then, take a drive in the car and enjoy your new head unit!

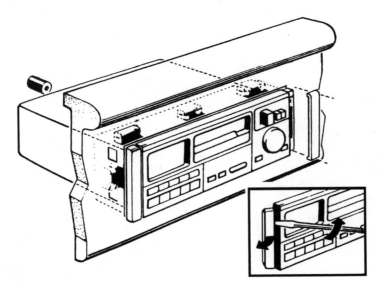

Fig. 3-29 *Push the head unit into the sleeve and lock it into place.* Philips

CONCLUSION

The head unit is truly the heart of any sound system. You should try to get the best-quality unit you can afford. There are a number of formats to choose from (cassette, compact disc, MiniDiscs, and eventually DVD), and it seems that all of these will continue strongly into the Twenty-first century, except for MiniDiscs, whose future is less certain.

4

SOUND PROCESSING

Equalizers and DSP devices are equipment that is used to alter the signal between the head unit and the speakers (or the head unit and the amplifier, if an amplifier is being used). Both devices are optional. Although a great system can be installed without any type of sound processing, it can be useful and make your system sound better.

But beware, a system with an equalizer requires more work and money than the standard "replace the speakers, replace the head unit system." When you by an equalizer, you are making a commitment to your car stereo system. The prerequisites are a head unit with preamplifier outputs and two amplifiers to power the system. The head unit's output power won't be used, the preamplifier signal from the head unit will feed to the equalizer. Then the low-level signal from the equalizer has two pairs of low-level outputs: one pair to feed an amplifier that will power the front speakers and another pair to feed an amplifier that will power the rear speakers. Other systems can be created, but these will all be more-complex variations (such as adding another amplifier and some subwoofers) of this basic system.

BASICS AND ANALOG EQUALIZERS

In contrast to the new, high-tech technology of the digital sound processor, the equalizer has been in common use in car stereo systems since they became popular several decades ago. The *equalizer* is a sort of analog sound-processing unit that controls the strength of the different audio-frequency bands. Instead of working with the bits of a digital medium, the standard equalizer is simply an array of variable slider resistors. Each resistor is a different value and has control over a particular audio frequency band. As a result, you can boost the audio response at lower or higher frequencies. Or if there is some hiss or other high-frequency noise, you can reduce the levels on the highest-frequency control to effectively cut back the effects of the interference.

Like many other features, equalizers appear in conjunction with various pieces of equipment. Occasionally, a three- or five-band equalizer is included on a head unit to allow the user to have a few extra controls over the final audio output.

Equalizers are also sometimes built into a floor unit with crossovers. These units generally are built into a flat box with the controls on the top, and instead of slider potentiometers, they only use the rotary types. In this case, the potentiometers aren't meant to be reset frequently; they are only used to tweak the system's overall sound. For more information, see the section "Parametric Equalizers" in this chapter.

Another type of equalizer is the *preamp equalizer* (Fig. 4-1). These units were fairly common in the late 1970s, when car stereo was making its first run in popularity. These days, preamp equalizers have become

Fig. 4-1 *A standard dash-mounted equalizer.* Pioneer

quite popular once again. However, these models are generally all tiny little boxes with a few rotary knobs on the thin front panel (Fig. 4-2). With them you can control about three to five different general frequency bands. Although these units are equalizers, I don't consider them to be true equalizers in the purest sense of the term.

I consider the real, grass-roots equalizer to be a black box with anywhere from about 5 to 12 slider potentiometers on the front panel. These units almost never do anything, except simply equalize the signals.

Equalizers are incredibly useful because they can be used to help alter the sound of a recording and to emphasize or deemphasize certain audio frequencies. When I was younger and had some really bad-sound-

Fig. 4-2 *A stack of equalizers from Cadence (top), and one from Coustic (bottom).* Cadence, Coustic

ing systems, I always liked to jack up the high frequencies on some of my third-generation tapes to try to perk them up a bit. However, to repeat a piece of advice that I have heard a number of times, equalizers are not a replacement for good-quality audio and they should not be used as such. If you need to alter the sound of a cassette with an equalizer, then you should re-record that cassette.

However, equalizers can be effectively used to balance out the negative effects of the car. Equalizers are often dismissed by the audiophiles in the home audio crowd who believe that final sound should be as close to the originally recorded audio as possible. Any divergence from this ideal is heresy. But the difference is that the audiophiles can create a nearly perfect listening room in their house. Face it, the car is far from being a perfect listening environment.

The first problem with the car listening environment is noise. Great strides have been made to reduce

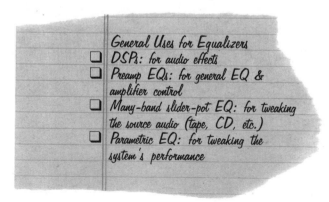

General Uses for Equalizers
☐ DSPs: for audio effects
☐ Preamp EQs: for general EQ & amplifier control
☐ Many-band slider-pot EQ: for tweaking the source audio (tape, CD, etc.)
☐ Parametric EQ: for tweaking the system's performance

95

the noise in cars, but they are still far from being noise-free. Noise alone is bad, not just because you have to "drown it out," but because it cancels out the audio frequencies of the music that you're listening to. So, if the road noise is around 100 to 200 Hz, it will cancel out (effectively removing) a good portion of the music's audio between 100 and 200 Hz. Of course, actual road noise is more complex than this, often consisting of a few different frequency ranges. With an equalizer, these frequencies can be raised to compensate for the road and car noise.

Next, an ideal listening environment is a relatively open area with no obstructions. A vehicle contains seats, people, and materials that both obstruct and absorb sound waves. Because the higher-frequency waves are so short in length, they are most susceptible to being absorbed by objects and materials. One advantage of using soft, padded ceilings, plush-covered doors, and carpeted seats are that they absorb road noise well, but they also absorb the audio from your stereo well. Although your system might sound great mounted in a room, you can bet that the obstructions and absorption will cause some frequencies to be reduced more than others (as opposed to lowering the levels of all of the different frequencies evenly). An equalizer can help overcome this sound absorption.

Finally, speakers can cause some problems that can be corrected with an equalizer. Sometimes, the speakers can't always be angled toward you properly. In general, this won't cause a problem that can be fixed with an equalizer. But, if you have use speakers for different frequencies (woofers or midranges and tweeters), an equalizer might be helpful. For example, if you use a kickpanel or in-dash midrange or woofer and a tweeter mounted in the front of the dash or around the sun visor, you might find that the sound is a bit bright because the tweeter is pointed directly at your ears, but the other speakers aren't. Also, even though on pair of your speakers might have cost $150, their frequency response is still not flat across the range (at least not where you're sitting). Most speakers at least have some curvature to their response (or even a few spikes). Rather than "playing it by ear," it's better to check the manufacturer's playback curves before tweaking the equalizer settings.

For more complex tweaking, it's best to choose an equalizer with more frequency bands (more slider potentiometers), such as an eight- or 10-band equalizer. The more bands it has, the tighter your control over the frequencies. For example, each band in a five-band equalizer is about twice as wide as those in a 10-band equalizer. See the section "Parametric Equalizers" for more information on tweaking your system to sound properly.

DIGITAL SIGNAL PROCESSORS AND EQUALIZERS

Digital signal processing (DSP) has been one of the fastest-growing aspects of all types of audio over the past few years. Among other things, DSP is used to reduce interference or noise in some applications, and to control time delays in others. In auto audio applications, DSP is primarily only used in coordination with various time delays to achieve different acoustic effects.

Some of the early DSP units, such as the Eclipse EQR-2140 DSP controller (Fig. 4-3), have five preset sound field configurations: concert hall, live night club, cathedral, stadium, and disco. In each of these settings, the reflected and direct sounds come from different general directions, are at various intensities in relation to each other, and all vary in time response.

Fig. 4-2 *The Linear Power PAII preamplifier/equalizer.*

Whenever you listen to a studio recording from a band, it generally sounds as if it was recorded in a studio (although this varies, depending on the overall effect that the producer was attempting to create). With the DSP unit, you can make the acoustics within your car sound like a cathedral, no less!

In addition to the available presettings, you generally have some manual control over the settings of the DSP so that you can set the audio to appeal to your personal tastes. Of course, the DSP could ruffle the feathers of any strict audiophile, who would hate to see the sounds manipulated in ways that weren't intended by the album's producer.

Many of the current DSP units are no longer novelty effects boxes; most are merged in with equalizers. The end result is a digital equalizer, with all of the special effects of DSP. Instead of the slider pots of the analog equalizers, these units have pushbuttons to control the levels of the different bands and the settings that are shown on the LED or LCD display. The digital equalizers are handy because you can program all of the different frequencies for all of the different bands, then everything can be stored into a memory. So, you could program all of the equalizer settings for different styles of music (one group of settings for blues, another for rock, another for hip-hop, for example), and then just press one button to change the equalizer settings when you change styles of music.

Digital equalizers with (or without) DSP generally have the highest number of bands (as many as 15 different) for dash-mounted units. As a result, the high-end digital equalizers offer the greatest amount of audio control and other tweaks to play with (such as the DSP settings), so they are the most attractive of the hands-on equalizers.

These days, many of the more-expensive head units offer DSP equalization. If you have one of these head units, you will probably find a DSP equalizer to be unnecessary. However, if you want to tweak your system, a parametric equalizer will still be necessary. Depending on the amount of frequency control that your head unit's DSP offers, you might also want a multiband analog equalizer in your system.

PARAMETRIC EQUALIZERS

For really complex tweaking, especially for compensating for the particular acoustics of your car, it's best to use a parametric equalizer. The parametric equalizer looks totally different from the others, so they're easy to spot. These equalizers use rotary potentiometers to adjust the settings, rather than either slider pots or pushbuttons. Also, the parametric equalizers are typically large, flat metal boxes with all of the controls on top (Fig. 4-4). From their design alone, they are meant to be mounted flat and adjusted very rarely. These units have many frequency bands (as many as 30!), so they are the ultimate in sound tweaking, and are intended to overcome the acoustics of the car and the performance of the speakers.

Fig. 4-4 *An AudioControl EQX Series II 13-band stereo equalizer, which also features a 24-dB crossover, a programmable-frequency match filter, and an isolated power supply.*

Parametric equalizers are typically only used in competition vehicles or by serious audiophiles, in part because they are very expensive (well into the hundreds of dollars) and because they are very difficult to adjust properly. Usually, specialized equipment (in particular, a real-time analyzer, which is also quite pricey) and a test CD are used to properly tweak the car for flat response. Because a real-time analyzer is specialized equipment and parametric equalizers are difficult to tune, so it is best left to a professional.

In general, parametric equalizers are necessary for high-level competition vehicles and can be helpful for audiophiles, but their cost is prohibitive for most people. Many small installation shops don't even have a real-time analyzer in the shop to tweak systems. In addition to the cost of the equipment itself, the added cost of tweaking the system by a professional will be prohibitive. It is possible to adjust a parametric equalizer "by ear" and improve the sound of a system, but it's impossible to set the levels perfectly this way (although some will surely argue that they can!).

INSTALLING EQUALIZERS

Installing equalizers can often be much more difficult than installing head units, even though they're both small boxes, and despite the fact that equalizers only require a few wires to run. The problem is that most cars have only one slot available for a head unit, and that's it. Back in the 1970s, it was common to see car audio systems with aftermarket preamp/equalizers screwed in under the dashboards. They looked terrible.

The standard dash-mounted equalizers almost always require custom installation work of some sort. The digital equalizers are often DIN sized, so they can fairly easily be installed if the vehicle has an extra DIN-sized hole. For example, some of the Plymouth Voyager minivans include an extra DIN-sized hole in the dash that can be used to hold extra CDs, cassettes, sunglasses, etc. Or a digital equalizer can be placed in the hole. In this particular instance, although the hole is DIN sized, it isn't premade for installing any equipment. As a result, holes must be drilled in the back of the plastic dashboard assembly so that power and audio wires can be passed through the hole to the rest of the system. If the equalizer comes with a slide-in Euro-DIN mounting sleeve, then drill a few holes into the sides of the plastic dashboard assembly so that the tabs of the mounting sleeve can be pushed out into the holes, locking it in place. Then the equalizer can be pushed into the sleeve until it locks in the sleeve.

Most analog (slider pot) equalizers are smaller than DIN sized, often only about 1 in. high. If your vehicle either has an extra DIN-sized hole or contains a 1 1/2 DIN hole (such as a GM or Plymouth), you're in luck. In the case of an extra DIN hole, it's necessary to screw the equalizer into place, cut an extra panel to cover the hole in the dash (not covered by the equalizer front panel), and cut a hole so that the wires can pass from the equalizer to the head unit and amplifiers (if necessary). The equalizer will need to be screwed into the inside of the plastic

molding, into a pre-existing hole in the metal dash frame, or into a hole in the metal dash frame that you need to drill yourself.

The tricky part is creating and installing an extra dash plate that matches and looks natural in the car. Most car dashboards use either vinyl or textured plastic in the dash. It's not easy to purchase materials to match exactly the original dashboard. The best materials are those that can be purchased from car modification companies, such as J.C. Whitney. With a little luck, you will find some materials that either match or complement the colors of the original dash.

In the case of the 1 1/2 DIN hole, the equalizer can probably be squeezed into place with the head unit. The problem is getting the sleeve to lock into a slot with nothing to lock to its top side (just the equalizer resting in place). You might have some problems locking the DIN sleeve in place.

If your vehicle has no extra DIN holes, mounting the equalizer can be a real problem. The most obvious and least problematic solution is to simply mount it under the dash. And some equalizers are even sold complete with an under-the-dash mounting kit. The under-dash mountings just don't look very good (and not just because they're a flashback of those bad 1970s systems), and many cars don't even have a feasible, accessible under-dash location for an equalizer. The problem is that if you don't have a good under-dash mounting location or an extra DIN hole in the dash, it could be very difficult to custom build a mounting location for the equalizer or any other equipment that you might want to include.

Sometimes the equalizers are installed in the glove compartment. The advantages of this mounting location are that it's easily accessible, that it can just be screwed in place and it will look fine, and no beautiful custom work is necessary. Best of all, most systems will equalizers in place include some pricey equipment. Currently, equalizers don't have removable faceplates, so they are a giveaway to thieves that the system is worth stealing. Keeping the equalizer in the glove compartment is a great stealth measure.

The final way to mount an in-dash equalizer is to build a separate unit that runs from the dash to the floor. The advantages of a custom unit are great: you can easily fit in an equalizer and another piece of equipment, add a door to hide your goodies, and even include some space to hold extra cassettes or CDs. The easiest method is to build the little "cabinet" out of wood and stretch vinyl, upholstery, or leather over the surface and staple it tight inside. Again, the problem is getting everything to match. A wood unit could be used, but unless you drive a Model T with an all-wood interior, it will look out of place. Just a little variance in the shade of color will cause the interior to clash.

An entire book could easily be written about creating custom equipment and speaker locations, pods, enclosures, and stacks, so there's not enough room to cover it all here. But, hopefully these paragraphs have given you a few ideas to create a useful system in your vehicle. Definitely the easiest methods are to install it in the dash or in the glove compartment, although the more-difficult methods can be used to create a better effect, be more useful, or simply be more fun for those in need of a challenge.

INSTALLING PARAMETRIC EQUALIZERS

Unlike in-dash equalizers, parametric equalizers are generally very easy to install. They are typically placed under one of the front seats. Then, they are screwed in place and the wire is run under the carpet. The real work begins with setting the levels of the parametric equalizer, not installing it.

The only concern is to be careful where you drill the holes for the screws to be placed. You could accidentally puncture something of importance in the car, such as its gas tank or some wires in the electrical system. So, be careful when drilling holes, and if you are still worried about hole placement, check with your mechanic to be sure that you're doing everything correctly.

CONCLUSION

Equalizers are often looked down upon, and sometimes for good reason. The old equalizer/preamp units were often shoddy. And for years, people have used preamps incorrectly, in an attempt to correct poor audio. Equalizers can be used effectively to improve the sound in a car, sometimes giving the final boost to turn a good-sounding system into a great-sounding one.

5

AMPLIFIERS

Car stereo enthusiasts, on the whole, seem to be a much different group from the traditional home stereo experimenters. Part of it is certainly the age of technology: home hi-fi equipment and experimentation has been popular since the 1950s, but car stereo only started to catch on in the late 1970s and early 1980s. The home audio market targets people who are above 30, have well-paying jobs, and spend plenty of time at home. Car audio manufacturers are much more upbeat. They target young, single people, who spend much of their recreational time in their cars. Whereas the home audiophiles are expected to like classical, jazz, and light pop, the car audioheads are expected to like rock, rap, hip-hop, and "alternative" rock. And these stereotypes appear to be somewhat accurate. The big difference is that where the home audiophiles love music that surrounds their senses and rushes past and through them, the car stereo enthusiasts want it LOUD and heavy.

The two major symbols of the differences between high-end car audio and home audio are the subwoofer and the 12-V dedicated amplifier. In home audio, the amplifier usually isn't dedicated; it is normally contained in the same cabinet as the AM/FM (MW/VHF) receiver and is simply called the *receiver*. In most cases, the only dedicated home amplifiers are in the high end (e.g., the proliferation of exaggeratedly expensive tube amplifiers that started cropping up several years ago).

For all intents and purposes, high-power car amplifiers must be dedicated because they will not fit in the dashboard of the average car. However, with the wave of miniaturization that has been sweeping the electronics industry, low-power car amplifiers have been manufactured that can be built into head units.

Even though miniaturization permits the actual dedicated amplifier circuit boards to easily fit in a dashboard, a few other problems make them impractical in most cases. The main problem is that no amplifier is 100% efficient. The output power of any given amplifier is nowhere near the same as the power that is drawn by the amplifier. In fact, most amplifiers are only about 50 to 80% efficient.

What happens to the other 20 to 50% of that energy? That is the problem; all of the extra energy turns to heat. The heat is very dangerous if it is not contained or controlled because it could burn someone, cause an electrical car fire, or simply destroy the components within the amplifier. One dangerous condition that occurs in these situations is known as *thermal runaway*, which occurs when the transistors continue to become hotter and hotter until they finally meltdown.

To protect the car's passengers and also the car itself, the high-power amplifiers are mounted in convenient locations away from people, usually under seats or in the trunk. Also, nearly every manufacturer uses massive heatsinks to dissipate the heat that is created by the amplifier. *Heatsinks* are a series of metal fins that are mounted on a part or around a circuit to dissipate heat (Fig. 5-1). Heatsinks operate properly

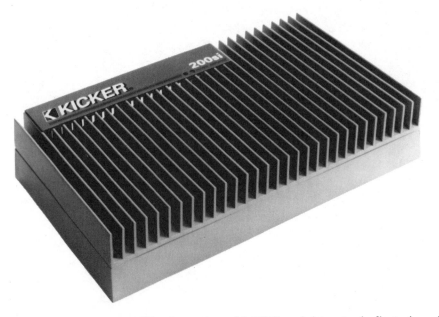

Fig. 5-1 *This Kicker amplifier from the mid-1990s might not win first place for having the largest and deepest heatsink fins, but it has to be close!* Stillwater Designs/ KICKER car audio systems

because metal generally conducts heat as well as it conducts electricity. As long as the fins are kept relatively thin and exposed to as much air as possible (a high surface-area to mass ratio), much of the heat in the metal fins will be transferred to the air molecules near the heatsink. Thus, the heat from inside of the amplifier will be transferred through the heatsink fins and into the air that surrounds the amplifier...and any internal destruction is prevented. Most dedicated amplifiers make efficient use of space and materials; in these amplifiers, the entire outside of the amplifier consists of a giant heatsink case. This technology is part of the "look" that has come to be associated with car audio systems. Even the amplifiers that don't have the ridged heatsink cases (to look different from the competition) have massive heatsinks inside of the amplifier case.

With some high-powered commercial amplifiers, heatsinks alone are not enough. These models also have a muffin fan mounted on top of the unit to suck the hot air out of the inside of the heatsink. Amplifiers with muffin fans are handy because they keep the circuits cool. On the other hand, some of these amplifiers use muffin fans as a requirement, not as a precaution. If that is the case, the amplifier will overheat and blow if the fan fails. Also, if these amplifiers are used within a very quiet car, the light whoosh of the fan(s) could be annoying; you would be much better off if you mounted them in the trunk.

PRINCIPLES OF AMPLIFICATION

Amplification might not appear to be a very exciting topic. After all, amplifiers are just "bigger components that make the sound louder," right? It's a bit more complicated than that, and precision is of key importance. Except for the stronger output, the signal exiting the amplifier should be as close as possible to the same as that which entered it.

If the previous "bigger components that make the sound louder" statement was entirely true, the issue of exact signal reproduction and amplification should not be difficult. However, as any signal is amplified and/or passes through more electrical stages, it is subject to being corrupted by various noise sources. For example, an electrically "dirty" amplifier power supply can add a hum to the audio; an inferior grade of components can alter the audio; or low-values of capacitors can cause distortion, especially at low frequencies. Also, there are several different ways in which a stereo signal can be powered, divided, and amplified. In addition, several different classes of amplification prove to be more useful for various applications.

This section is only intended to provide some basic background information behind how amplifiers work and nothing more. A number of books were written on the theories and design examples of amplifier and high-fidelity circuits several decades ago. These days, however, few people ever consider picking up a book and experimenting with building their own stereo equipment. Even fewer people would build their own car audio system. So, rather than being a guide to the theory that could enable you to build an amplifier for your car, this section is intended to provide you with a few of the interesting theories that could help you to purchase an amplifier to suit your tastes.

Years ago the key to amplification was the electron tube (also known as an *audion* or *valve*), which has since been virtually replaced by the transistor and the integrated circuit. Typical electron tubes are glass envelopes with anywhere from four to eight steel pins at the bottom. Early receiving tubes were approximately 8 in. (20.32 cm) high and 2 in. (5.08 cm) to 3 in. (7.62 cm) wide, but as the industry miniaturized, receiving tubes were reduced to about 1.5 in. (3.81 cm) high and 0.75 in. (1.9 cm) wide. The very early tubes looked something like a lightbulb, but later on the appearance changed considerably (Fig. 5-2).

The first real tube, the diode, was invented by Lee DeForest in the early

Fig. 5-2 *A size comparison among (from left) a relatively early four-pin audio tube, an integrated circuit, and a transistor.*

1900s and it was a breakthrough that helped propel radio into the beginning of its glory in the next decade. As radio technology progressed, other more complicated tubes, such as the triode, tetrode, and pentode, were invented. These tubes were used for a variety of applications, such as regulating voltages and controlling the direction of signal flow, but they were essential as the key element in amplifiers.

Amplifier tubes could raise the input signal level many times. To generate the power to amplify the signal, the tube required high voltages at various pins. As a result, it could, in effect, change electricity into audio impulses.

Several decades ago, it was discovered that some elements with a high resistance to electricity could be used in applications to regulate and amplify signals. These elements, such as silicon, germanium, selenium, arsenic, etc., were known as *semiconductors* and were later used to make diodes and transistors. By the mid-1950s, these devices started to appear in consumer products instead of tubes. This sort of hybrid tube/transistor equipment was often of strange design. The relatively tiny transistors were used to save space wherever possible, but transistors had not yet replaced tubes in every function. Also, transistors did not "behave" like tubes: they had different requirements, were sometimes less stable, and required different types of biasing. The end result was something like a patchwork quilt of new and old technologies.

By the early 1960s, not only were transistors becoming widespread, but transistors were being built into a package with several other parts like diodes, capacitors, resistors, etc. Before long, small circuits were being integrated into a small semiconductor chip, hence the name *integrated circuit (IC)*. Today, technology has miniaturized to the point where large circuits and even some power amplifier stages can be built into a single, small IC chip. Because of this miniaturization, a very powerful high-fidelity auto amplifier can be built into a very small case. For that matter, because audio amplifiers can now be built into an integrated circuit, some low- to medium-powered amplifiers can be assimilated into head units.

One misconception is that tubes are an inferior technological joke. This is not the case. Transistors replaced tubes, not so much because of superior performance, but rather because of the tiny amount of space that transistors required. One difference in performance is that tubes slowly degrade with use; they gradually become weak. Transistors, on the other hand, either work or they don't. For all intended purposes, transistors will last forever. The problem is that semiconductors can easily be destroyed by such conditions as overvoltage. This is a severe dilemma, considering that a very small amount of electricity can cause catastrophic damage. Even the static electricity on your hands that is generated from walking across a carpeted room is powerful enough to destroy most modern semiconductors. To combat these problems, anyone who works with semiconductors should wear a grounded wrist strap, which will funnel all of the static electricity to ground.

Because of the miniaturization and problems of catastrophic destruction, electronic equipment is increasingly looked upon as being a "throw away" commodity. When one tiny part is destroyed, a number of parts are likely to have been taken along with it. This is compounded by the fact that so many of the surface-mounted parts are tightly squeezed together that many electronics service centers simply replace the entire circuit board, rather than repair the equipment. In years past, radios and audio equipment were built to withstand most any kind of physical or electrical abuse. Even after they were severely damaged, they could be repaired. In no means should this imply that older electronics equipment was better than the that of today, just that some of it was more useful in different applications. And, yes, one of these applications is often in tube amplifiers.

If you read the stereo magazines, you will notice that a large number of small American companies currently build high-end home-stereo tube amplifiers. Transistors and integrated circuits were all the rage throughout the 1960s and 1970s. But, by the 1980s, some people became vocal about how they still liked how the old tube amplifiers sounded better than the solid-state ones. And some musicians prefer the sound of tube guitar amplifiers better, too. As a result of this publicity and some comparisons, audio enthusiasts began to pull out their old audiophile amplifiers manufactured by such companies as McIntosh, Leak, Marantz, Western Electric, etc. And dozens of tiny companies began producing handmade audiophile-quality tube amplifiers. Many people seem to think that tube equipment sounds "warmer." Whether it does or not, it certainly does *feel* warmer!

The trend toward tube audio has even started to spread across to auto audio. Milbert entered the car audio market with a few tube amplifiers and preamplifiers, including a pricey mobile audiophile tube amplifier that currently lists at $995 (Fig. 5-3). A few years later, Calcell also

Fig. 5-3 *The warm glow of electron tubes in a Milbert amplifier. The unit is temporarily powered via alligator clip leads.* Milbert Amplifers, Inc.

began selling a high-end tube amplifier, and Tube Driver has entered the market with a full line of hybrid tube/solid-state car stereo amplifiers.

Although I believe that some more mobile tube amplifiers will appear in the marketplace, I do not believe that they will displace the many hundreds of different models of dedicated amplifiers that use semiconductors. Nearly all of these power amplifiers are now using *metal-oxide-semiconductor field-effect transistors (MOSFETs)* to amplify the input signals. MOSFETs have been an amazing electronics breakthrough because they are inexpensive, can be used in high-power applications, and are well known for their ability to amplify a signal to a much higher level. Also, some professionals and hobbyists say that MOSFETs are much more stable than transistors and that their behavior in circuits is much closer to that of tubes.

CLASSES OF AUDIO AMPLIFICATION

The different classes of amplification are based on how much of the input signal cycle (to the amplifier) the output current passes through the amplifying device. This is an extremely complicated theoretical process. For the most part, you can assume that if the output current flows over a longer amount of the cycle (in degrees), the amplifier will be correspondingly less efficient, but it will be capable of producing low-distortion audio. Likewise, you can also assume that if the output current flows over a shorter amount of the cycle (in degrees), the amplifier will be correspondingly more efficient, but it will not be as capable

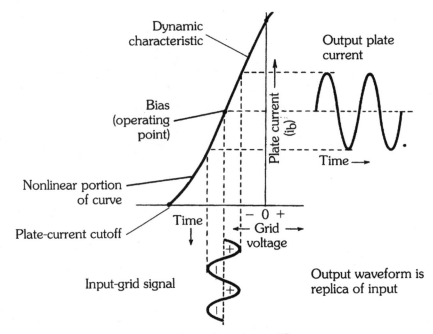

Fig. 5-4 *The amplification waves for a class-A amplifier.*

of producing low-distortion audio.

Class A Class-A amplifiers operate in a manner that is similar to the first assumption in the previous paragraph; the class-A amplifier has a very clean output, but the efficiency is poor. In fact, most class-A amplifiers operate only at about 20 to 30% efficiency (Fig. 5-4). That is, if the amplifier requires about 100 W of input power from the battery, it will only output about 20 to 30 W of audio signal to the speakers. The power-crazed car audio fiend would avoid any class-A amplifier simply because the power output is so low. And if the output was raised on the class-A amplifier, it would suck down all of the juice from the alternator and possibly even the battery. Few people would want an amplifier like this, so the amp designer will usually move on to another class of amplification.

Class B In class-B amplifiers, the output current of the amplifier only flows through 180 degrees of the input signal cycle (instead of the full 360 degrees, as in the case of class-A amplifiers). Theoretically, this class of amplifier is two times more efficient than a class-A amplifier, although in operation, those figures aren't quite met (Fig. 5-5). With the great increase in efficiency, it appears that class-B amplification would be the ideal choice for audio amplifiers. But the problem is that class-B amplifiers is that they take the other extreme and cause audio

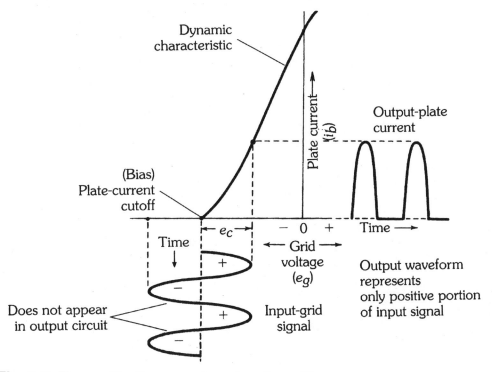

Fig. 5-5 *The amplification waves for a class-B amplifier.*

distortion. One attempt to avoid this problem is to run two output transistors in a push-pull configuration: each one applies current for an opposite half cycle. Operated in this manner, the push-pull class-B amplifier can be effective for power amplifier applications, but distortion still exists at the points where the transistors turn on and off. As a result, the amp designer will more than likely use a different class of modulation.

Class C In class-C amplifiers (Fig. 5-6), the output current of the amplifier only flows through approximately 120 degrees of the input signal cycle (instead of the full 360 degrees or even through 180 degrees). As you can imagine, the class-C amplifier is even more efficient than the class-B amp, but it also adds that much more distortion to the audio. A class-C amplifier can reach an efficiency level of up to about 75%, so they do have some obvious advantages, but they still aren't particularly useful in applications where high fidelity is a requirement.

These are the three groupings of audio classifications. So, if class-A operations are too inefficient and class-B and -C are too distorted, what is the alternative? Modify the existing classes.

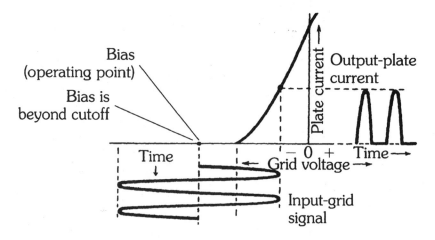

Fig. 5-6 *The amplification waves for a class-AB amplifier.*

Class AB Class-AB amplification is the last of the four original classifications, and it is considered to be a separate class, rather than a merely subset of a class. By developing the amplifier so that it is between the A and B classifications, it will be more efficient than a class-A amplifier, yet will have better fidelity than a class-B amplifier (Fig. 5-7). Most high-fidelity audio power amplifiers use class-AB amplification.

Class D Class-D amplification is a relatively new finding in the amplification frontier, which was thought to already have been thoroughly scouted. Instead of a traditionally designed analog amplifier, the class-D amplifier is digital. Instead of developing output current during the complete input wave or part of it, the class-D amplifier switches on and off, hundreds of thousands of times per second—in keeping with the digital data that is being output from a compact disc, MiniDisc, and DVD audio player. For this reason, class-D amplifiers are sometimes called *switching amplifiers*. These amplifiers are amazing because the amplifier turns on and off so quickly that it is very efficient. As a result, the class-D amplifiers are much smaller than most other amplifiers that are in a comparable power class.

These classes of amplifiers are used for many different applications: Classes AB, B, and C are used frequently for a variety of transmitter circuits. Class AB is typically used for high-fidelity audio amplification, and class A is used for voltage amplification. Of course, these are only a few of the different applications for amplifier circuits.

As far as car stereo is concerned, class AB seems to be the most fre-

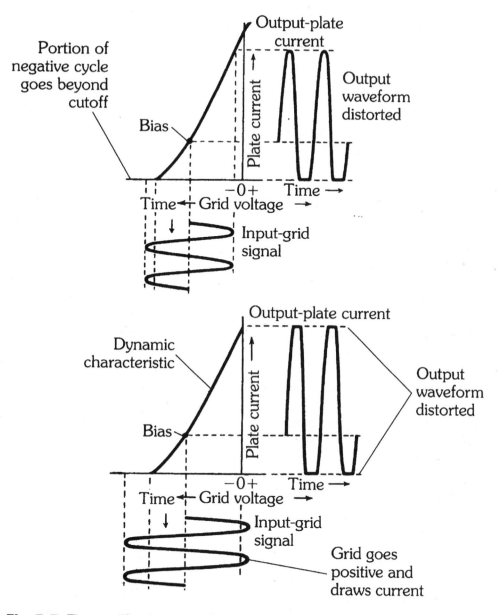

Fig. 5-7 *The amplification waves for a class-AB amplifier.*

quently used class of amplification. Class A is also occasionally used, like tube amplifiers, in costly high-end applications, such as in several amplifiers from Furi, Premiere, and Tube Driver, which all list for $1,000 (or more) apiece. Several of the MARS amplifiers can even be switched between class-A and class-AB amplification for precise sound control.

Interestingly enough, according to Joseph Carr in *Mastering Solid-State Amplifiers*, nearly all of the lo-fi car radios in the 1950s and 1960s used class-A amplification. They were not built to handle large amounts of power, so efficiency was not a problem, and the alternators developed so much power that plenty was available. It's funny how the features and techniques used in supposedly antiquated equipment sometimes becomes sought after!

General Amplifier Class Info
- ❑ *Class A: High-quality sound, but expensive*
- ❑ *Class AB: Most amps are class AB.*
- ❑ *Class C: Unusable for audio applications*
- ❑ *Class D: Very efficient, but often expensive in car audio. Seldom used.*

Once again, like the tube amplifiers, class-A amplifier operation is not going to rule the world. For a while, it was thought that class-D amplification could revolutionize the market with smaller, lower-cost high-quality amplifiers. However, many have come to regard class-D amplifiers as being most appropriate for applications where extremely high efficiency is necessary and low quality is acceptable. Instead of car amplifiers, class-D modulation is now most commonly used in computer audio applications. However, several companies, such as the class-D innovator, Infinity, Calcell, and MMATS, have continued to offer high-end class-D amplifiers.

FEEDBACK

Feedback occurs whenever a signal is fed from the output of a circuit back into the input of the same circuit. The most common type of feedback (or at least the type that most people immediately think of) is when the sound of an electric guitar returns (feeds back) through the pickups of the guitar. If the feedback is strong enough, the guitar will oscillate and a high-pitched sound will squeal through the speakers. This sort of feedback distorts the audio and it can be either desirable or undesirable, depending on the situation. Now, however, most rock musicians seem to avoid feedback (by using amplifiers with built-in anti-feedback circuits) because it is much harder to control than other types of distorting effects. Of course, the musicians who aren't afraid to lose control have more fun!

One of the important terms in the principles of amplifier operation is that of *loop gain*. Any amplifier has a particular amount of gain; that is, it will amplify a signal by any given factor. Unfortunately, every amplifier also has a certain amount of distortion and noise. These audio impurities are quite disruptive in the basic building-block amplifier. In order for any amplifier to be useful, the designer must implement any of several different distortion-reducing methods.

The most common method is to use feedback. However, the signal doesn't feed back through pickups to the point of oscillation (obviously). Instead, the signal is directed through the power stage, where it is amplified. Then, part of this signal is then fed back around the power amplifier stage and into the line. Instead of causing any feedback squeals, the two signals are combined and, for the most part, the noise and distortion are cancelled out of the signal.

The catch when using feedback in amplifiers is that the desired audio signals are also cancelled out to some extent (i.e., the final output of the amplifier is lower than the original loop gain). And amplifier designers are stuck with the dilemma of choosing between more power or increased clarity. Of course, it isn't that easy, either. The designer must choose between different circuits and feedback situations to obtain an optimum power versus clarity ratio.

In the example from the previous paragraph, feedback was used to help eliminate the noise and distortion. This circuit didn't oscillate because it was using *negative feeback*. *Positive feedback*, on the other hand when used in this example, would have caused the traditional squeal over the speakers. The difference is that although negative feedback reduces the final output signal, positive feedback actually increases it. Positive feedback is more limited in its uses for hi-fi audio amplifiers.

VARIOUS AMPLIFIER RATINGS AND SPECIFICATIONS
POWER RATINGS

Power ratings for dedicated power amplifiers are the one piece of technical information that consumers base most of their purchases on. And, it makes sense. Sound quality is subjective. You just want to fill your car with good-quality sound (or perhaps blast music through the downtown). Either way, the major concern is the sound level from your speakers. You shouldn't have to worry about the sound quality because the amplifier merely boosts the sound level, right? Yes and no.

As covered earlier in this chapter, power amplifiers *do* color the sound that passes through them. Because most amplifiers are designed fairly well, choosing a fair-quality amplifier won't make your system sound bad, but it could make an otherwise great-sounding system merely sound good. Most people think of amplifier wattages as being linear. When they buy, they get a 100-W amplifier because it is twice as loud as a 50-W amp, and so on. The problem is that sound levels are not based on a linear system of measurement. Instead, sound levels double, based on orders of magnitude. For example, if your amplifier is rated to output 100 W, adding another 100-W amplifier will not double the *sound pressure level*, which is normally measured in decibels (dB). Instead, to double the loudness of the system, you would need to replace the 100-W amplifier with a 1000-W system of amplifiers!

As you can see by the difference between wattage and actual sound levels, you will not normally notice the difference between a few watts here or there if the systems are rated for over 25 W per channel. More than likely, you will notice more of a difference in loudness just from the different means that manufacturers use to determine the amplifier power ratings. To inject some advice at this point, it is better to purchase a high-quality medium-power amplifier than it is to buy a cheaply built high-powered amplifier. Chances are that the audio will be a bit better on the higher-quality amplifier, it will have more features, and it might be rated for less power than it is actually capable of (although the "high-powered" amp might actually be capable of less power than it is rated for).

Depending on how the equipment is rated, the amplifier could sound differently than you would expect for the level that it is rated at. For example, most audio amplification stages will distort at an increasingly higher level if they are driven beyond a certain point. For the 2 x 100-W amplifier that you just picked up, do you know what the percentage of distortion was when those 100 W per channel were measured? Perhaps it was 0.01% or perhaps it was 10%. The difference is incredible. If the distortion was only 0.01%, it should still sound good above 100 W per channel. But if the distortion was 10% at 100 W out, the actual usable power would be more like 50 W per channel—that amount of distortion is just too great for listening by people who aren't even interested in good audio.

Thus, the rated amount of power in an amplifier depends, in part, on how much distortion that the designers believe is allowable. Not only is the maximum amount of allowable signal distortion subjective, but it is not based on a standard amount. As a result, some amplifiers perform as the examples in the previous paragraph: one 2 x 100-W amplifier might be capable of well over 100 W per channel, although another 2 x 100-W amplifier might actually only be capable of 50 "clean" W per channel. The first time I noted this difference was when shopping for a home stereo tuner/amplifier when I was in high school. I had to choose from some major brands with many extra features and basic offerings from a higher-end brand. The salesman showed me how the 50-W per channel amplifier actually didn't sound as loud as the conservatively rated 35-W per channel amplifier, in part because the former was much noisier and it began to distort after a certain volume. Incidentally, this story isn't just based on good salesmanship; the amplifier that he was pushing was a cheaper model than the one that he was telling me to avoid.

SHOPPING FOR AMPLIFIER SPECIFICATIONS

So, how do you know what to expect from an amplifier? The last thing you want to do is search for an amplifier that fits your needs for power, only to find that it can't deliver the power that you purchased it for. As you might suspect, these power ratings can be used to deceive consumers, and unfortunately, some companies seem to purposefully mislead their customers. Very few people have the resources to test and rate the amplifiers on the market for power ratings and sound quality. However, my favorite source of information on the subject are the amplifier reviews in *Car Stereo Review*. The reviewers give the specifications they find in their laboratory and then rate the equipment on a scale for such classifications as sound quality, noise and distortion, ease of installation, etc. These reviews are interesting and helpful; most importantly, they seem to be unbiased and based on their actual findings and not by what companies spend the most money advertising in their magazine. A method that is less scientific is to find a car stereo installation center that has a working audio display so that you can compare different components.

Average output power is only one way in which amplifier power can be rated. The ratings covered so far have generally been for average output power. Amplifiers, as well as most other electronic devices, can also be rated in average input power, peak input power, peak output power, and several other means. *Input power* is the amount of power that is consumed by an amplifier. Depending on the class of amplifier that is used, the amount of output will vary considerably from the amount of power that is input to an amplifier. As a result, *input power* is a nebulous term. *Input power* is not frequently used to describe car audio amplifiers, but it is a common manufacturers' specification for some other types of electronics equipment. Breaking this term down further, *peak input power* is the maximum input power that the amplifier can safely handle

WHAT AMPLIFIER TERMS MEAN	
Input power	Power required to operate amplifier
Peak output power	Power that the speakers must readily accept
Average ouput power	Operating output power of the amplifier
THD	Percentage of distortion in audio
Impedance	If 2 ohms or less, the outputs cn be bridged

and *average input power* is the average amount of power that is used by an amplifier during its course of operation. Likewise, *average output power* is the average amount of power that an amplifier outputs to the speakers during its course of operation and the *peak output power* is the maximum power that the amplifier can safely deliver to the speakers. Because the only rating that matters is one based on what you hear, only average output power is useful for determining how much power you need for your system. Peak and average input power are both important for determining whether your electrical system can tolerate the power-eating requirements of your amplifier. Peak output power can be used to determine what power ratings you must have for your speakers so that they won't blowout on a peak.

LOAD IMPEDANCE AND STABILITY

The issue of load impedance transcends the topics of output power and the quality of construction in the power supply. *Impedance* is the opposition to an alternating current, which is inherent in a line, component, or circuit. This amount of impedance must be closely matched when the signal source is connected to another component. For example, if your amplifier is rated to output into a 4-ohm load, you must use 4-ohm speakers or an impedance-matching system. Otherwise, heat will build up at various points and you could damage the amplifier as a result of the impedance mismatch. Impedance mismatching is also touched upon in Chapter 6, which covers speakers.

Some amplifiers are capable of being used at lower impedances. It might seem strange that anyone would want to run an amplifier with a peculiar output inductance, but the answer lies in Ohm's law. Ohm's law is:

$$E = I \times R$$

Where:
E = voltage (in volts)
I = current (in amperes)
R = resistance (in ohms)

and it has a place in most any electronics application that you can imagine.

The attraction of audio enthusiasts to lower the impedance is twofold. Impedance consists of resistance and inductive reactance. Rather than ramble on an extensive technical diatribe on inductive reactance, resistance, capacitive reactance, and their relationships, let's be flexible and use imagination for a little bit. Even though resistance and impedance are not the same, interchange them in Ohm's Law. If the voltage is constant from the battery and the resistance (impedance) is lowered, then the current must increase. In turn, wattage can be determined by multiplying current times voltage. Thus, if the resistance (impedance) is lowered, then the wattage from the amplifier increases. Following Ohm's Law theoretically, if any given amplifier is rated for a 4-ohm output, it will output twice as many watts into a 2-ohm load (speakers). In reality, however, one manifestation of the differences between impedance and resistance is that the amplifier won't actually output twice as much power into the load. But lowering the impedance is still somewhat effective; for example, if a 100-W amplifer that is rated at for output into a 4-ohm load is operated at 2 ohms, it should still output between 140 and 170 W.

The second reason for implementing a lower output impedance occurs, in part, because of the major problem that arises when using this method of power boosting. When you lowered the resistance (impedance) in the system and, using Ohm's law, the current increased, that current had to come from somewhere. It had to be built up through and regulated by the amplifier. If the amplifier is not built solidly, with better-than-minimum components and specifications in the power supply and power output stages, it will become unstable and be unable to function at this level. Thus, you can use the low-impedance output specification as a benchmark for how solidly the amplifier is built and designed (Fig. 5-8). Many of the high-end amplifiers are specified to operate properly down to 1 ohm and some real "tanks" in the amplifier world can go down to 0.5 ohm!

NOISE

One problem that occurs during the process of amplification is *noise*.

Fig. 5-8 *A stack of Cadence Ultradrive amplifiers. The bottom three are bridgeable and all four can be operated into 2-ohm loads.* Cadence

This term can easily be confused with *distortion*, which occurs because the amplifier alters the signal as it amplifies it. Noise is sometimes called *line noise* because it is a low-level sound, usually a hiss or maybe a hum, that is present in the source and is amplified by the amplifier. Also, some line noise develops in the amplifier because no electronic circuits are perfect, although digital audio certainly improves upon this problem. You can check various amplifiers in this regard. Just check the rated specifications for the *signal-to-noise (S/N) ratio* of the particular amp.

You should look for the highest S/N ratio possible because that is the ratio of actual amplified signal to the amount of noise that is developed in the amplifier. The signal-to-noise ratio is rated in decibels (dB), so it is quite easy to determine which amplifier has the best ratio—just look for the highest numbers! According to the 1998 equipment directory from *Car Audio and Electronics*, the signal-to-noise ratio figures for amplifiers available in North America range from 50 to 120. Although every amplifier differs and each have their own strengths and weaknesses, most of the units with S/N ratios under 80 are the low-end models (ranging in price from $20 to $100) and those that have S/N ratios over 100 are generally high-end models (ranging in price from $250 to several thousand dollars).

The only problem with this rating is that the rating must have a specific reference or the figure is worthless. The typical reference signal for amplifiers is 1 W. If any figure above 1 W is used, the number of dB above 1 W must be subtracted from the listed S/N figure to find the standard S/N ratio. If you are worried about signal-to-noise ratios, check the manufacturer's box, the reviews in the car audio magazines, or call the manufacturer for exact information.

DISTORTION

One of the figures that you will commonly see listed in the amplifier specifications is *THD (total harmonic distortion)*. Any amplifier will cause some distortion to the audio signal. In the case of THD, the amplifier distorts the audio by producing harmonics of the input signal. These harmonics are not "clean" representations of the audio; rather, they make it sound more ragged.

Like the signal-to-noise ratio, the THD depends upon a reference (in this case, a reference power and a reference bandwidth) or the figure is virtually useless. The standard range that THD is measured in ranges across the entire audio frequency from 20 Hz to 20 kHz. Most amplifiers will have a higher or lower THD at different frequencies, so if the THD is only rated for one particular frequency or for one portion of the entire audio frequency range, beware. The THD will most certainly be higher for other frequencies inside of the audio range because any manufacturer who lists in this manner would pick a low THD in order to get a better figure.

AMPLIFIER DESIGN CONFIGURATIONS

MONO OR STEREO

You might be surprised that anyone would consider using a mono (single channel) amplifier. In this day and age, the only people who listen to music in mono are still singing along with Mitch Miller. But alas, mono amplifiers are yet another one of those technological throwbacks to an age where the boys wore coonskin hats and the girls thought that poodle skirts were all the rage.

However, unlike like those days long past, mono amplifiers are not normally used alone. For that matter, the only time a mono amplifier will be useful is when it is used in conjunction with other amplifiers.

LEFT OR RIGHT

The one popular use for mono amplifiers is a crossover method from audiophiles who have used it in their home systems for decades. One option when picking out a car system is to buy a single stereo amplifier that might have trouble keeping the left and right audio channels separate. Although some people might not notice the separation of left and right channels, the audiophile *will* notice the difference (for example, if the cello is coming from 30° to the right instead of from 45°). This difference in stereo separation is disconcerting to someone who expects to hear *everything* exactly as it was recorded.

The audiophilic option to tolerating less-than-precise stereo separation is to use one mono amplifier to boost all signals from the left channel and another mono amplifier to boost all signals from the left channel (Fig. 5-9). In this configuration, the signals will probably be cleaner than with one stereo amplifier. Also, with the separate power supplies, PC boards, and enclosures, the system would be less likely to overheat or blow up.

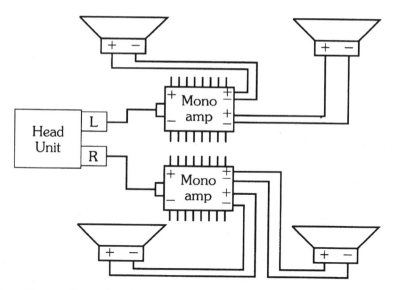

Fig. 5-9 *The configuration for using two mono amplifiers in stereo..*

CENTER CHANNEL

The other use of a mono amplifier is to provide a center audio channel to "beef up" the sound. The center channel is generally a nonphysical entity, an image that is created by having audio reproduced in both the right and left channels. Important information, such as the vocals, are contained on the imaginary center channel. In some cases, the stereo effect of a system will be so prominent that the center channel image will be weak. In order to develop a strong center, where one previously was not present, some people install a physical center channel (Fig. 5-10). This technique can be effective to boost a weak center channel, but if it is not tweaked properly, it could cause some of the stereo effect to disappear. So, if installed improperly, the center-channel technique can degrade the audio quality more than it would boost it.

MONO SUBWOOFERS

Mono amplifiers are especially effective when they drive woofer or subwoofer systems. The wavelength of low frequencies is so long that it is longer than the entire inside of the car (e.g., the wavelength of a sound wave at 50 Hz is 22' or 6.7 m). As a result, the sound pressure wave is virtually the same at all distances, compared to the wavelength (22' or 6.7 m, as was given in the previous example). For that reason, stereo subwoofers within a car are virtually useless. The benefit of the

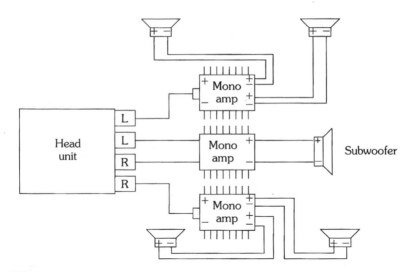

Fig. 5-10 *Using a mono amplifier to amplify a center-channel mono subwoofer.*

"directionless" bass is that you can install a subwoofer most anywhere in the car and not have to worry about the sound noticeably emanating from one particular location. Considering the size of most subwoofers and their enclosures, this is a great relief!

For lower powered systems, you can often bridge a subwoofer across the negative side of one of the stereo output channels to the positive side of the other output channel (Fig. 5-11). Check your amplifier or the one that you are considering purchasing to see if it is possible to bridge it in this manner. If you can't do it, then a dedicated subwoofer amplifier might be in order (Fig. 5-12). Even so, the high-powered systems require separate subwoofer amplifiers because bridging the subwoofers across the outputs of the other amplifiers probably won't drive the subwoofers properly. Another downside to bridging subwoofers across the outputs of the stereo amplifier is that you lose the volume control on the bass. With a dedicated woofer or subwoofer amplifier, you can tweak the low frequencies to the levels that sound great to you.

A large number of dedicated mono amplifiers on the market are made specifically for subwoofers, so they are more efficient at amplifying the low (and not the other) frequencies. If you need more power for your woofer or subwoofer, then a step into the post-Mickey Mantle days of mono amps might be right for you.

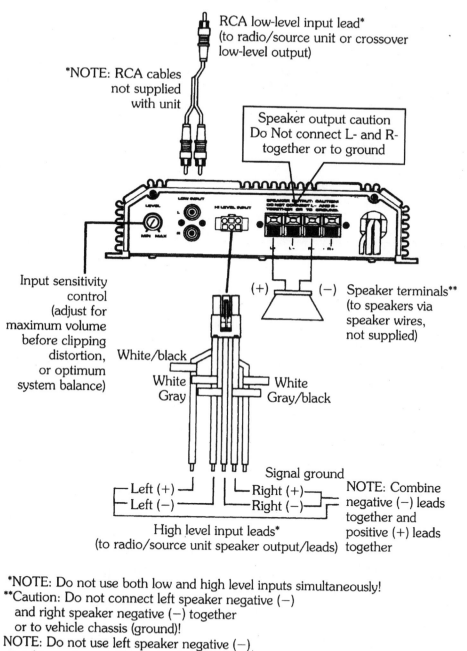

RCA low-level input lead*
(to radio/source unit or crossover
low-level output)

*NOTE: RCA cables
not supplied
with unit

Speaker output caution
Do Not connect L- and R-
together or to ground

Input sensitivity
control
(adjust for
maximum volume
before clipping
distortion,
or optimum
system balance)

(+)   (−) Speaker terminals**
(to speakers via
speaker wires,
not supplied)

White/black
White
Gray
White
Gray/black

Signal ground

Left (+)
Left (−)
Right (+)
Right (−)

NOTE: Combine
negative (−) leads
together and
positive (+) leads
together

High level input leads*
(to radio/source unit speaker output/leads)

*NOTE: Do not use both low and high level inputs simultaneously!
**Caution: Do not connect left speaker negative (−)
and right speaker negative (−) together
or to vehicle chassis (ground)!
NOTE: Do not use left speaker negative (−)
or right speaker positive (+) in bridged mode.

Fig. 5-11 *The system configuration and wiring connections for runnng an amplifier in bridged mono mode.* Jensen

Fig. 5-12 *Becoming more popular are mono amplifiers, for better stereo separation or for amplifying subwoofers.*
Alpine

POWER SUPPLIES

The words "power supply" can mean several different things to different people. For home power, the supply would be related to the wall sockets, the power lines, or the power generators that are operated by the local utility company. The parallel to all of this would be the alternator and the battery in your vehicle.

The *power supply* of any piece of electronic equipment is a device that regulates and supplies the proper voltages to the various circuits that are contained within. This definition of a *power supply* is often contrary to what the average non-electronics-minded person thinks of. Before you start thinking of whoever came up with this term as being a clueless dweeb, think of the power supply for any given piece of electronic equipment as being the input stage or the stage that supplies power to the rest of the amplifier.

Because the power supply has nothing to do with providing the power to the system and everything to do with altering and regulating that power, building a bigger power supply for an amplifier will not solve the problems of having the battery die when the audio system pulls too much power. Where you will find that the power supply should be built more solidly is in the condition where the amplifier clips the audio when it peaks above a certain level. In this condition, in which the amplifier is sometimes said to be "current starved," the amplifier cannot instantaneously react and amplify to the sudden peaks of audio power that burst through from the head unit or preamplifier.

To solve the problem of "current-starved" amplifier, audio engineers use higher-rated capacitors to handle the extra power that is necessary for the audio peaks. Capacitors are one of the basic building blocks in electronics, and they can be used to perform a variety of functions (Fig. 5-13). In this case, the capacitors build up a charge and they function somewhat like a battery. Rather than completely draining, leaving no extra charge for the rest of the peak signal, and causing the audio to clip, the higher-rated capacitors are filled with a larger charge and they have enough power stored to be able to dump a sufficient charge to power the amplifier during the peaks. Because the "current-starved"

Fig. 5-13 *The top view of the main circuit board in a well-built amplifier.*

condition is best avoided, some audio manuals list the amount of capacitance in microfarads throughout the entire amplifier. This capacitance rating doesn't necessarily mean that an amplifier is better built or that it can provide plenty of power to avoid audio clipping. It merely means that it has a large amount of capacitance. If the amplifier is poorly designed, this means nothing. In all, it is much better to read the amplifier reviews in the magazines than to tally up the amount of capacitance in an amplifier.

When an amplifier is clipping, it is being overdriven, whether it has reached its specified output or not. Clipping is not just a problem because the condition distorts the audio, but because it can easily blow out the speakers. The chopped off waveforms can cause the voice coils in the speakers to overheat and subsequently be destroyed. The only solutions to the problem are to either listen to music well within the means of the amplifier (which might mean listening at lower volumes than you would like) or buying another amplifier that you could use in conjunction with the first one.

STEREO SEPARATION

Another problem than can occur with the power supplies in amplifiers is interaction between the power and audio stages. Sometimes the audio will draw power from the power supply, but instead of supplying a steady energy source, the voltage will fluctuate. The voltage fluctuates along with the audio signal, and it makes a sort of duplicate of the audio signal. This duplicate voltage signal can interfere with the two real audio signals. Of course, there is only one source of power; so, when the audio signal modulates the voltage, and it in turn interferes with the audio, the stereo separation will become less prominent. In one magazine article that I read a few years ago, the audio experts involved isolated the dc power in an amplifier (that was in operation) and they were actually able to demodulate it to the point where the songs were recognizable!

The standard for rating stereo separation in *Car Audio and Electronics* is in dB at 1000 Hz, which is within the midrange and where the difference is most important. In some of the recently rated amplifiers, the stereo separation has ranged from 33 to 78 dB—quite a difference. Even so, stereo separation, although helpful in establishing a great sound, is not nearly as important as some figures (such as THD) and some of the features (such as built-in crossovers).

Fig. 5-14 *The Clarion APA1200 mono power amplifier, which offers an average output power of 200 watts with a 0.04 THD.* Clarion

Still, stereo separation is a factor for audiophiles to consider. One of the best ways to clean up the problems with separation between the left and right channels is to use two (or more) mono amplifiers, one (or more) for each channel. Another solution is to purchase one of the high-end amplifiers that solved the problem by building in either a separate power supply for each channel (such as the Monolithic PRO-2000-DM) or building two separate mono amplifiers into the same cabinet (such as the Audison HR-100) to achieve virtually the same results (Fig. 5-14).

Stereo separation is of no concern if you are just using the amplifier to run one or more subwoofers, which typically aren't run in stereo anyway.

ADDITIONAL AMPLIFIER FEATURES

In the high-tech world of car stereo, you can expect that more features will be jammed into an dedicated amplifier than just an amplifier. Today's amplifiers not only include extra features, they also put a spin on some of the standard, boring parts, such as the connectors.

CROSSOVERS

One of the beneficial add-ons to dedicated power amplifiers is a cross-over system. Crossovers are covered throughout this book, so look in Chapter 6, which covers various filters and crossovers, if you need more information about the subject. Power amplifiers are a perfect location for crossovers because they must be placed between the speakers and the amplifier. Unless the crossovers will be installed within an enclosed speaker box, they will need to be built into an enclosure and mounted somewhere in the car or they will bounce around in the trunk or back seat. A much neater solution is to purchase an amplifier with a built-in crossover network. In addition to the neatness benefits, some of the amplifier manufacturers dedicate a great amount of time perfecting their crossovers. As a result, some of the best crossovers available are built into amplifiers (Fig. 5-15). Some of the built-in crossovers are even tunable; that is the high-pass and low-pass positions can be set and altered via a control knob. This feature is particularly useful because you can tune the crossover to match the frequency ratings of your speaker system.

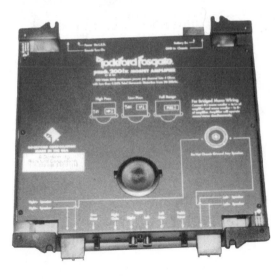

Fig. 5-15 *The underside of the Rockford Fosgate Punch 200ix amplifier, showing inputs, outputs, and the hole through which you can control variable the variable crossover.*

NUMBER OF AVAILABLE CHANNELS

The amplifiers of today aren't merely the in-dash black-box boosters, which defined the technology of the 1970s. Now, many cars are filled with speakers and anywhere from one to eight channels of amplified output are available. The number of amplifier channels is nearly as important as the output power for determining what you need.

For example, if you are in the market for an amplifier to be dedicated to running a single subwoofer that you are mounting in the rear deck, then you would probably be most interested in a mono subwoofer amplifier or a two-channel stereo amplifier that you could bridge for a high-power mono output (Fig. 5-16). If you are an audiophile who is attempting to maximize the "wall of sound" in the car, you will probably want to place as many speakers around the car as possible. For these requirements, you could get as many as eight channels of audio. If you are just interested in setting up a standard, affordable, but great-sounding system, a four-channel amplifier would be best so that you could mount two speakers in the front and two in the rear. Of course, your channel requirements will be more flexible if you will be using several amplifiers and can add the number of channels.

PLUG-IN MODULES

Because of the varied requirements of car audio enthusiasts, one company has even developed a line of plug-in amplifiers so that you can

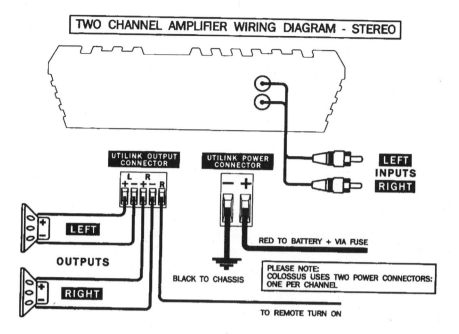

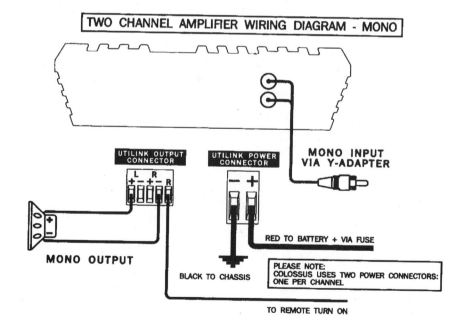

Fig. 5-16 *Connecting an amplifier in stereo or mono.* HiFonics

arrange an amplification system to suit your tastes. Canton has two chassis available that can hold from three to five of their stereo or mono amplifier modules that will plug into the slots. This system is really sharp, but it works well only if you want to stick with Canton-brand amplifiers; no other company builds amplifier modules to fit into the Canton chassis assemblies. Some other amplifier companies use plug-in filters (Fig. 5-17).

GOLD PLATING

Some metals are better conductors than others; that is, power flows

Fig. 5-17 *A plug-in circuit board module plugged into the main amplifier circuit board (center).*

through with less natural line resistance. Also, some metals are more inert (corrosion resistant) than others. Obviously, corrosion resistance is of key importance, given the harsh car environments. So, the key method of reaching maximum corrosion resistance and maximum signal transfer between amplifiers and the interconnects is to use connectors that are plated with a material that is both very highly corrosion resistant and conductive. It just so happens that two of the best metals for these purposes, gold and silver, are also ancient symbols of wealth. So, if you want to maximize your signal transfer with gold-plated connectors, you will have to pay for it. Like many of the car stereo features, you don't need gold plating to have a much better-than-average-sounding car stereo system, but you might notice a difference years from now if the connector begin to have a corrosion problem. The terminals at the forefront (bottom) of Fig. 5-17 are gold plated.

SIZE

Size doesn't seem like much of a feature until you start stuffing amplifiers under the seats, and on the walls and all over the floor of the trunk. A typical amplifier case is approximately 8 x 8 x 2 in. (20.32 x 20.32 x 5.08 cm.), although the higher-powered amplifiers run much larger than this and the lower-powered ones are often much smaller. Depending on your car's available space, size could make a real difference in which amplifier you choose. For example, if you were initially considering an Audison HR-100 amplifier, you might find its 9 x 29 5/8 x 2 in. (22.86 x 75.24 cm) size to be intimidating. Then again, if you were ready to shell out the $6,000 to own one, you might just as soon buy a larger car for it to fit into!

EQUALIZATION

Although equalizers are more often equated with preamps than with dedicated power amplifiers, a number of those on the market do have some type of equalization system. As you can imagine, the equalizers on dedicated power amplifiers, which are normally stuffed somewhere out of sight and out of reach, are not overly complex. Most are merely a "bass boost" or a "treble boost" switch that is mounted on the front panel. The bass boost control is especially handy if the amplifier will be put into dedicated service with one or more woofers or subwoofers. Some amplifiers have several tone controls that you can adjust for a general type of sound that you want to get from your system. Other than the bass boost, the equalization controls aren't very important if you plan to also use a separate equalizer.

NOISE REDUCTION

A few amplifiers on the market actually have built-in noise reduction circuits. None of these circuits are the standard Dolby B, C, or DBX circuits, which are used to decode or modify the audio signals during the recording and playback processes. Instead, these amplifier noise-reduction circuits are all used to prevent ground loops. Rather than decode the information that they receive, they prevent ground loops by using differential inputs, which subtract ground noise from the inputs and break the ground loops that induce noise. Each different company seems to have designed each particular amplifier noise-reduction system specifically for their own amplifiers because it seems that each company uses a different system. For example, Blaupunkt uses the HUSH noise reduction system, Philips uses a CMR (common-mode rejection) circuit, and LA Sound uses a buffered active noise canceller to eliminate ground loop noise problems. Not having ever used these products, I can't say whether or not they are effective or useful. However, one audio expert has told me that these noise-reduction techniques are very effective, particularly if using a high-powered or a very complicated system.

SPEAKER-LEVEL INPUTS

As was stated early on in this chapter, head units are becoming increasingly higher powered. 2 x 25 and even 4 x 25-W head units are becoming common. What if you want still more power? Although many of these head units are high powered, not all of them have line-level outputs. Likewise, not all amplifiers have speaker-level inputs. If you connect speaker-level outputs from a head unit to line-level inputs on a dedicated power amplifier, you could cause severe damage to your equipment. Of course, it is possible to buy speaker-level to line-level adapters, which are currently available for less than $15 from Parts Express. Depending on your situation, speaker-level inputs could be a very important feature.

BRIDGEABILITY

As stated previously in this chapter, an amplifier can produce more power (usually more than twice as much) if the outputs are bridged. This method is particularly useful if you want to bridge an amplifier for dedicated use on either a single (right or left) channel or for a woofer or subwoofer. Most dedicated power amplifiers are bridgeable, but about 10 to 20% percent aren't. This could be a factor if you plan to buy one amplifier, then gradually add more amplifiers and put them into bridged service (Fig. 5-18).

THERMAL AND OVERLOAD PROTECTION

Thermal protection is the ability of a piece of equipment to shut down or blow a fuse if the circuit is overheating and on the verge of being destroyed. *Overload protection* is the same thing, except that it protects the circuit against being overloaded/overdriven, rather than against overheating. Nearly every dedicated power amplifier has both of these form of protection. For the most part, the only amplifiers on the market without these forms of protection are the low-end amplifiers that are built as cheaply as possible. Unless you won't be taxing your amplifier's capabilities and you cannot afford a better amplifier, avoid those without thermal and overload protection. Otherwise, your amplifier could self-destruct before its mission had been completed (Fig. 5-19).

Fig. 5-18 *The end of an amplifier, showing the bridgeable outputs.* Blaupunkt

GAIN CONTROL

Most amplifiers have a gain control knob on the front panel so that you can control the level of amplification (Figs. 5-20 and 5-21). This control is useful because if you set it at a proper level that neither causes the amplifier to be overdriven nor the head unit to be cranked out (causing the signal-to-noise ratio to worsen). Also, amplifiers induce less noise into the audio output if they are being operated at a lower level. For more information on setting the gain control on an amplifier, see the section "Amplifier level tweaking" later on in this chapter.

PRACTICAL AMPLIFIER TIPS AND TRICKS

Dedicated power amplifiers are more along the lines of custom units than head units and their treatment is also more flexible. Of course, you are not expected to modify the equipment, as if you would be if constructing from a kit. Still, you do have the flexibility to mount the amplifier most anywhere in the car, and the ability to adjust the crossover rates, amplifier input levels, and the choice of whether to add a stiffening capacitor.

INSTALLATION LOCATIONS

Dedicated power amplifiers aren't the most difficult pieces of equipment

Fig. 5-19 *This isn't a thermal-overload circuit, but this circuitry is manufactured to reduce the heat in an amplifier. In the center is a metal bar that is screwed down to the heatsink. Under the metal bar is a row of power-amplifier transistors. Good heatsinking will reduce the need for actions from the thermal-overload circuitry.*

to install. Just plug in a few wires and screw the amplifier down and your audio system is in business. However, there are a number of difficulties that spring up and can cause some slight problems in preparation.

For an example of preparatory problems, the most common installation locations for a dedicated power amplifier are in the trunk and under the front seat. You can mount under the front seat, but depending on how hot the amplifier will get, it might not get enough ventilation. You probably won't know if the amplifier gets enough air until you have installed it and see how hot it gets.

If the space is tight, you run the amplifier cranked up, and the case gets very hot to the touch, then you should probably move it to an open area in the trunk. One exception to this rule is in the case of running an amplifier into a load less than 4 ohms (normally, these low-impedance systems run at 2 ohms). In this case, you should *always* install the amplifier in a maximum-ventilation location.

Often the under-the-seat location is difficult because you must remove

Fig. 5-20 *The back side of an amplifier, showing the inputs and gain control.*
Clarion

Fig. 5-21 *A separate volume control that can be screwed in place under the dash for easier access.* Coustic

the seat in order to install it. In some cases, such as with a VW Rabbit, the seat removal is relatively simple. Unscrew a few bolts and then pull out the lightweight seat. However, many other cars have a bench-type front seat that fills most of the front of the passenger space. Depending on the size of the front seat and the manner in which it is installed, it could cause a number of hassles with trying to pull it out.

Amplifiers could be mounted in other locations in the passenger area of the car, but in most cases they are not the optimum. In-dash or under-dash amplifiers ("signal boosters") are common low-end units that were especially typical in the 1970s. These models were often combined with equalizers and they were not known for impressive fidelity. If you are working on a low budget, you might want to find one of these amplifiers and mount it under the dash. Because of the odd sizes that these models were built in, you probably won't be able to find a location in your dashboard to cleanly mount it. If the sound and low cost are more important than the looks, you would probably want to go with the under-dash mount; it's much more convenient to install and operate.

AMPLIFIERS

Depending on the size of the dedicated power amplifier and the amount of space in the passenger area, it might be possible to mount it up in the kick panel on the passenger's side. Not only should the car be roomy and the amplifier be small for this type of installation, but you should run the system at lower level so you don't cause the amplifier to become hot and burn the passenger in your car. For this reason, you shouldn't mount a dedicated power amplifier under the dash board. Your system could very possibly burn the legs of the passenger.

If you decide that a trunk-mounted amplifier is the only way to go, you have a few other options and problems. It is very easy to mount the amplifier on the floor of the trunk or against the back seat, if you have a pickup truck or a sedan. If your car is a hatchback, then you are stuck with mounting either on the floor or on one of the side walls of the vehicle. To install the amplifier on the trunk floor or on the back of the seat, just screw it down.

Be sure that you are screwing into something that is solid. The back seats of many cars are made with dense foam rubber. This type of mount is feasible so long as you use longer screws or butterfly nuts that spread out as you screw them in place. Also, you shouldn't run the amplifier at a level so high that it makes the unit hot to the touch: you might melt the back of the seat!

Also be sure that you will be mounting the amplifier in an area that is clear of any wires or important auto parts. I haven't yet heard of anyone who's done it, but I'm sure that someone somewhere has accidentally mounted their power amplifier over (or over part of) the spare tire in the trunk. The all-important question is whether they realized it soon after doing so or if the moment of realization came moments after getting a flat tire.

Another trunk-mounting option is the side wall of the rear fender. This is a great location, but it requires more work than all of the other simple locations that have been mentioned in this section thus far. If you own a newer car, there might be a layer of carpeting along the inside walls of the rear fenders of the trunk. This material will only get in your way when you go to mount the amplifier.

Because only a thin steel wall separates the back of the trunk from the outside world, you cannot screw the amplifier directly into place. Instead, cut a thick piece of plywood into a shape that is larger than the amplifer and yet will still mount on the hole in the side wall of the rear fender.

Screw the amplifier onto the board and determine the direction that you want it to face. Be sure to place the amplifier in a position that the controls will be accessible. Once you have a position set, consider how the mounting straps should be cut and laid out so that they can securely hold the mounting board in place.

A typical set of mounting straps consist of several strips of metal that have had a few holes drilled in so that screws can hold the mounting board tight against the fender. You could improvise some metal strips (such as side supports from a metal shelving unit) or you could cut your own strips with a pair of tin snips or aviation snips from a piece of sheet metal. If you take this route, be sure to file off any sharp edges or burrs.

Then, bend the mounting straps so that they will fit in nicely with the supports and ensure a tight fit. You will need to drill holes into areas near the panel (such as the floor or a piece of metal that helps support the fender, yet isn't part of what you see on the outside) to hold it in place. When you drill the holes, make sure of where you are drilling; otherwise, you might drill a hole into or through the fender.

Next, use a heavy-duty adhesive, such as Liquid Nails, to glue the mounting board to the trunk wall. While the adhesive is still wet, add the mounting straps and screw them to the board, then into the holes that you drilled earlier. Then, let the adhesive set and try to avoid bumpy drives (railroad tracks, speed bumps, offroad driving, etc.) for the next 24 hours or so. Otherwise, you might bounce the amplifier loose.

The job isn't necessarily easy, but at least it is quite simple. Actually, the wiring for the amplifier will be as or possibly more difficult than installing the amplifier. For more information on cables and cable installations, see Chapter 9, which covers wire, cable, connectors, and transmissions systems, and Chapter 11, which covers several specific installations.

AMPLIFIER LEVEL TWEAKING

When I was a teenager, one of my best friends and I used to copy albums for each other. He had a good component system for someone in their early teens and I had...well, for a while I had my parents' Zenith AM/FM/phono console (no recording capabilities there) and later I could use my parents' average-grade component system. With an audio system under his belt and a father who taught electronics at the local vocational/technical school, he was the audiophile between the two of us. He was also very nice and graciously taped quite a bit of music for me when I was unable to record anything in return. When he recorded, he would usually use some of those snazzy effects, such as Dolby B or C and he would be very careful about the levels of the analog dB meters. A hair into the red and he would back the levels off.

On the other hand, whenever I recorded and still do record (using a less-sensitive digital LED dB meter), I keep the peaks at the next-to-last LED (yes, into the red) of the display. It didn't take me long to notice that my friend's cassettes were always low in volume and I had to crank them up in order to hear them. Even then, the tape hiss would sometimes become quite an annoyance. On the other hand, my friend complained several times about how I pushed the levels. Admittedly, some of the recordings slightly distorted on high-frequency peaks, such as cymbal crashes. A good-sounding level to the average person would probably be in between our two recording-level choices.

More than just a nostalgic trip down memory lane for me, this story illustrates setting the levels in an auto audio system. The recorded material, as compared to the background hiss, represents the signal-to-noise ratio. My recordings have a great signal-to-noise ratio. However, often the peaks of my recordings are clipped as the audio goes beyond the sound "ceiling." My friend's recordings, on the other hand, had no trouble with distortion because the levels were well below the dB "ceiling."

When you set the gain on your car stereo amplifier (or amplifiers), you will be doing exactly the same thing, plus a few extra steps. If you set the gain on the amplifier too low, you will have to turn the volume control of the head unit way up, which will cause more noise to be amplified. As a result, the extra noise will probably be annoying. On the other hand, if you set the gain too high, your amplifier might clip and cause distortion. Chances are, however, that it won't distort, it will just be LOUD! This excessive volume is a real problem if turning the volume knob up to "1" makes it difficult to hold a conversation in the car. The opposite is true if you have to turn the head unit volume control up to "10" and the system still isn't loud enough.

In order to tweak up the system's amplifier gain, pull out a recording (either cassette, compact disc, or MiniDisc) that is representative of the audio levels that you will be listening to. Turn the level of the amplifier to the "0" position (all of the way counterclockwise) and pop in the recording. If necessary, turn the gain on the amplifier up so that you can hear the audio from the source. Then, raise the volume on the head unit until it starts to distort. Back off the level on the head unit until the audio is no longer distorting. Then, turn the gain up on the amplifier until the audio either becomes distorted or is too loud for you to tolerate. At this point, the settings of the amplifier gain are probably close to where you would want them to be, but they might require some final tweaking (such as were described in the previous paragraph).

It's also worth noting that it's important to have a head unit with a high S/N ratio if you are using an amplifier. With an amplifier, you are making all of that system noise sound that much louder. Especially with cassette head units, which vary considerably in S/N ratio, it's important to buy something with as high of a ratio as possible.

USING STIFFENING CAPACITORS IN CONJUNC-TION WITH DEDICATED POWER AMPLIFIERS

One of the hottest fads in auto audio has got to be the stiffening capacitor (Fig. 5-22). Although you can attain some definite system improvements with a stiffening capacitor in certain applications, there are also some

Fig. 5-22 *Stiffening capacitors: 0.5 farad (left) and 1.0 farad (right).*

myths that are floating along. Fortunately, stiffening capacitors and the theories behind them are both quite simple and the tall tales are easy to dispel.

A *stiffening capacitor* is merely a very high-valued capacitor that is used in conjunction with dedicated power amplifiers to temporarily store electricity. When a large power-drawing signal peak drains all available power, the stiffening capacitor discharges in order to fill the power requirement of the amplifier. When the stiffening capacitor unloads, it helps prevent clipping—especially in the bass frequencies, which require much more power to boost the signal to an appropriate-sounding level. So, a sign that you might need a stiffening capacitor in your system is if the bass frequencies distort at high volumes.

ELECTRICAL CONNECTIONS AND SAFETY CONSIDERATIONS

The stiffening capacitor is placed in the power circuit by the dedicated power amplifier (Fig. 5-23). The positive terminal should be connected

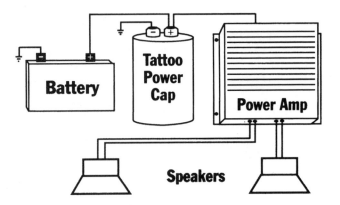

Fig. 5-23 *An installation diagram for installing stiffening capacitors.*
Authorized Parts Company

to the positive lead (in the circuit between the amplifier and the battery. The negative terminal should be connected to ground. Because the capacitor is in the circuit that supplies power to the amplifier, you should follow the same wire gauge specifications for the capacitor's wiring that you did for the power amplifier. Also, the can should be strapped down to the floor or sidewall so that it is secure, won't tip over, and won't short out.

You must be sure that the polarity is not reversed or, just like trying to jump start a car battery with the polarities reversed, you could have a nasty explosion in your car.

One manufacturer specifies that you should charge and discharge the capacitor with a 25-ohm 1/2-W resistor in line with a 12-Vdc power supply. The resistor isn't necessary to charge the capacitor; the alternator will charge it just fine. However, you should discharge the stiffening capacitor with that resistor so that it will unload slowly and not all at once. It's not dangerous in itself to have the capacitor discharge immediately, but you'll probably make fewer mistakes if you connect the resistor across the leads, rather than zap them together with a screwdriver. Just make sure that you aren't also bridging the capacitor's leads or you could be in for a *nasty* shock!

Although the high-current 12-Vdc from the stiffening capacitors is generally not considered to be lethal, they are very dangerous nonetheless. One of my electronics teachers said that some of the guys that he worked with liked to play practical jokes on each other. These jokes sometimes involved loaded high-value capacitors (but not as high-valued as auto stiffening capacitors). In one case, someone threw a charged capacitor to a coworker; in another, several high-value capacitors were charged and placed in a drawer full of capacitors; and in the last joke, a charged capacitor was thrown in a toilet while someone was doing his business (these are not where the term *stiffening capacitor* originated)! The end result was that one of the practical jokers wound up visiting the doctor for second-degree burns and a few other problems. Be careful around capacitors; they can be very dangerous.

Because of the dangers of stiffening capacitors, most companies very clearly mark the polarity on the terminals so that you won't accidentally reverse the wires. As an extra safety precaution, Harrison Laboratory even includes an LED to show when the capacitor is charged so that you won't improperly handle a "hot" capacitor.

When installing the capacitor, you should keep it as close to the amplifier as possible. If your amplifier is close to a highly used area in the car, you should probably place an insulating cap over the top of the capacitor to prevent the terminals from being inadvertently shorted together.

Some audio enthusiasts protect their amplifier and capacitor by installing a fuse between the two. However, this practice only prevents the high current from instantly reaching the amplifier. Instead of protecting the equipment, it defeats the purpose of the stiffening capacitors.

CONNECTING SEVERAL STIFFENING CAPACITORS TO-GETHER

Because of the power requirements for an enormous competition-caliber system are so large, you just might need to use several stiffening capacitors in parallel to supply the necessary instantaneous power to the amplifiers. The group of stiffening capacitors can either be connected via heavy power cables or via a bus bar. The bus bar is a flat metal piece that snaps onto the top of the capacitors and greatly simplifies the connection process. Some companies even sell large gold-plated bus bars for expensive, high-powered systems.

ARE STIFFENING CAPACITORS NECESSARY?

Like any fad, you have to eventually question how many of the positive words are appropriate and how many are just hype. The truth is that stiffening capacitors are necessary to prevent distortion at the low frequencies when the amplifier is being driven hard. Some of the problems can be reduced by using a power amplifier with a more stoutly built power supply. In other cases (such as in super-powered competition vehicles), the capacitors are still necessary.

One factor to consider is cost. Most stiffening capacitors run anywhere from $60 to $220; quite a high price just to remove some low-frequency distortion at high levels. For people who want high power and thundering bass and who are on a budget, it might be more attractive to spend that extra $100 or $200 on another amplifier so that it could be dedicated to operating the subwoofers. And for the price of three 1-F stiffening capacitors are connected to a gold-plated bus bar, you could easily purchase a McIntosh MC420 (4 x 50 W) amplifier, an Alpine 7987 compact disc player, or a Mobile ES MDX-C8900 MiniDisc player. Personally, I'd take the toys and spare a bit of volume, but that's just my preference.

The bottom line is that stiffening capacitors are essential for competition vehicles and for bass boomers, but not necessarily for the audiophile or the average in-car listener. Take some time to listen to your system and get to know it before you shell out the big bucks for those big, shiny cans of electrolyte.

CONCLUSION

For such an apparently simple device, dedicated power amplifiers are fairly complex. To make matters worse, well over 1100 different models were on the market for the 1998 year alone. In order for the amplifiers to be competitive, each company has to create a niche with different features so that they can have their own angle on the market. Chances are that when you go amplifier shopping, you will not even come across half of the models that are available. There are just too many for any distributor to be able to sell them all. Unless you contact some of the companies directly, particularly for the very small, high-end manufacturers, you probably will wind up purchasing something from one of the very large companies that can afford to have their entire line sold by dealers.

6 SPEAKERS

Although some elements of car audio and its components might be foreign to you, speakers should be familiar turf. Probably over half the pieces of electronic equipment on the market are equipped with a speaker of some sort. As common as speakers are, there is still a huge difference between the various grades of quality that are available. Some speakers cost as little as 99 cents, yet others cost hundreds of dollars. What is the difference? Before throwing out some numbers (but not too many), here are a few basics behind speaker theory.

SOME SIMPLIFIED SOUND BASICS

A speaker is just one part of a broad category of components that are known as *transducers*. Transducers change one form of energy into another. One of the other very common types of audio transducers is the microphone. Understanding what a transducer does is a very important part of understanding how high-fidelity audio systems work and can be improved upon.

Whenever a microphone picks up a sound, it changes sound vibrations into electrical impulses (Fig. 6-1). The sound waves strike a thin element that is called a *diaphragm, ribbon*, etc. There are a number of methods by which the sound waves are converted, but in one of the common techniques the diaphragm is held within a magnetic field. Whenever the diaphragm vibrates, it moves within the magnetic field. These movements create an electromagnetic signal that travels through the line cord. In some cases, the microphones contain preamplifiers to boost the signals up to a more usable level.

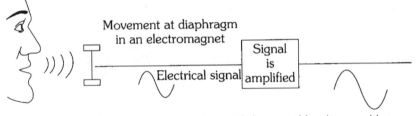

Fig. 6-1 *The traditional analog process by which sound is changed into electrical impulses.*

With the phonographic record (which is used here because it illustrates the point more clearly than the other methods), the same vibrational pattern that the diaphragm made is translated back from an electromagnetic pulse into physical vibrations. These vibrations are cut into a wax disc, and they exactly match the vibrations that the diaphragm made (with the time factor added). After the records have been pressed, the sound process takes an opposite route (Fig. 6-2). The record needle bounces up and down within the groove. The depth of the groove controls the volume of the recording and the width controls the frequencies (wide grooves for low frequencies and narrower for higher frequencies). As with a microphone, the phono cartridge contains an element that vibrates within an electromagnetic field when the needle bounces along in the grooves. These electrical impulses travel to an amplifier, where they are considerably boosted in strength. These signals travel through the speaker wire to the speaker inputs. There, a coil of wire known as the *voice coil* is suspended between a powerful permanent magnet and an iron core. The voice coil is directly connected to the speaker cone (often made from paper), which is what most people

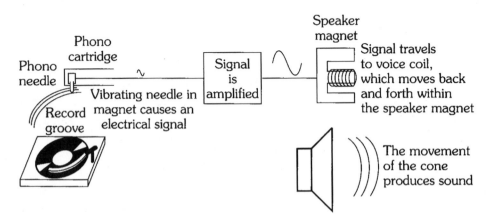

Fig. 6-2 *The process by which the grooves on a record are changed into sound.*

assume the actual speaker to be. The electrical impulses cause the voice coil to pump in and out within the magnet and the iron core. Because the voice coil is connected to the speaker cone, the cone vibrates in and out from the center of the speaker, sort of like the action that a piston makes.

As peculiar as it might seem, the audio from a radio, stereo, television, etc., is produced entirely because the thin paper cones are being pushed in and out. Even after years of using speakers and understanding the basic concepts behind how they work, it still amazes me that speakers can work that way and that they can sound as clear and loud as they do. These vibrations from the speaker cones are, in turn, transmitted through the air.

Sound waves, like any form of energy, will dissipate slowly. Fortunately, because of the enormous wavelengths across the voice frequency range, sound has a very limited range. If it didn't, you would constantly be hearing noise from all around the world. Instead, most sounds are restricted to a range of a few hundred feet or less, and only extremely loud sounds will travel for longer than one mile. Because of this aspect of sound, it is best to know the limitations of the environment that you will be designing a system for. Car stereos basically fit within a big, closed box, so this factor is less important than the acoustics in your particular vehicle. However, you will notice a difference in the sound levels between the same system in a car with less room than if it is installed in one with more room (or the difference between a convertible with the top down and the windows rolled up, and when the top is down). For these reasons, you might have to use more power and more speakers or speakers with higher power ratings, depending on the size of the vehicle's interior.

THE SOUND STAGE

One very important aspect of audio that is almost entirely based on the speakers and their stereo separation is the *sound stage*. The sound stage is the positioning of the sound, as you hear it. The positions that affect the sound stage are front and back (depth), up and down (height), and left and right (width). The sound stage is very important when designing and installing any audio system because it is the key to making music from head unit sound real and lifelike.

The combination of the physical speaker locations, the stereo effects of the recordings that you listen to, and the combination of audio signals in the air creates the sound stage, which is much different than the physical speaker locations alone. When you have four widely separated speaker locations in car, the audio will not sound like it is coming from each of the sources. Instead, it will spread out and fill the car. If all of your speakers are mounted in the front dash, the sound stage will be decidedly to the front, which is generally good, but without rear speakers, the sound will not be as realistic because the audio will lack depth. As a result, it is best to have a balanced set of speakers around the vehicle. With some creative speaker placement and acoustic design, you can create several different sound stages (Fig. 6-3).

For example, as I am writing this, I am listening to a cassette recording on a portable stereo (affectionately known as a "box" around these parts) that is about 4 ft. (approximately 1.3 m) away at a 45° angle to my front left. The sound stage is small and to my lower left. Although the music is clear and in stereo, it does not sound like a real band—it sounds like some music that is coming from a small box a few feet away from me. This sound stage is very narrow and unbalanced and is what you should try to avoid in your vehicle.

On the other hand, I can go out to my car and experience an entirely differ-ent sound stage. With the wonders of faders, I can move the sound stage around me. My personal favorite type of sound stage is to place the settings so that the sounds are hitting me from all angles and it seems as if I am in the middle of the band, but still am facing most of the members. The speaker system consists of one speaker in each side of the dashboard and one in each side of the rear deck. The speakers in the rear deck are built to handle more bass that the speakers in the front. As a result, the sound is three-dimensional—a sort of artificial quad sound. The front/back ratio is set so that the audio from the front and back is almost the same volume from where I am sitting in the driver's seat. Thus, bassier instruments sound as if they are coming from the back somewhere, but everything else seems to be coming from very slightly in front of me. By setting the faders this way, I am sacrificing the audio that would sound as if it was coming from far in front of me (and as a result, all of the points of origin for up-front sounds seem to be very close).

Many sound experts would say that I have shortened the frontal sound stage too much with my settings, but I like it this way and it's my system. Like-wise, with some experimentation, you can set the sound stage in a manner that suits your tastes.

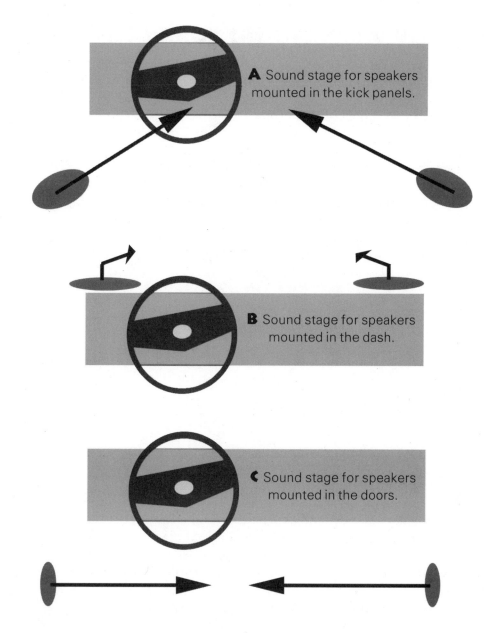

A Sound stage for speakers mounted in the kick panels.

B Sound stage for speakers mounted in the dash.

C Sound stage for speakers mounted in the doors.

Fig. 6-3 *Several different sound stages for the front of a car. The kick-panel sound stage (A) offers the greatest distance between speakers, and thus the best stereo separation, but it is more difficult to properly aim the speakers. The top dash-mounted speaker arrangement (B) is most common because the sound is good, no speaker alignment is required, and most dashboards have open space left over for speakers. Mounting speakers in doors (C) is not often recommended because great effort is required to keep them from firing audio into legs and mounting holes often interfere with winding the windows.*

SPEAKER ACTION AND COMPONENTS

Any speaker consists of a number of components that must work together as a team (Fig. 6-4).

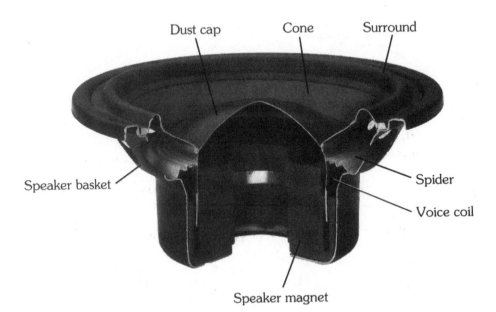

Fig. 6-4 *A cutaway view of a speaker that shows its individual parts.* Morel Acoustics

MAGNETS

As stated in the previous section, the voice coil is a coil of wire that moves within the speaker magnet and an iron core in the center. Because the magnet (Fig. 6-4) is the key to the magnetic field that the voice coil moves in, a stronger magnetic field is necessary for the speaker to be able to handle greater amounts of power. Generally, with the speakers from one particular manufacturer (or from a particular product line), you can go by the rule: the larger and heavier that the magnets are, the better the speakers are. This isn't always the case because some magnets have a stronger pull per pound than others. Most speaker magnets are made from ferrite, a form of powdered iron, and ceramic magnets, although some of the high-power handling speakers have strontium magnets.

Although most people can deduce whether or not they would be satisfied with a particular speaker system just from the catalog specifications, it is always best to preview any potential purchases beforehand, especially if you are an audiophile. Some speakers are not designed as well or use materials of lower quality, but still have heavy magnets. This difference will generally occur in the higher-end speaker class; large speaker magnets are expensive and few manufacturers will blow their profits on overstocking a speaker with extra magnet material.

Another problem with judging speaker quality by sheer magnet weight alone is damping. *Damping* is the reduction in the speaker cone's ability to move properly. The problem is that a large magnet with a strong pull is necessary to handle a large amount of power, yet too much magnet strength will restrict the movement of the speaker cone and will in turn reduce its low-frequency response. The engineering trade-off is to design a heavy-duty speaker that can handle the power output of a small nuclear reactor and yet still be able to produce thundering low frequencies that could crack the former Presidents' ears on Mt. Rushmore.

So, you can deduce quite a bit from the magnet size and composition, but not everything. That is part of the difficulty with choosing speakers: you can choose by price, by manufacturer, by advice, or by the features in the catalog descriptions, but you won't know what any given speaker sounds like until you listen to it.

VOICE COILS

The speaker *voice coil* (Fig. 6-4) generally consists of a very fine gauge of enameled copper wire wound around a bobbin, which fits in between the permanent magnet and the iron core in the center (Fig. 6-4). The bobbin must slide straight back and forth within this space without grinding against the magnet and the iron core or it will hang up and fail. For this reason, you should be very careful to clean up any metal tailings or wood chips when cutting holes during the installation process. If you leave them behind, they could work their way into the voice coil of the speaker and destroy it.

The most common cause of speaker damage is voice coil failure. When a speaker is driven by more power than it can safely handle, the voice coil will overheat and then short. Some high-powered speakers use air-ventilated or liquid-cooling methods to prevent the voice coil from becoming too hot and opening. This is an excellent method to prevent speaker damage. Tweeters are the most fragile of all speakers. The voice coils in woofers and subwoofers must move across large distances, and they are often pumped with huge amounts of power. If possible, purchase tweeters, coaxial speakers, woofers, and subwoofers with liquid-cooled voice coils if you plan to install a high-power system. But the liquid-cooled speakers are more expensive than speakers without additional cooling, so they might be out of your budget.

DUAL VOICE COILS

A handful of the more expensive speakers on the market contain dual voice coils (nearly always in woofers and subwoofers). Each speaker coil (Fig. 6-5) is an equal length of coiled wire of the same gauge and wire loop spacing.

Fig. 6-5 *A dual voice coil subwoofer. Notice the pairs of speaker input terminals mounted on opposite sides of the speaker basket.*

Then, one coil is placed inside of the other. Rather than being entirely independent, both voice coils are connected to the same speaker cone and both pump it in and out. Also, these speakers have two sets of connections, one for each voice coil. Otherwise, the performance is similar to a standard single voice coil speaker.

The peculiar aspect of the dual voice coil speaker is that the performance is not really affected by having the extra coil. In fact, if the two voice coil connections are hooked up to a stereo amplifier, one voice coil will be operating from the right channel and the other will be operating from the left. Because they are both operating the same speaker cone, the voice coils will push and pull out of synch with each other and cancel out. The cancellation is on par with standing waves in speaker boxes or weak, flexible walls in a speaker enclosure, where some of the frequencies are cancelled out and the response is uneven. In other words, they are not meant to be hooked up in stereo.

The usefulness of dual voice coil speakers lies in the flexible ways to install and connect the speakers because of the impedance and the extra speaker terminals. For more information on dual voice coil speakers and their advantages, see the section on speaker impedance and connections at the end of this chapter.

SPEAKER CONES

Although the voice coils do most of the actual work in a speaker, the speaker cones (Fig. 5-4D) account for the sound that you hear.

CONE MATERIALS

For years, speaker cones have been made from paper or cloth. The improvements in speaker cone materials are one of the great advances in car audio speaker design over the past decade. Presently, a number of different materials are used to make speaker cones, including polypropylene, polymerized paper, corrugated fiber, Kelvar-reinforced paper, titanium, titanium/polymer composite, Mylar film, etc.

Any particular cone material is chosen over another type for reasons of cost, speaker type, sound quality, sound environment, and durability. For example, paper speaker cones are commonly used in home audio systems. However, if speakers with paper cones are used in car stereo applications, they could easily warp from dampness or degrade in the Sun's ultraviolet light. Instead, many of the speakers for the car use polypropylene or other resistant material cones (Fig. 6-6) because they will not warp as a result of dampness in the car (Fig. 6-7). On the downside, polypropylene is not touted at the world's best-sounding speaker material; but when it comes to having good-sounding speakers or having an expensive pile of steel and paper that used to sound fabulous, I think the choice is easy.

I might be overdramatizing the difference in durability between paper cones and the other types, but some of that depends on the car that you own. My family's cars vary quite a bit. Our 1981 Volkswagen Rabbit is not at all watertight, after every rain, the carpet along the floor is wet and musty. In this case, the polypropylene speaker cones (Fig. 6-8) are the best bet (either

Fig. 6-6 *This speaker cone consists of woven fiberglass.* Polydax

that or spending a few dollars to get the car watertight). On the other hand, our Plymouth Voyager is in much better condition, from a waterproofing standpoint, than the Rabbit. Rather than fill with condensation after every rain, the Voyager is always dry, and I would be more apt to choose paper cone speakers for this car.

Fig. 6-7 *The close-up of this speaker shows the pattern of woven carbon strands.* Altec Lansing

Fig. 6-8 *A speaker with a polypropylene speaker cone.* Madisound

The materials for speaker cones are also chosen for the frequency range of the speaker that they will be used in. Heavier cone materials are used in the low-frequency speakers and thinner, stiffer cone materials are used in the high-frequency speakers. For example, thick, polymerized paper cones are often used in woofers and subwoofers because the thick material is strong and flexible. Its representation of high-frequency signals is poor, but that's fine because it is only intended to radiate the low end of the audio spectrum. Titanium (Fig. 6-9) and other very stiff materials are used in tweeters because they are strong and reproduce shrill sounds very well. These materials cannot tolerate the low-frequency sounds because they would be quickly destroyed by the long, deep movements that are required to reproduce sound at these wavelengths. Because of the medium range of the mid-range drivers, they are often a

Fig. 6-9 *A tweeter that uses a titanium speaker cone.* Polydax

Fig. 6-10 *The Velodyne DF-10SC. The aluminum-coned sub is on the left and the servo controller is on the right.* Velodyne Acoustics

compromise in materials between the woofer and the tweeter.

One interesting switch from the normal use of metal cones for only tweeters is theVelodyne DF-10SC subwoofer (Fig. 6-10). The subwoofer uses an aluminum cone and requires a model-specific servo controller box, to which the audio signal inputs are fed. It seems like a lot of extra electronics, just to produce some good bass, but the idea is interesting.

Dust caps

Dust caps are merely dome-shaped caps that are sealed around the center of the speaker cone over the area of the voice coil (Fig. 6-4). The dust cap is primarily intended to prevent dust, dirt, and debris from entering the small space around the voice coil and, consequently, destroying it.

Dust caps can have an impact on the sound, and they do push in and out along with the speaker cones. As a result, they are also often made of the same material that the speaker cone was constructed from, although some other materials are sometimes used. In auto woofers and subwoofers, one of the prime applications of dust caps is as a bright "billboard advertisement" for the speakers (Fig. 6-11).

Fig. 6-11 *The MTX "Black Gold" series of woofers with flashy logos on the dust caps.* MTX

SUSPENSIONS

SURROUNDS

As the speaker cones are pumping like pistons in a car engine, the surround is flexing and holding the cone to the speaker's frame (Fig. 6-4). The surround consists of a thin ring of polyester foam, polyether foam, rubber butyl rubber, paper, or cloth that attaches the outer edge of the speaker cone to the top outer edge of the metal basket. The surround helps to control the speaker movement and it also absorbs energy from the speaker cone. This combination is flexible enough to allow the speaker cone to move and produce high-quality sound, yet it is tough

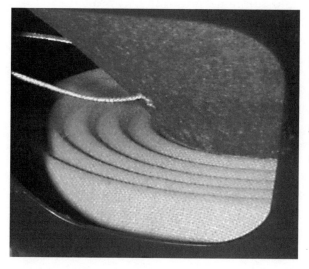

Fig. 6-12 *A close-up view of the spider, which fills the gap between the cone and the basket. Also visible in the photo are the two braided wires that run from the terminals to the cone.*

enough to keep the cone in place without tearing away.

The surrounds take the worst physical beating in the speaker and are also one of the few weak links in speakers over the course of years. The problem is that the material must be flexible enough to bounce in and out smoothly. This requirement alone generally reduces the possible materials down to some synthetic foams (although, as mentioned, cloth and paper surrounds are sometimes used). The problem is that these materials have not been able to withstand damage from ultraviolet light in the past. After a few years of sitting in strong sunlight, they have broken down and cracked. Then, they are usually thrown out or replaced. Recently, some companies and small speaker repair shops have begun to replace speaker surrounds, and Parts Express offers do-it-yourself surround replacement kits. More information on speaker repair is contained in Chapter 11.

SPIDER

Contrary to unpopular beliefs, the speaker *spider* was neither named after a Fiat nor because this form of suspension is made out of ground spiders. Frankly, I have no idea why this ribbed, circular, piece of cloth mesh is so named (Figs. 6-4 and 6-12). My wife believes that it's because spiders were often found in hardened resin and were fashioned into jewelry. Either way, the spider of a speaker is a piece of cloth that has been soaked in resin, so it is still and it holds its shape, yet it is still flexible. Like the surround, the spider is connected to the speaker cone and the speaker basket. Likewise, the spider also helps to control the speaker cone and prevent it from distorting in shape (and, in turn, in sound quality). In spite of its colorful name, the spider is a mostly ignored part of the speaker.

SPEAKER BASKET

The *speaker basket* looks and functions like the name implies—it is a metal basket that holds the speaker components (Figs. 6-4 and 6-12). If the speaker was an animal, the basket would be the exoskeleton; it provides the necessary strength and rigidity to hold the entire unit together (and it is all on the exterior). It is important for the speaker baskets to be constructed out of one piece of metal to prevent any rattling at high volumes. Many of the high-end speaker baskets are even cast out of aluminum for extra strength with less weight.

SPEAKER CONNECTIONS

Most speakers have a pair of lugs that are mounted on a small piece of circuit board material (Fig. 6-13). This board is then mounted on the side of the speaker basket. Nearly all speaker companies use standard

Fig. 6-13 *A close-up of a pair of lug-type speaker terminals. Also clearly visible are the surround and the polypropylene cone.*

lugs that mate with slide-on connectors. However, a few of the high-end companies, such as Hart Professional and AVI, use gold-plated screw terminals. Considering that few speaker companies use gold-plated terminals, it is difficult to recommend that your speakers have them. However, it does make sense that if you are going to spend the extra money on gold-plated amplifier terminals, power distribution blocks, and RCA plugs, that the final interconnections (the speaker terminals) would be gold plated as well. Gold is an efficient conductor, but it is also quite expensive.

SPEAKER CLASSIFICATIONS (BY FREQUENCY)

To some extent, speakers can be classified by size or maybe even by the materials that they are built with. But, a more-accurate method of classification is to sort the speakers out by the frequencies that each model is most capable of reproducing accurately.

Other than woofers and subwoofers, no speakers can fit into more than one classification. It just wouldn't be accurate for a speaker to be listed as a "tweeter/midrange/woofer." In that case, it would simply be a midrange. Most speakers in stock car audio systems simply use one inexpensive, all-purpose midrange speaker. These speakers will reproduce audio frequencies across much of the hearing range, but they are deficient in several ways. Frequency-wise, these stock midranges are most lacking in their response at the lower frequencies. Because of the small wavelength of the much higher frequencies, they can be reproduced via small speakers that require fewer materials and are much less expensive to build. However, to reproduce the bass and low bass frequencies, a much larger speaker is necessary. The larger speaker is much more expensive to build, so the typical stock auto audio system only has a relatively small set of basic midrange speakers.

TWEETER

A *tweeter* is a speaker that is designed to reproduce high-frequency audio (Fig. 6-14). The general frequency-reproducing specifications of

Fig. 6-14 *A tweeter.* Polydax

tweeters are from 4 to over 20 kHz. One of the most important actions of a tweeter's speaker cone is to move very quickly; otherwise, it will not be capable of reproducing the high frequencies. Because of this need, tweeter cones are often made of stiffer materials than those intended for lower frequencies. Some of the speaker cone materials used in tweeters are paper, aluminum, titanium, polymer, ceramics, silk, polymide, cloth, and graphite. Tweeters are much smaller (often as small as 2 in. in diameter) and more fragile than the other speaker types. Tweeters must be used in conjunction with other speakers.

Midrange

Midrange speakers are designed to reproduce audio in the middle frequencies (Fig. 6-15). Midranges are a bit less interesting because the

Fig. 6-15 *A midrange speaker.* Polydax

woofers and tweeters operate in a specialized manner, but the midranges are much more of a compromise between the two designs. To classify as a midrange, the speaker should produce audio frequencies in the range from about 400 Hz to 5 kHz. These frequencies overlap a bit with the tweeters and woofers because every speaker varies a bit in the styling and the frequency range that it is intended for. Most midrange speakers are approximately 4" to 6" (10.16 cm to 15.24 cm) wide, so they are somewhat convenient for mounting in cars, unlike woofers.

For many years, audio enthusiasts concentrated on the bass and treble frequencies because they were at the edge of the hearing range and were more difficult to reproduce than those in the middle. Times have changed and people are realizing the importance of the once-forgotten midranges. Most of the human hearing lies within the midrange frequencies. If you concentrate on the high and low frequencies, you will be emphasizing frequencies that humans don't hear as well at and also ones that aren't as critical musically. As a result, if you are working from a separate speaker standpoint, it is best to first buy a good set of midrange speakers, and then build the system from there. After all, if you have great speakers, it's best to use those that operate in a frequency range where you can best hear them.

MIDBASS

Midbass speakers aren't especially common, but they are designed to reproduce audio in the upper end of the woofer region/lower end of the midrange region. Most midbass speakers will cover anywhere from approximately from 200 Hz to 3 kHz, which is anywhere from the bass region up through the midrange. Most midbass speakers are approximately 6 in. (15.24 cm) in diameter, which could be a prohibitive size, depending on where you plan to mount them. Overall, most midbass speakers are designed in the same style as woofers, except smaller. The mid-range speaker in Fig. 6-15 is called a *bass-midrange speaker* in the Audax catalog, so it would also work here.

For your system, midbass speakers might be handy. They should work best in systems where separate speakers (not multiple-drive speakers) are used. Midbass speakers work well without any woofers, but they work better in conjunction with subwoofers or crossovers. That way, you can prevent the subwoofer and the midbass speakers from reproducing the same sounds, which will probably make the bass sound boomy and less crisp. Otherwise, you could use a crossover (either a separate unit or one that is built into the amplifier) to make sure that the frequencies that are intended for each speaker don't overlap.

Overall, midbass speakers are not particularly common in auto sound systems, but they are somewhat common in the more specialized audiophile systems. Audiophiles are great at tweaking, and with a set of specialized well-made speakers, the midbasses are perfect for high-end systems.

WOOFER

Woofers reproduce bass frequencies, generally in the range from approximately 30 Hz to 2 kHz (however, they do much better in the lower end of their collective range). Woofers are characterized by their large sizes and heavy-duty construction (see Figs. 6-11 and 6-12). Most woofers range in size from about 8 to 18 in., although the most favored woofer sizes are 10 in. (20.54 cm), 12 in. (30.48 cm), and 15 in. (38.1 cm)(in diameter). As was mentioned previously, the speaker cone materials are often (but not always) thicker and tougher than those for high-frequency applications. Some of the woofer speaker cone materials include paper, polypropylene, "organic" fiber, glass fiber, Kevlar, graphite, carbon, etc. The overall favorite for woofers and subwoofers seems to be paper or some combination of paper and another material.

In general, woofers are placed in the back of the vehicle; in the trunk, behind the seat, or on the hatchback. Part of the reason for this is to improve the sound stage and part is just because it is so much more convenient to stuff the huge speakers in the trunk. Speaker placement is covered further in this chapter and speaker installation is covered in Chapter 10.

SUBWOOFER

A microcosm of woofers, *subwoofers* reproduce the low bass frequencies, generally in the range from approximately 20 Hz to 1 kHz. In many cases, subwoofers are not considered to be a separate grouping, but are instead considered to be a subset or just lower-range woofers. There is some basis for this lack of a separate grouping because the frequency specifications for subwoofers are not significantly different from those of woofers, and also because the size and construction of the two types are very similar.

Fig. 6-16 *A pair of bass tubes, shown from both ends.* Collins USA

In car stereo applications, it seems as though a subwoofer is any type of woofer that is mounted separately in a such a position as in the trunk or in a "bass tube" (Fig. 6-16). In all, the term *subwoofer* has become synonymous with the deep bass sound that is especially sought after for rap and hip-hop recordings. So, when you hear someone talking about subs, it could be anything from a "true" subwoofer to a standard woofer.

MULTIPLE-DRIVER SPEAKERS

If you don't drive a 1975 Ford Grenada with enough space inside to hold a rock concert, then you might become discouraged about installing a good-sounding speaker system into your car. If you decide to go with a pair of tweeters and midranges in the front and a pair of tweeters, a pair of midranges, and a pair of woofers in the back, then you need to account for 10 speaker holes in your car. Most newer cars simply cannot handle such a large amount of speaker holes in the car.

Fig. 6-17 *A whole series of Blaupunkt multiple-driver speakers, showing the various sizes, shapes, and configurations available.* Blaupunkt

The only alternative with placing one speaker in each stock speaker location is to use four full-range/midrange speakers, but the sound quality is not as good as if you used separate speakers. Another possibility is to alter the positions of the speaker holes without cutting anything: take your car to an auto stereo installation shop and have custom fiberglass speaker panels built to match your car. As you can imagine, custom panel work at an installation center is very expensive—it would probably cost about as much as the entire price tag of my used car. So, if you want to get the multiple-speaker sound from only the stock mounting holes, the only option is to have several speakers mounted together. Multiple-driver speakers have several speakers that are built into one basket (Fig. 6-17). The most common type of multiple-driver speaker is the *three-way* arrangement, which has one midrange and two different frequencies of tweeters built onto the frame above the midrange cone. Other possibilities are the standard two-way (coaxial) speaker and even the four-way speaker.

Multiple-driver speakers are designed with the tweeter (or tweeters) mounted in the center of the midrange speaker cone. This is tough because the tweeters must be mounted to something solid, yet if they extend out into the edges of the midrange speaker, its sound will be muffled. To solve this dilemma, the tweeters are bonded together on a plastic "shelf" and they are in turn mounted on a post that runs to the center of the midrange speaker. This creates further problems because, referring back to Fig. 6-17, the post runs straight through the area where the dust cap should be. Instead, the dust cap is not used and the post is connected to the center of the voice coil. The fit around the center post must be close to prevent dirt and dust from getting in the space between the voice coil and the magnet. Some multiple-driver speakers even attach a piece of felt to the middle of the midrange cone or a piece of foam wrapped around the center post to prevent this from occurring.

Otherwise, most multiple-driver speakers operate as autonomous speakers. In these cases, each of the tweeters has their own magnets, etc. They are merely three speakers that have their input leads connected together—usually in parallel, but possibly in other configurations, depending on the whims of the engineers.

Some multiple-driver speakers include a parasitic passive "speaker" (Fig. 6-18). In this case, the parasitic speaker is a small tweeter that is mounted above the midrange, usually beside a real tweeter, to make a sort of three-way speaker. The parasitic tweeter is merely the cone of a tweeter. The sound waves from the midrange are caught by the tweeter cone, and it, in turn, vibrates at a higher frequency. These parasitic

Fig. 6-18 *A multiple-driver speaker that uses a parasitic passive "speaker."*

speakers have the advantage of being a bit cheaper to build than traditional three-way speakers, but the sound quality generally isn't quite as good as with "real" speakers. Of course, I bought a used pair of three-way speakers with parasitic tweeters for only a few dollars, so it was worth the sacrifice.

Multiple-driver speakers were an excellent breakthrough in speaker technology because the sound could be improved considerably, compared to the amount of extra custom car work that would need to be done otherwise.

Buying speakers

Buying speakers can be a big problem because, as far as sound quality is concerned, speakers are the most important components in your system. Yet, you can't necessarily rate speaker quality by looks, size, size of the magnet, speaker cone materials, or price. Because of the variables in speaker construction and design, it is somewhat common for most people to give a better rating to a speaker that costs half as much as another. Notice that I said "most." Beyond a point, good-quality audio is completely subjective. Although the ultimate goal of most people is to have a system that *exactly* reproduces the music that was produced as it was being recorded, some actually would rather have a system that is inaccurate. One example of this are the "bassheads," who would rather boost the bass higher than the proportion at which they were recorded. When it gets down to intricacies such as these, it's your system and you have to buy it. Pick the sound that you like.

Similar to the situation with amplifiers, one of the worst problems with picking out what speakers to use in your vehicle is the sheer number of speakers on the market. According to the most recent *Car Audio and Electronics* buyer's guide, there are 969 different models of multiple-driver speakers, 452 different models of enclosed speakers, and 1,774 different models of "raw" speakers currently available. That means that 3,195 different speakers were available in one year alone. Which ones will you pick for your car?

When it comes right down to it, the main factors that will affect your choice of speakers are cost and availability. With so many different speaker varieties available, chances are that you will not be able to find some of the brands and models. No car stereo stores have the facilities to buy every model that's on the market; very few would even have 1/20 of those in stock. Pricewise, chances are the you will get the most for your money from the large companies that sell in such volume that they can afford to offer lower prices or to offer special discounts to the distributors who buy many of their units. Of course, many auto audio enthusiasts will also note that some of the larger companies use their big name to sell substandard equipment. So, where do you turn to?

If you just want something that sounds better than the stock speakers in your car, and you don't care much about the sound quality otherwise, just purchase a set of four multiple-driver speakers. There's no reason to waste time and money if you won't even notice a difference in the sound quality. You will save much more money if you shop around for a discounted price. If you are lucky, you might even be able to find a complete set of discontinued speakers or maybe a set of floor model speakers.

On the other hand, if you care at all about the sound in your car, re-search anywhere you can and gather as much information as possible. Read the car auto magazine reviews and tests for all of the speakers that might catch your interest. Rather than just feature one speaker and talk up its good points, *Car Audio and Electronics* actually laboratory tests a handful (maybe eight, for example) of speakers (and other stereo components) from time to time. The *CA&E* equipment testing team discusses the various strong and weak points of each component, shows graphs that represent various specifications, and finally rates the components in terms of best overall performance. These reviews command a great deal of respect among auto audio enthusiasts, and they are a great source of information when shopping for equipment.

Next, go to audio stores and local installation shops and listen to as many different speakers as you can. Some of these shops have their own sound rooms so that you can test out the various speakers on your own. Of course, the speakers will all sound differently when they are mounted in a car (they won't even sound the same if you have the same speakers mounted in different cars) than in an acoustically sound test room. Still, they will give you an idea of what you can expect from a set of speakers. Make sure that you go to each testing session adequately prepared. Take a few examples of music that have excellent audio/recording quality and that you know very well. Listen closely to the various parts of the songs and see how well the speakers reproduce the sound. If you have a home stereo system that you are satisfied with, listen to the test tracks at home to get a feel for what you should be listening for. Listen to the tracks at home as close to your listening test trips as possible. Unless you have been doing installations and tweaking for a few years, you will probably not have the experience to automatically *know* what a system is lacking.

While you are at the audio stores and installation shops, ask the salespeople as many questions as possible. Ask questions about installation, system designing, repairs, warranty information, and anything else that might come to mind. Also ask for opinions because chances are that the salesperson knows these speakers far better than you do. Remember that anything that the salesperson says is going to be colored by the fact that they will be getting a commission off of their sales (possibly from you). They will be biased toward any product that their store carries, and they will generally lean toward the more expensive products that they sell. It is very rare, but if the salesperson recommends equipment that is sold elsewhere, be sure to take the advice; the salesperson is going against store policy and personal interests to give you honest advice.

Next, if you have any friends who have aftermarket car stereo systems, talk to them about their systems—get their opinions on most any audio subject. Like the salespeople at the car stereo shops and installation centers, remember the potential biases and altered opinions that these people might have. For example, one person might have bought a set of low-end speakers from Konopasek Audio. After some bad experiences with this set of speakers, your friend sounds like Beavis or Butthead and constantly says "Konopasek Audio sucks!" every time that the subject of auto audio comes up. Little does he know that that particular type of speakers was an inexpensive offering, made to get the company shelf space in a discount department store. And the rest of Konopasek Audio's line consists of competition- and near-competition quality equipment.

Or the near-opposite could happen: perhaps your friend picked up a McCandless Speakers' pair of 6 x 9s (15.24 x 22.86 cm) a few years ago and he thinks that they are the greatest thing since head-cleaning cassette leader tape. Little does he know that the company was bought out by Amalgamated Stereo two years ago, and it was decided that the company should focus on low-end audio instead. As a result, several of the innovative audio engineers from McCandless Speakers quit and the design department has been in shambles as a result. Now, McCandless Speakers is dumping out inferior speakers that are more suitable as coffee table coasters, yet your friend *loves* his speakers—and he can even let you hear them to *prove* how great they sound! So, listen to your friends' advice and opinions, but be sure to balance this information out with information from these other sources. (Just in case you're wondering, Konopasek Audio, McCandless Speakers, and Amalgamated Stereo are fictional names, created specifically for this illustration.)

If you have a computer, be sure to check into the computer bulletin boards and networks for some of the best and timeliest auto audio information available. The computer bulletin boards that specialize in auto audio are operated by people who are dedicated to the hobby on a noncommercial basis. In most cases, they are participating because they love the hobby and not because they will benefit financially from any transactions in cyberspace. For information on calling the different computer bulletins that are dedicated to auto audio, flip back to the Appendix, which covers various sources of helpful information.

At this point, the Internet is beginning to make its way into the news on a regular basis, but yet a number of people still don't know what it is. The Internet is a computer system that connects an estimated 1.5 to 2 million computers around the world. Many of these connections are to universities and military installations, but personal subscriptions to various systems that connect to the Internet (such as via Delphi and America On-Line) are becoming much more common. Also, some of the large local computer bulletin boards are setting up subscriptions to different parts of the Internet. The charges for connection time are usually vary from about $40 to $200 per year (plus any applicable long-distance charges) for a subscription to part or all of the Internet.

The Internet has a number of features, including different newsgroups (known as *Usenet*), electronic mail (known as *e-mail*), and connections to a number of different university libraries. Some entire books are even on line! As far as its benefits to auto audio are concerned, I have found that the Usenet group rec.audio.car is loaded with beneficial information. Hobbyists post questions or talk about various experiences and others provide answers or opinions. In general, the users are good-natured and helpful, although the exchanges sometimes get heated over some subjects, such as "Are Kenwood head units better than Pioneer head units." This is a great place to receive noncommercial tips and information about a variety of manufacturers and products from those who have had experience with the equipment. Also, audio enthusiasts frequently post "equipment for sale" messages; just remember to follow the basic conservative approaches to buying used equipment that were covered more extensively in Chapter 1.

FULL-RANGE SPEAKERS, MULTIPLE SPEAKERS, ENCLOSED SPEAKERS, OR MULTIPLE-DRIVER SPEAKERS?

One of the big dilemmas in purchasing a speaker system for your car is what to stick in those holes after you have ripped out the stock speakers. The answer is usually speakers, but what type? This debate rages on from time to time, but it is generally believed that multiple speakers provide a more realistic sound than multiple-driver speakers. Of course, there are also some people who would rather spend the money that they would allocate for the rear speakers on two excellent-quality full-range (or midrange) speakers than on a set of lesser-quality tweeters and midrange speakers or on a set of multiple-driver speakers.

Each of these methods is a feasible approach for piping good music into your vehicle. But which approach is best for you? In general, given good-quality speakers, the best-sounding approach is to use separate speakers instead of the other options (Fig. 6-19). Even if the quality of all of the speakers is the same, the separates will have the advantage because they can be tweaked and moved into positions so that you will have the best imaging possible and exact type of sound stage that you want.

On the other hand, the rear speakers are often used more as a fill for the back end of the sound stage. If your intentions are to fill out the sound from the rear with high-quality midrange and bass, you might opt for a good set of full-range or midbass speakers for the rear deck. A system like this would be especially useful for someone who wants a strong frontal soundstage—especially if passengers will only be sitting in the front seat. This route would be the cheapest of the three methods if all of the speakers were of the same caliber.

The enclosed speaker option is less of a separate option than a subset of the multiple speakers option. Either way, enclosed speakers have some sort of speaker cabinet and multiple speakers don't. If you buy the speakers as separates, you have the choice of building an enclosure for them, building or buying fiberglass panels for them, or cutting holes in the car. If you want your speakers to be built into cabinets, pre-enclosed speakers have an advantage over homemade cabinets in that they have been made at the factory (Fig. 6-20). Unless you are a professional

Fig. 6-20 *Two subwoofers in a commercially manufactured enclosure.* MTX

upholsterer or car stereo installer, your cabinets probably won't look as nice as those made at the factory. The enclosure will also be designed specifically to work for those speakers. On the other hand, if you decide to build your own cabinets, you will have the flexibility of designing them as you please, to fit perfectly into your car. Also, the commercially enclosed speakers cost much more than building your own cabinets. I personally lean toward building speaker enclosures, but if you want a very professional look, have more money than time, and distrust your acoustical engineering talents, then you are probably better off buying commercially enclosed speakers.

The last method is to go with multiple-driver speakers in the rear. Whether out of habit or because of the true benefits, I am partial to this method. With multiple-driver speakers, as was covered in a previous section, all of the speakers (two, three, or four) are contained within the speaker basket area of the woofer/midrange (the largest of the set). The benefits are lower cost for the set, ease of installation, no need to cut holes in the car or to build special external enclosures, and less space required than the other types (except for the single-speaker midbass or full-range types).

OTHER SPEAKER SPECIFICATIONS

In addition to the frequency ratings, several other ratings are important when you are considering a group of speakers to purchase for your system. The power specifications are even more critical than the frequency ratings, so read and choose carefully.

INPUT SENSITIVITY

The *input sensitivity* is the sound pressure level in dB that is output when 1 W is delivered to the speaker. This measurement is taken at a range of 1 m from the front of the speaker, at a given frequency (usually 1 kHz). The input sensitivity is important because if the level is lower than average, you will need more power (and possibly a higher powered amplifier) to reach the same sound level in your car. Also, if you have mixed and matched your speakers, some might have a much higher sensitivity than others. This being the case, some of your speakers might overpower others in the system and you might need to attenuate each of the more sensitive speakers with a resistor. Typical input sensitivity ratings for speakers are generally all between 87 and 101 dB. Woofers, tweeters, midranges, etc., are found throughout the range, although the woofers and subwoofers are on average a bit higher.

A higher input sensitivity rating does not necessarily mean that the speaker is better than another; it only means that it is more efficient with its output power. The input sensitivity rating might be a factor in determining the best speaker for your system *after* you have compared speakers and they sound just as good to your ears. Otherwise, a solid, clean-sounding speaker with a flat response is much more important than a loud speaker.

To confuse matters further, not all speakers are measured by the manufacturers at a frequency of 1 kHz. Some of the cheaper speakers do not have a flat response and the level will vary across the frequency spectrum. Some of the less-honest manufacturers have been known to rate their speakers' input sensitivity at one of the spikes in the response, which obviously is not accurate.

RESPONSE

The *response* of a speaker is a graph of its output across the entire frequency range. To understand speaker response, imagine if the input sensitivity measurements for a speaker were taken across the entire frequency range, then all of those measurements were listed on a graph. That's it. The best speakers will have a plateau-shaped response with a fairly sharp roll-off on either end. Most speakers have somewhat sloping responses, etc., but as long as they are relatively flat, they should do fairly well. Beware of speakers with many spikes and valleys throughout their response graphs; they will not accurately represent the sound of your recordings. Unlike the sensitivity rating, the response graph is very important when determining whether the sound of a particular speaker will be worthy of being installed in your car.

The frequency response of a speaker is also known as the range within which the speaker will output within a certain power rating. The high and low points, where the response drops below the predetermined level (usually +/- 3 dB), determine the specified frequency response for a given speaker.

NOMINAL POWER HANDLING

The *nominal power handling* rating of speakers is the amount of power that a speaker can handle continuously. The nominal power handling rating is the practical power limit that you should ever consider inputting from your amplifier. For that matter, if the amplifier is driven at high levels, a system is much better off with speakers that are rated approximately 10% higher (in watts) than the power output of the amplifier, just to be safe.

PEAK POWER HANDLING

Not to be confused with nominal power handling, the *peak power handling* rating is the instantaneous amount of power that a speaker can safely tolerate. The peak power handling rating is more of an academic figure than one that you could use to design a system. In many cases, you will not know the output levels of your amplifier on peaks while you use it unless you have electronic measuring equipment. Rating a system by the peak power and not the nominal power would be pushing the system for a little more. It's much safer to use the nominal figure and play it safe.

SPEAKER POLARITY

If you look closely, you will notice that every set of speaker terminals has a + sign on one side and a - sign on the other side. Likewise, the amplifier will also either have these same markings or a red terminal (positive) and a black terminal (negative). These markings are to enable you to match the polarity of the speakers to the amplifier and to the other speakers, if they are connected in series or in parallel.

However, the speaker polarity is nothing like the polarity of capacitors; they won't be destroyed or explode in your face if you connect the speakers to the wrong polarity. In fact, if you connect the speakers to the wrong polarity from the amplifier, you might not even notice a difference in sound quality. The speaker polarity actually is the phase in which the audio signals arrive at the speakers. The speaker polarity is marked on the speakers and the amplifiers because if the two signals arrive at the speakers out of phase, some of the audio frequencies will cancel and will thus reduce the frequency response. But the phase of the signals might have even been altered by an amplifier, an equalizer, or by some other piece of equipment before this point. As a result, the signal could already be out of phase (i.e., the polarity would be the opposite from what is shown at the speaker terminals) and following the directions for connecting them would be incorrect.

Speaker polarity is one of those "if it sounds good, do it" subjects. Connect your speakers and if you think that they don't sound quite as good as they should, try reversing the connections and listen for a difference. Chances are, you will notice only a slight difference, at best.

IMPEDANCE AND INTERCONNECTING SPEAKERS

When technology becomes more complicated, it is much more difficult to come up with a working system. However, these complications also make it much easier for you to be able to work around your problems and modify a system to fit your requirements.

One of these complications broaches the topics of speakers, amplifiers, and sheer power. As was covered in Chapter 5, all amplifiers are rated to output power into a load with a certain impedance value. The normal value is 8 ohms for home stereo applications and 4 ohm for auto audio use, although a few companies use other impedances, such as 6 and 10 ohm.

As was explained in Chapter 5, the reason that some people experiment with using particularly lower speaker impedances is because the amplifier will theoretically output twice as much power into a load with half as much impedance. Of course, using real-world components and the effects of such factors as capacitive reactance and inductive reactance, the power output will be much less than the twice-the-original figure. The actual figures for an amplifier running into half of the impedance are usually between approximately 1.5 to 1.7 times higher than the original power output. This difference might not meet the simplified theoretical standards, but the differences in output power in these systems are significant and worth experimenting with.

One problem is that some amplifiers can't tolerate being running into a lower impedance load than was specified in the manual. By running the amplifier into too low of an impedance, you can easily overheat and destroy its power output circuitry. You must determine from the manufacturer's specifications what the lowest impedance is that the amplifier will safely operate into. These specifications are listed in terms of stability (e.g., an amplifier that is "2-ohms stable" can operate safely into a 2-ohm load). Some amplifiers are rated with stability as low as 0.5 ohm, but you really shouldn't use a speaker system that pushes your amplifier to its limits because you might take a few years off of its life.

Connecting Speakers in Parallel

You won't find many 1- or 2-ohm speakers around anywhere, so you might wonder how the sound-off competitors crank thousands of watts into a wall of speakers at 2 ohm. The wonderful thing about electronics is that the values can be added or subtracted, sometimes using simple means. In this case, it is simple. By wiring the speakers together in parallel (Fig. 6-21), the impedances drop according to the following equation:

$$Z_t = \cfrac{1}{\left(\dfrac{1}{Z_1}\right) + \left(\dfrac{1}{Z_2}\right)} \,\cdots$$

where:

Z_t is the total impedance (in ohms)

Z_1 is the impedance of the first speaker (in ohms)

Z_2 is the impedance of the second speaker (in ohms)

etc.

One of the easiest and most common examples of wiring speakers in parallel is running two 4-ohm speakers in parallel off of the same amplifier channel. To determine the impedance of the parallel speaker connection:

$$Z_t = \cfrac{1}{\left(\dfrac{1}{4}\right) + \left(\dfrac{1}{4}\right)}$$

$$Z_t = \cfrac{1}{\dfrac{1}{2}}$$

$$Z_t = \frac{1}{0.5}$$

$$Z_t = 2 \text{ ohms}$$

As you can see from this value, you can quickly pull the impedance down to almost nothing. It's very handy because very little effort is required to draw a huge amount of power from the amplifier. But the problem is that many amplifiers are not stable below 4 ohms, and few of even the well-built

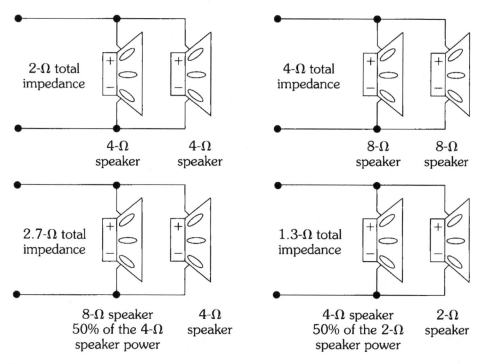

Fig. 6-21 *Various arrangements for wiring speakers in parallel.*

amplifiers will operate without becoming *very hot* below 2 ohms. So, it is nearly impossible to install and safely use a complicated speaker configuration that only uses parallel speaker connections and no other impedance-matching techniques.

CONNECTING SPEAKERS IN SERIES

Another method of connecting speakers together from the same amplifier channel is to wire them in series. However, unlike parallel speaker connections, series connections don't decrease in impedance, they increase it (Fig. 6-22). To determine the impedance of a series speaker connection:

$$Z_t = Z_1 + Z_2 \ldots$$

where:

Z_t is the total impedance (in ohms)

Z_1 is the impedance of the first speaker (in ohms)

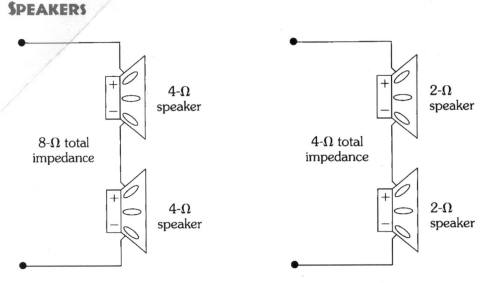

Fig. 6-22 *Speakers connected in series with equal power sharing.*

Z_2 is the impedance of the second speaker (in ohms)

etc.

Series speaker connections are not nearly as common as parallel connections, but you might care to wire to 4-ohm speakers in series. Perhaps you want to pull your old 4-ohm speakers out of your car and use them with a stereo system, which are often rated at 8 ohms. To determine the impedance of the series speaker connection:

$$Z_t = 4 + 4$$

$$Z_t = 8 \text{ ohms}$$

As you can see, determining the impedance of speakers connected in series is not nearly as difficult as determining a parallel connection. Unfortunately, series connections on their own are not particularly useful on their own. Most car amplifiers are intended for 4-ohms and using higher-impedance speakers will mean that they will receive less power from your amplifier. Perhaps the most interesting and beneficial use for series speaker connections in car stereo applications is when they are used in line with parallel connections to increase the impedance to a safe level.

CONNECTING SPEAKERS TOGETHER IN SERIES AND PARALLEL

Because connecting speakers in series will quickly add impedances and connecting speakers in parallel will quickly diminish the impedances, it would be great to be able to balance the two effects out. You can do this by running speakers in parallel and series from the same audio channel (Fig. 6-23). By wiring the speakers together in parallel and in series, the impedances drop according to the following equation:

$$Z_t = \cfrac{1}{\left(\cfrac{1}{Z_1 + Z_2}\right) + \left(\cfrac{1}{Z_3 + Z_4}\right)}$$

where:

Z_t is the total impedance (in ohms)
Z_1 is the impedance of the first speaker (in ohms)
Z_2 is the impedance of the second speaker (in ohms)
Z_3 is the impedance of the third speaker (in ohms)
Z_4 is the impedance of the fourth speaker (in ohms)

etc.

One of the easiest and most common examples of wiring speakers in parallel is running two 4-ohm speakers in series, but also in parallel with two other 4-ohm speakers that are also in series with each other. This set of four speakers can be run off of the same amplifier channel. To determine the impedance of the parallel/series speaker connection:

$$Z_t = \cfrac{1}{\left(\cfrac{1}{4 + 4}\right) + \left(\cfrac{1}{4 + 4}\right)}$$

$$Z_t = \cfrac{1}{\left(\cfrac{1}{8}\right) + \left(\cfrac{1}{8}\right)}$$

$$Z_t = \cfrac{1}{\cfrac{1}{4}}$$

$$Z_t = \frac{1}{0.25}$$

$$Z_t = 4 \text{ ohms}$$

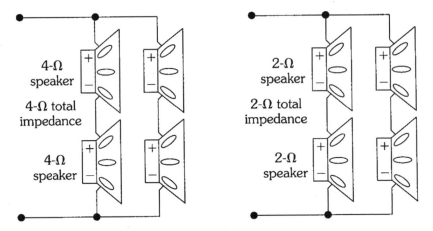

Fig. 6-23 *Wiring in series with equal power sharing.*

The series/parallel connections are a bit more complicated than the other two interconnection methods to determine on paper and also to install. Still, they are a viable alternative to the higher cost of dual-voice coil speakers.

CONNECTING DUAL VOICE COIL SPEAKERS

As stated earlier in this chapter, dual voice coil speakers are those that have two voice coils and each one can be separately connected to an amplifier output. The advantages of dual voice coil speakers are that an array of these speakers can easily be connected together and installed because they offer three different possible wiring combinations.

In the first method, the two voice coils are connected in parallel. In this case, if each coil is rated at 4 ohms, then the impedance that will be "seen" by the amplifier is 2 ohms (Fig. 6-24). Thus, one dual voice coil subwoofer could be operated at 2 ohms, which would otherwise not be possible.

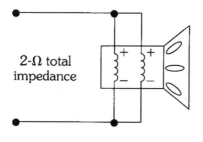

Fig. 6-24 *Wiring both coils of a dual-voice coil speaker in parallel.*

In the second method, the two voice coils are connected in series. In this case, if each coil is rated at 4 ohms, then the impedance that will be "seen" by the amplifier is 8 ohms (Fig. 6-25). Thus, the dual voice coil subwoofer could also be operated at 8 ohms, which is no big deal, but it could be handy when making a large array of subwoofers.

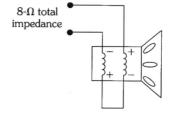

Fig. 6-25 *Wiring both coils of a dual-voice coil speaker in series.*

In the last method, the two voice coils are independently wired to separate channels of a mono amplifier (the channels must be in mono to prevent the voice coil cancellation that was mentioned earlier). Alternatively, it can be connected to a single stereo amplifier that is operating in mono. In this case, if each coil is rated at 4 ohms, then the impedance that will be "seen" by the amplifier will still be 4 ohms (Fig. 6-26). Thus, the dual voice coil subwoofer could also be operated at 4 ohms, which is also not big deal, but it still provides you with more flexibility and allows you to use a less-expensive stereo amplifier.

A simple two-speaker arrangement could be used in place of the dual voice coil speakers. The two windings on each speaker would be connected in parallel, which would make the impedance at each speaker 2 ohms. Then, each speaker could be connected in series, which would yield a total impedance of 4 ohms. This rating is fine for auto audio applications, but you might as well just connect two 8-ohm speakers in parallel to get that 4-ohm rating.

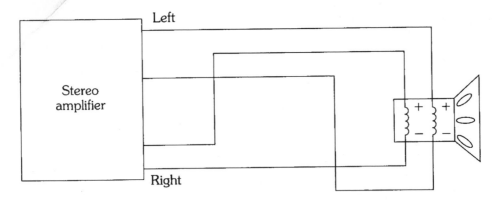

Fig. 6-26 *Connecting one voice coil per channel of a stereo amplifier for a mono subwoofer.*

However, one dual voice coil speaker design that is more interesting is an array of four 8-ohm speakers. The coils of each of the speakers are bridged together, which produces an impedance of 16 ohms at each speaker. These four speakers are then connected in parallel, which produces an impedance of 4 ohms at the amplifier for the woofer wall (Fig. 6-27).

INSTALLING SPEAKERS

In general, installing speakers is the easiest upgrade that you can make to a car audio system. Just check the size of the speakers that you have in your car and purchase new speakers that are exactly the same mounting size as those that you are replacing. Then pop off the grill cover. The grill covers are usually held in place with screws or they just snap in place. Look over the covers for screws. Remove the screws and lift the cover up. If it's not pulling right out, check to see where it's catching. If you don't find any screws, try prying gently with a screwdriver.

Once the covers are removed, you can access the speakers (Fig. 6-28). Most speakers screw directly into the metal or plastic edge that surrounds it (such as the dash, rear deck, door, etc.). Unscrew these screws and unclip the wire leads from the speakers. It's more annoying if the car uses a special plastic connector to match the wire to the speaker. If this is the case, it's best to find a matching connector so that you don't have to cut up the wiring. In the case of clip leads, just clip the leads on to the new speaker, replace the screws and the grill cover and you're finished. If the speaker has screw terminals, snip off the clip leads and

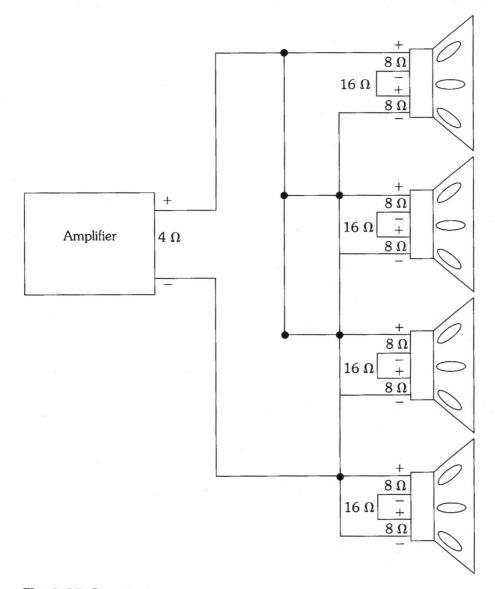

Fig. 6-27 *Four dual-voice coil speakers connected together for a 3-ohm output.*

use a wire-stripping tool to remove about 1/2" of the insulation from the wire. Then insert the wire and screw it shut tightly.

If you replace all of the speakers and have problems with the speaker grilles rattling, first try tightening the grill screws. Chances are that this won't work, but it's worth a shot. A more effective method with the

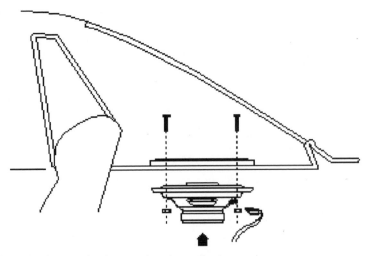

Fig. 6-28 *A typical rear deck speaker installation.* Blaupunkt

plastic grooved grills is to buy some artist's modeling clay and lightly rub some across the underside of the plastic. The key is to add enough clay that it will prevent the grill from resonating, but not so much that it is visible. With the metal screen grill panels, you can run a strip of modeling clay around the inside of the plastic lip, including the edge where the screen fits in. If the problem is that the screen is loose, you could try a light application of caulking or adhesive (such as rubber cement).

You start running into problems mounting speakers when you pick speakers that are too large for the mounting location or if you want to mount them in a nonstandard location. A good example of this is my VW Rabbit. The stock front speakers are mounted in the dashboard and are a mere 3.5-in. (circular). I first tried a pretty good (comparatively) pair of 3.5-in. speakers. One problem is that the response of most 3.5-in. speakers won't even go down to 120 Hz, and mine were no different. Installed, the rear speakers blasted and the front speakers emitted a faint, tinny sound under those from behind.

I checked the door-mounting positions. One speaker position was available, a circular 5 1/4-in. hole. A 5 1/4-in. speaker can be capable of a lot of power and low frequencies...but the window slides through this area. So, I could have mounted the speaker in the position, but I could never open the windows!

Aside from only using the rear speakers, I thought that the best solution was to use a front-dash mounting position. There's no way to tear the dash apart to open enough space to for a 4-x-6-in. plate speaker set to fit in. The only direction to go is up, and to either build or buy a speaker enclosure attachment. Some companies, such as Kicker and Q Logic, manufacture molded speaker kick panels and subwoofer boxes that match the interiors of different vehicles.

In the case of my VW Rabbit, the car is too old for any company to manufacture specialty enclosures for. So, my only recourse was to make them myself. For more information on fiberglass and homemade enclosures, see Chapter 8, "Building with Fiberglass."

CONCLUSION

Speakers are the most important component, as far as sound is concerned, in any audio system. They are also very complicated and potentially expensive, so it is a must to choose your speakers carefully so that you can get the best sound for the money. However, just buying great speakers is only half of the ballgame. Next, you've got to install them, choose speaker cabinets, if necessary, and decide if you want to use crossovers. A good installation can make your system sound great, but a bad installation can make those $50 speakers sound like you scrounged around a junkyard, pulling them out of old television sets. See Chapter 7 for more details.

SPEAKER ENCLOSURES

The all-encompassing topic of speakers is one of the most important factors in any type of audio system. You can spend a relatively small amount of money purchasing a head unit and much more on the speakers. Chances are that you will have a better system than someone who spent a great deal of cash on the head unit and little on the speakers. Part of this difference lies in the fact that the overall sound quality difference between assorted head units is not that great. Most of the difference in price is because of the extra features: skipless CDs, memory presets, RDS systems, removable faceplates, autoreverse, remote control, etc. You might find these features to be very desirable, but the fact is that they don't alter the sound quality under normal listening conditions. The same argument holds true for speaker wiring, amplifiers, equalizers, signal processors, etc.

Although good-quality speakers are very important, they still must be properly installed and positioned. In fact, expensive speakers can still sound lousy if they are not installed properly.

The standard speaker enclosure consists of a solid rectangular box with the speakers mounted in the front of one of the two long, wide sides. In spite of their normal uses for subwoofers, portable systems, or sport/utility vehicles, a good speaker cabinet is not just intended to be portable; the cabinet is intended to improve the actual frequency response from the speakers. Thus, the purpose of a speaker cabinet is to isolate the air mass that is in front of the speaker from that which is behind it. Without the cabinet, the lower-frequency waves will cancel out and the audio will be much weaker, with a tinny, thin sound.

In addition to shielding the front air mass from the back, the walls of the enclosure should also be solid. If they aren't, the walls will vibrate and these waves will, in turn, cancel out more audible frequencies. The best speaker enclosure should be dead: the walls should be solid and virtually flawless, the enclosure should be physically strong, and the joints should be sealed.

ENCLOSURE MATERIALS

A number of materials can be used to make speaker enclosures, but some work much better than others. If you go to a stereo shop, you will notice that the more expensive home audio speakers often use expensive wood, such as oak, to build the enclosures, yet commercial auto audio enclosures are usually covered with carpeting. This difference is merely cosmetic: fine wood is used in home systems to fit in with the decor of a house, not because of any desirable acoustic qualities. Likewise, carpet is used to cover auto audio enclosures because it matches the car's interior and because its finish won't scratch like a stained or painted surface, not because of any beneficial sound-damping qualities.

Although wood covers nearly all of the home speaker enclosures, the wood is not a part of the actual box. Instead, the wood is veneered or a board is glued to the enclosure. Wood is not normally used for enclosures because the grain and knots provide an uneven surface density. The grain lines and knots are much denser than the wood that is in between. As a result, the surface of the wood won't be "dead;" it will vary, depending on the grain. Strangely enough, for a good-sounding, "dead" box enclosure, you'll get the best results from getting one of the cheapest, least-expensive materials that's available from hardware stores and lumber yards: particle board, also called *MDF* (Fig. 7-1). It's ugly and cheap to make, but a length particle board is also evenly dense and about as heavy as a refrigerator. All of these qualities make it a great pick for speaker enclosures. Sometimes other materials, such as thick plywood, are used, but plywood is much more expensive than particle board and only the best grades of it are somewhat evenly dense. Cheap grades of plywood will often contain gaps in the layers that can buzz and absorb sound energy. Multi-ply subflooring is another option that would work well, but it is also very expensive. For more information on building materials, see Chapter 9.

Fig. 7-1 *This unassembled subwoofer box kit from Harrison Labs consists of eight pieces of precut MDF boards and all of the necessary hardware. Yes, the finished enclosure is heavy!*

ALTERNATIVE ENCLOSURE MATERIALS

As you might guess, many other materials have been used to build speaker enclosures. Some of these have been peculiar, but if you have a taste for experimentation, they might provide some interesting tests. Because one of the most important qualities for speaker enclosures is sound deadness, very dense materials that are not easily vibrated by sound are desirable. Metals are normally out of the question, unless you can cast a 1 in. or 2 in. (2.54 cm or 5.08 cm) thick aluminum box that would cost more time and effort than it would be worth. Stone or brick enclosures would also normally be out of the question, unless you commute to Bedrock everyday to work. But, the Flintstones-style enclosure is along the line of three of the more interesting enclosure experiments that I have seen.

The first is a very feasible project that is included in *Great Sound Stereo Speaker Manual with Projects* by David B. Weems. In this case, the author made a diagonal cut through one piece of ceramic flue tile to produce two potential enclosures with sloping front sides (Fig. 7-2). The insides of the tiles were carpeted, special crossovers were built, the boxes were braced on the inside with pieces of wood, and pieces of special heavy-duty 13-ply plywood were cut for the front and back of each speaker. Then, the speakers were installed and wired, and the front and back plywood sides were glued to the flue tiles and sealed with silicone caulking. The author said that the sound is very natural, which is good and bad. The bass is a bit lighter than that from most larger speaker enclosures, but they do well whenever the recordings have deep bass. Otherwise, they will not compensate and beef up the bass. You might run into some problems solidly mounting these speaker enclosures in a vehicle, however.

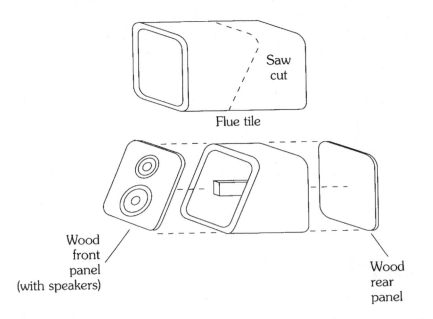

Saw cut

Flue tile

Wood front panel (with speakers)

Wood rear panel

Fig. 7-2 *A diagram for speaker enclosures using alternative materials: flue tile!*

The Weems ceramic tile enclosures are at the opposite end of the practicality/usefulness chart from a pair of concrete subwoofer enclosures that were used in a 1986 Mercury Cougar that was featured in *Car Audio and Electronics* (see "Heavy Weight Mercury Cougar," February 1994, p. 36-44). The subwoofer boxes weighed 260 lb. and were set into the trunk just behind the back seats. Because of the extra weight, the owner had to replace the rear suspension with one from a Ford F-150 pickup truck. The owner said that the concrete has tightened the sound of the bass. If you plan to win car sound-off competitions, concrete might be the route to take. Otherwise, drop the idea like a ton of bricks.

Along the fiberglass method of speaker enclosure materials, some audio enthusiasts have used different synthetic materials. For example, in the concrete enclosure, five of the walls were concrete, but the sixth wall consisted of a sheet of nearly 1-in. (2.54 cm) thick clear acrylic so that interested parties could see inside. These materials seem to be commonly used in audio competition show cars, so it seems that they do quite well as far as being a dead material. The prohibitive factor in using thick slabs of Lucite, Plexiglass, fiberglass, or some other material is certainly cost. It's much less expensive to build your enclosures out of particle board.

SPEAKER ENCLOSURE SHAPES

The shape of the speaker enclosure does not make as much difference in the sound quality as the materials that the box is made from, but it is still very important. Because speaker enclosure shapes combine the technological aspect of audio design with physical beauty, many arguments spring forth over the topic.

The name of the game for enclosure shapes is *standing waves*. Standing waves occur when sound waves build up at a particular frequency as a result of the resonance of the speaker enclosure. The standing waves can null out other audio waves and produce a weak response at a particular frequency or frequencies. As a result, the frequency response of the enclosed speakers will be uneven or lacking, particularly at the bass frequencies. Because of the negative effect of standing waves, it is desirable to prevent the speaker from being in a location (in the enclosure) where it is equidistant from the speaker walls. Thus, the shape of a cube, with one speaker mounted in the center of one side, is one of the worst possible geometric configurations (Fig. 7-3).

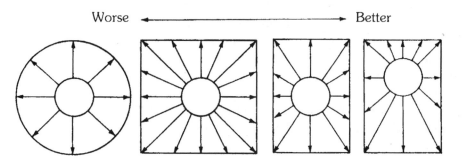

Fig. 7-3 *The distances from the speaker to the enclosure wall.*

For some time, I assumed that a perfect cube would be one of the best enclosure shapes because the waves would all reflect back at the same time, aiding the movement of the speaker and making the sound stronger and tighter. Whoops, nearly the opposite is true; those reflected waves are fighting against those that are currently being produced by the speaker. As a result, the best sound occurs when the waves are permitted to reflect back at different distances.

One of the best speaker enclosure shapes is a rectangular box with the speaker mounted off center. This box is rather impractical for auto audio applications because of the size and the shape. Few people would have the room to mount their rear drivers using this method, although two woofers or subwoofers mounted in evenly spaced positions in one side would work well. So, it is time for some creativity.

Speaker enclosure shapes for auto audio applications are beginning to take off on their own, away from the traditional home audio arena. One example of this creativity is in the design of woofer and subwoofer enclosures. Recently, more people are using the available space to shape a subwoofer enclosure to fit within that cavity. Thus, if space was much more important to the owner than money, it might be an option to construct a mold that would fit into the odd-shaped cavities of the trunk. Then, the mold for the enclosure could be cast with a thick layer of fiberglass resin. I have never seen nor read about any DIYer who used this approach to saving trunk space, but I'm sure that someone some-where must have done it. Now, as mentioned in the last chapter, some companies, such as Kicker and Q Logic, now manufacture odd-shaped subwoofer enclosures for some of the more popular, newer cars.

With or without fiberglass resin, it is still possible to at least use most of this space by building a particleboard box to fit inside. Just measure the inside of the space, design the subwoofer enclosure so that it will be solid and durable, and make sure that the interior space is enough to accommodate the size of the speaker (more information on this topic occurs later in this chapter).

Another nonstandard shape for speaker enclosures (i.e., a nonbox shape) is the trapezoid. In case the information from your high-school geometry class has slipped away with the names of the actors from "The Love Boat" or if you decided not to bore yourself by taking that class in the first place, a *trapezoid* is any four-sided figure that has non-90° angles at the corners. The most useful enclosures that use the trapezoi-dal shape are those that have a large front panel (where the speaker fits into), then either the top or both the top and bottom slope in toward the back. For the 6-x-9-in. (15.24 x 22.86-cm) three-way rear speakers in my VW Rabbit, I used a set of unfinished trapezoidal enclosures from Parts Express (Fig. 7-4), but this is covered more extensively later on in this chapter.

I have also heard some arguments and read differing (pro and con) accounts of some speaker enclosure shapes, such as the sphere. The sphere is a particularly interesting shape because many people have

Fig. 7-4 *A truckload of dirt-cheap speaker enclosures from Parts Express at the Dayton Hamvention.*

argued that it is either the very best or the very worst shape for a speaker enclosure. It is sometimes considered to be the worst shape because a number of distances from the speaker would be the same length, so waves would return to the speaker at the same time. This would set up an ultimate worst case for standing waves in a speaker enclosure. However, this standing wave problem would only occur if the speaker was actually in the center of the sphere, so proponents of this shape say that it is actually the best of the bunch. In my opinion, the point is moot as far as auto audio is concerned: the shape is totally impractical for anyone to build a spherical enclosure (the only real possibility would be to cast it out of fiberglass), and even if it wasn't, the shape wastes valuable car space and the enclosure would roll around in your trunk or back seat, unless it was bolted down.

Another geometric possibility would be the pyramid. This design would be much easier to build than the sphere for obvious reasons. However, on the downside, the pyramid would require much more space than any of the other enclosure designs, so it probably will not be useful to most people.

Although a number of different speaker shapes are possible in auto audio applications, the most useful will be the rectangular and trapezoidal boxes because of the good-quality sound, the ease of construction, and the relatively small amount of space that they require. As a result, these two basic types are covered almost exclusively throughout this chapter and in Chapter 13, which covers system installation.

SPEAKER ENCLOSURE DAMPING

As has been mentioned, the volume of and the materials in a speaker enclosure are crucial to the sound that the speakers will produce. The sound can, in turn, be either enhanced or degraded by using damping materials inside the box. *Damping materials* are sound-absorbing layers that are added to the inside of a speaker box to reduce the reflections and "tighten" the sound. Another quality of damping materials are that they can effectively make a smaller enclosure sound as if it is much larger (to a certain point). Considering the cost of materials and tiny amount of space that can be allocated to auto audio applications, damping materials are very popular!

It is somewhat common for speaker enclosures that require very light damping to have the insides of the box covered with a very thin layer of carpeting. However, it seems that larger amounts of damping are required for most speakers—especially now that people are becoming more mobile and living space is shrinking. These days, most commercial speakers seem to be undersized models that have been padded with damping materials to compensate.

Some of the most common sound damping materials are acoustic polyfill and unbacked fiberglass insulation. After insulating a few houses with fiberglass insulation, I try to avoid the stuff, but it isn't so bad to install such a small amount in a speaker enclosure (Fig. 7-5). Another possibility is polyester quilt backing. It has less damping ability, but it is also a bit more fun to work with and you can buy it in smaller quantities than fiberglass insulation. You can purchase acoustic polyfill at some local audio stores or mail-order companies, rolls of fiberglass insulation from building supply companies, and quilt backing from fabric stores.

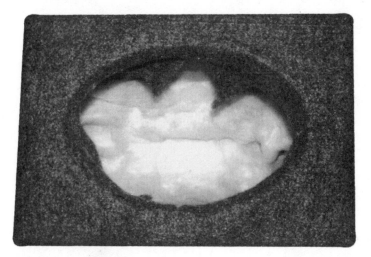

Fig. 7-5 *Fiberglass insulation glued into an enclosure to serve as dampening material.*

To install damping material, just staple a layer of it to the inside of the speaker box—either to the back wall or just so the sheet is squashed in across the back and covering some of the other inside walls as well. If you don't have a staple gun, try spraying the inside with adhesive, such as that which is used to hold carpet on an enclosure. Next, put the front plate on the box or insert the speaker (depending on the type that you have) and listen to the way that the bass sounds decay. If the sounds aren't tight, add another layer and try it again. If the bass frequencies seem to be absorbed, remove some of the damping material and try it again. After a few tries, you will have the damping material/speaker enclosures tweaked for optimum performance.

SPEAKER ENCLOSURE DESIGNS AND TECHNIQUES

It might seem as though the this section's topic is a repeat of what was just featured in the last section. Nope, those were all speaker enclosure shapes, whereas this section covers different designs that are all modeled around the rectangular box shape. Speaker enclosure designs can be very complicated, involving multiple speakers in various arrangements, large speaker boxes, tuned ports, etc. Fortunately, some of the best designs for speaker boxes are also some of the least complicated.

THE CLOSED-BOX ENCLOSURE

Because of the absolute simplicity, good performance, and difficulty in botching up the sound quality, I prefer the closed-box (sealed) enclosure. The *closed-box enclosure* is a simple speaker enclosure that is sealed on all sides so that the air mass behind the speaker is entirely separated from that which is behind it (Fig. 7-6).

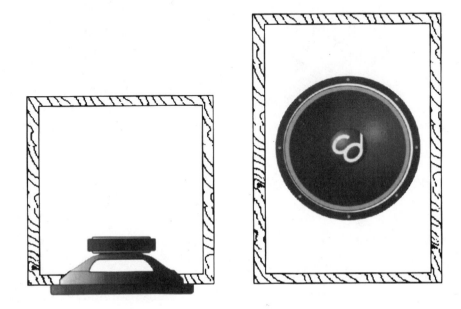

Fig. 7-6 *A sealed enclosure.*

The volume of each box has a particular frequency range for which a speaker of a particular size will operate well. The box will generally work well for all audio frequencies that the particular speaker is rated for. However, if the box has a smaller volume than is required for the size of the speaker that is in it, the sound pressure will be even higher within the box. As the pressure level increases within the speaker enclosure, some of the lower frequencies are dropped out. And, as the size of the enclosure is reduced, the pressure level within the box is increased, and even more of the lower frequencies are cutoff. But, not all of the low frequencies are removed, as is the case when a speaker is in a free-air position. Instead, some of the frequencies are removed and others peak, which results in a "boomy" bass sound, instead of a tight, clean bass sound.

As a result of this action, larger speakers require larger box volumes to be able to accurately reproduce the low frequencies properly. Because of this speaker law, very small woofers, such as the 8-in. models, are quite popular among people who want to have bass, yet can't or don't want to waste the speaker and enclosure space that would be required to support a larger system, such as one for 12- or 15-in. woofers or subwoofers.

Because speaker enclosures can "stiffen" the sound waves and cause the low bass to drop out if the area inside is too small, you might want to make the box larger than is specified. I have heard some varying opinions on the subject of larger-than-specified box enclosures. Some people have said that the lower bass frequencies will drop out, and others have said that they won't, but that a larger box has little "bass boost" over one with the specified box size. The arguments are usually pointless because your vehicle probably will not have the space to handle a massive, oversized enclosure anyway.

Speaker Enclosure Types

❑ *Sealed enclosures*
❑ *Aperiodic enclosures*
❑ *Ported-box enclosures*
❑ *Band-pass enclosures*
❑ *Transmission-line enclosures*

Regardless, by varying the size of the enclosure, you will produce a different sound, perhaps one that is more to your liking than the specified enclosure volume. So, it is very helpful to use speaker enclosures, and it's even better to have ones that are near the proper volume so that you can get the maximum sound quality from your system.

Unfortunately, the volume of a closed-box speaker depends on a number of factors: Q is the magnification of the resonance factor of any resonant device or circuit, Q_T is the total Q factor of the speaker, f_S is the free-air resonance of the speaker (frequency), and V_{AS} is the compliance of the speaker. These calculations and few other factors are used in a number of different equations to determine the exact best volume for a closed-box enclosure.

To design a closed speaker box, you must know three of the terms from the previous paragraph: f_S, Q_T (often listed in manufacturer's specifications as Q_{TS}), and V_{AS}. These values should be available from the manufacturer, and they are often printed right on the box (or in the manual or product information sheets), next to the other specifications, such as the power ratings.

For a sealed box design, all you really need to know is "the bigger, the better" until the box volume exceeds (time to get out that calculator):

Maximum box volume $= 1.1 \times V_{AS} \times Q_T^2$

The total volume will be in cubic feet if V_{AS} is in cubic feet or in liters if V_{AS} is in liters. If you need to covert this information:

1 cubic foot $= 28.3$ liters

Making the box much larger than this size is just a waste of particle board.

For more advanced mathematicians, you can now calculate how the bass will be (for any size of box) using the following equation:

Cutoff frequency $= 0.8 \times f_S \times \sqrt{V_{AS}/\text{box volume}}$

For this equation, V_{as} and box volume must both be in either cubic feet or both in liters. These equations are just approximations, but they should be accurate to within 10% of the actual value.

For example, unless you are an audiophile or a hard-core experimenter, you might be better off by using a chart of approximate specifications. To get the simplified volume specifications for closed-box speaker systems, see Table 7-1, which shows the approximate volumes for most speakers that would be enclosed in a car system.

In all, the only major concerns with building a closed-box enclosure are to achieve the proper volume inside, to make it solid and airtight, and to use an off-center speaker mounting position or an odd-shaped box (if possible).

CLOSED-BOX ARRANGEMENTS

A number of different speaker arrangements are possible with the

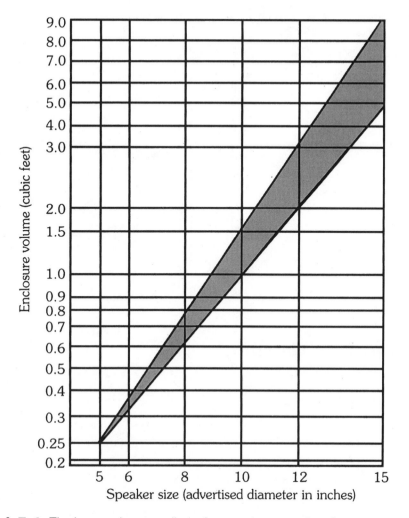

Graph 7-1 *The box enclosure volume for any given speaker diameter.*

closed-box speaker design. Two woofers can be placed in one box, side by side, to double the bass force; the full range of speakers (woofer, tweeter, midrange) can all be placed in one box; or different arrangements of woofers can be placed in the box, such as the many variations on the push-pull theme (Fig. 7-7), where two woofers are mounted in line to "drive" each other. The possibilities are numerous, so if you want to read further on the subject, read the books that are listed in the conclusion for the section "Speaker enclosure designs and techniques" or read some of the books and magazine articles that are listed in the Bibliography.

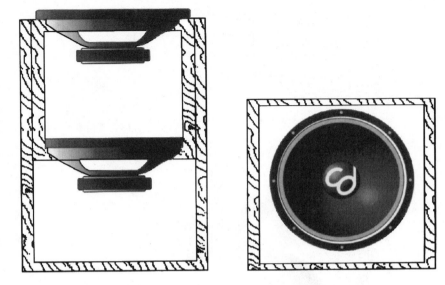

Fig. 7-7 *An isobaric enclosure.*

APERIODIC ENCLOSURES

Because of the amount of pressure that exists in a closed-box enclosure, some people have experimented with removing that pressure without making the box "leaky." The result is the *aperiodic enclosure*, which is a closed-box design with a screened hole that is covered with an acoustic damping material (Fig. 7-8). Thus, the pressure inside of the box is released, yet the box is still acoustically sealed. Normally, the pressure vent is a square or rectangular hole that is anywhere from approximately 1 x 1 in. (2.54 x 2.54 cm) to 3 x 3 in. (7.62 cm x 7.62 cm). Although the aperiodic enclosure is a serious standard speaker enclosure, it is outperformed in nearly every way by a comparable closed box enclosure.

Typically the pressure vent is located in the back of aperiodic enclosures for cosmetic reasons. Because the amount of damping material will determine how acoustically tight the box really is, you should experiment with how much material you use over the hole so that you can tweak the sound to your liking. Likewise, you should also tweak the amount of damping material that is in the box. For the most part, the same procedures and rules that apply to closed-box enclosures also apply to aperiodic enclosures, except that the internal pressure has been released.

In general, the aperiodic enclosure is not a favorite of audio enthusiasts and some people look upon it disparagingly.

Fig. 7-8 *An aperiodic enclosure.*

PORTED-BOX ENCLOSURES

Complicated ported box enclosures have been in the audio world for decades, although they generally only see service in home audio applications and not in the car. I am not sure why ported-box enclosures have not been more popular in the past, but it might be because auto audio has not been taken seriously until recently.

Audio enthusiasts choose ported-box speaker enclosures over the other types because they believe that these designs have an edge in frequency response over the others. Not being an audiophile, I would choose the closed-box enclosures for the sake of simplicity. In my opinion, the extra work and frustrations would not be worth the price to pay for slightly better audio quality. But, of course, they are worth price for some people to pay, so for these people, and for the sake of covering the most popular types of enclosure designs, they are included here.

A typical *ported-box enclosure* is a type of speaker enclosure that features a port in which a tuned pipe can be fitted (Fig. 7-9). If a tuned pipe is used in the design, its diameter, length, and the way in which it is mounted are crucial. In the second type of ported-box enclosure (a double-chamber reflex), the top part of the enclosure is exactly the same

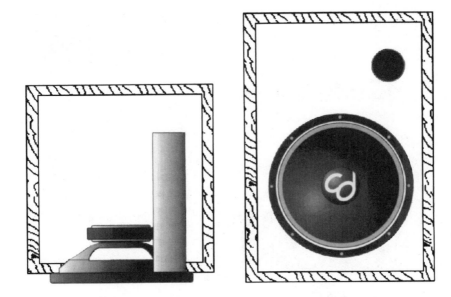

Fig. 7-9 *A ported enclosure.*

as the typical ported box. However, it is also ported into another, smaller enclosure, which also has a separate port to the outside. Thus, the speaker "sees" the chambers as being either separate area or as a united air mass, which permits it to be much more flexible in terms of frequency response. The last type of ported-box enclosure is another design that uses a parasitic speaker. If you read the section that covered multiple-driver speakers in Chapter 6, you might remember that the one type of speaker array used a parasitic tweeter without a magnet or voice coil to capture and reradiate sound. The parasitic ported-box enclosure uses a parasitic speaker (often called a *passive radiator*) instead of a port to function. This style of enclosure would be very interesting and inexpensive to experiment with, except that the most auto audio manufacturers do not sell parasitic speakers. However, Madisound does have several of these models available for home experimentation.

One design that uses a tuned port, yet isn't normally considered to be a common ported-box enclosure, is the *bandpass enclosure*. In this design, the speaker is not visible—the sound can only reach the outside via the tuned port (Fig. 7-10). I can't say that I know of many people who are building bandpass enclosures, but it is a very popular style among the commercial subwoofer system designers. A very complex Polk C-4 Isobaric bandpass subwoofer is shown in Fig. 7-11.

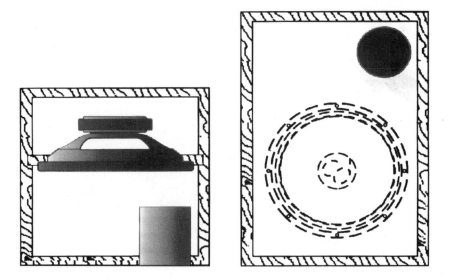

Fig. 7-10 *A band-pass enclosure.*

The tuned port in ported-box enclosures alters the resonant frequency of the enclosure. By adding a port with a larger diameter, the resonant frequency will be increased. You can see the same effect by making an "owl whistle" with your cupped hands. To raise the pitch of the whistle,

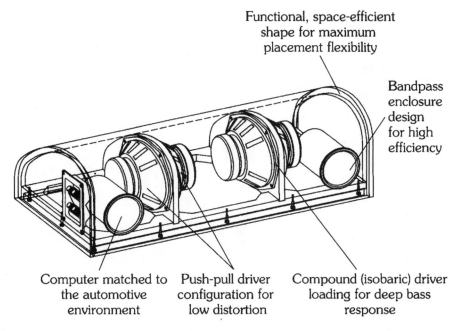

Functional, space-efficient shape for maximum placement flexibility

Bandpass enclosure design for high efficiency

Computer matched to the automotive environment

Push-pull driver configuration for low distortion

Compound (isobaric) driver loading for deep bass response

Fig. 7-11 *A diagram of the Polk CA isobaric bandpass enclosure.* Polk

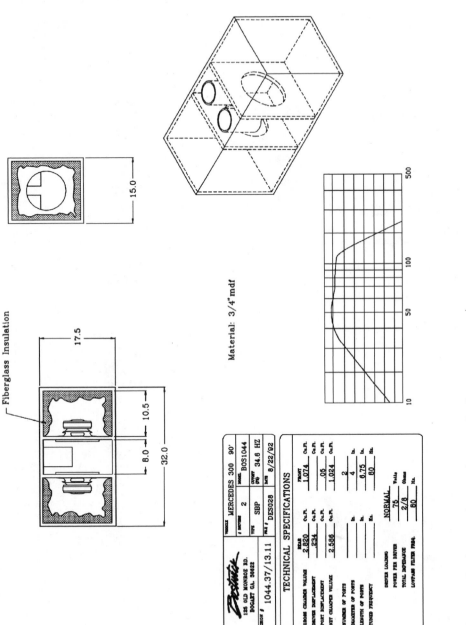

Fiberglass Insulation

17.5

10.5

8.0

32.0

15.0

Material: 3/4"mdf

10   50   100   500

Bostwick
125 OLD MONROE RD.
BOGART GA. 30622

DESIGN # 1044.37/13.11

VEHICLE	MERCEDES 300 90'		
# DRIVERS	2	MODEL	BOS1044
TYPE	SBP	OUTPUT SPL	34.8 HZ
FILE #	DES028	DATE	8/22/92

TECHNICAL SPECIFICATIONS

	REAR		FRONT	
GROSS CHAMBER VOLUME	2.820	CU.FT.	1.074	CU.FT.
DRIVER DISPLACEMENT	.234	CU.FT.	.05	CU.FT.
NET CHAMBER VOLUME	2.586	CU.FT.	1.024	CU.FT.
NUMBER OF PORTS			2	
DIAMETER OF PORTS		IN.	4	IN.
LENGTH OF PORTS		IN.	6.75	IN.
TUNED FREQUENCY		HZ.	80	HZ.

	NORMAL		
DRIVER LOADING			
POWER PER DRIVER	75	Watts	
TOTAL IMPEDANCE	2/8	Ohms	
LOWPASS FILTER FREQ.	80	Hz.	

Fig. 7-12 *A complex enclosure design.* Bostwick

you merely open your outside hand, which covers the back of the enclosure. This open area that is covered by your back hand operates as a variable simple port to alter the pitch of your whistle. The speaker duct is only used to tune air within the enclosure, not to focus the energy from the speakers. As a result, the duct can either run straight toward the back of the enclosure or it can be bent upward. Also, the frequency of the box can in turn be lowered by adding a length of pipe (or a square-shaped duct) to the port. As a result, the port roughly determines the frequency of the box and the duct is used to fine tune the system.

In addition to the variables that are encountered in determining the proper specifications for a closed-box enclosure, the port size and duct length are also necessary to determine the proper specifications for a ported-box enclosure. Many pages could easily be filled just with the material constants, duct specifications, and design parameters (for two examples of complicated ported speaker enclosures, see Figs. 7-12 and 7-13). Instead of covering every aspect of ported-box enclosures, some basic design information is covered in the following section.

PORTED-BOX DESIGN AND EQUATIONS

The same variables that were necessary to determine the size of the closed-box enclosure are also required to find the proper specifications for the ported-box enclosures. If you haven't already read the section on determining the closed-box speaker enclosures, read it, and find the f_S, Q_T, and V_{AS} for your speakers. If you are planning to use a ported box, you must use the following equation to roughly estimate the box size.

Use a port when the box volume $> 2 \times V_{AS} \times Q_T^2$

If you can tolerate having enclosures with a volume of this size or larger, you will probably benefit from using a ported box. Otherwise, you should probably stick with the closed-box enclosure. As was the case with the closed-box enclosure, the box should be as large as possible until it reaches its maximum volume. Once again, pull out that calculator:

Maximum box volume $= 11 \times V_{AS} \times Q_T^2$

The result is in cubic feet if V_{AS} is in cubic feet and it will be in liters if V_{AS} is in liters.

You can now calculate how low the bass will be for any size of box using

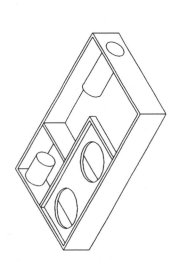

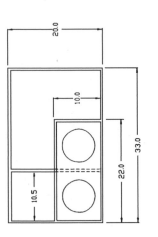

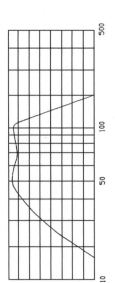

VIEWS SHOWN WITH TOP OFF

USE 1/2" MDF

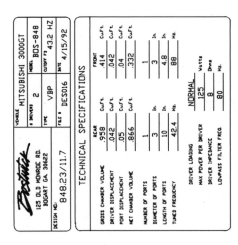

Bostwick
125 OLD MONROE RD.
BOGART GA. 30622

DESIGN NO: 848.23/11.7

VEHICLE	MITSUBISHI 3000GT		MODEL	BOS-848
# DRIVERS	2		OUTPUT F3	43.2 HZ
TYPE	VBP			
FILE #	DES016		DATE	4/15/92

TECHNICAL SPECIFICATIONS

	REAR		FRONT	
GROSS CHAMBER VOLUME	.958	cu.ft.	.414	cu.ft.
DRIVER DISPLACEMENT	.042	cu.ft.	.042	cu.ft.
PORT DISPLACEMENT	.05	cu.ft.	.04	cu.ft.
NET CHAMBER VOLUME	.866	cu.ft.	.332	cu.ft.
NUMBER OF PORTS	1		1	
DIAMETER OF PORTS	3	in.	3	in.
LENGTH OF PORTS	10	in.	4.8	in.
TUNED FREQUENCY	42.4	Hz.	88	Hz.

NORMAL

DRIVER LOADING		
MAX POWER PER DRIVER	125	Watts
DRIVER IMPEDANCE	8	Ohms
LOWPASS FILTER FREQ.	80	Hz.

Fig. 7-13 *A peculiar thin enclosure that was designed specifically for the Mitsubishi 3000GT.* Bostwick

the following equation:

$$Cutoff\ frequency = f_s \times \sqrt{V_{AS}/box\ volume}$$

For this equation, V_{AS} and *box volume* must both be in either cubic feet or liters. These equations are just approximations, but they should be accurate to within 10% of the actual value.

Once you have chosen the box volume that you feel would work best in your car and with your speakers, you must then design the port itself. First calculate the box frequency (the frequency that the port is tuned to):

$$Box\ frequency = 0.39 \times \frac{f_S}{Q_T}$$

To calculate the length of the port:

$$Port\ length = \frac{2117 \times D^2}{box\ frequency^2 \times box\ volume} - (0.732 \times D)$$

In this equation, the port length and the port inner diameter (D) must be in inches and the box volume must be in cubic feet.

Most ports for these enclosures are made with 2- or 3-in. PVC pipe because of it low cost, strength, availability, and ease of use. Calculate the port length for each diameter of pipe that you are considering and choose one that is not too short (less than 3 in. or so) or too long (so that it won't fit within the box or comes within a few inches of the back wall of the box).

TRANSMISSION-LINE ENCLOSURES

A *transmission line* is a cable, usually coaxial cable, where a radio signal flows (either transmitter to antenna or antenna to receiver). Thus, the coaxial cable that connects the car radio antenna to the head unit is transmission line. In terms of speaker systems, a *transmission-line enclosure* is one in which the air pressure is forced to travel through a long maze until it is relieved through a small duct at the bottom of the enclosure. Transmission-line enclosures have some of the same advantages and disadvantages that were mentioned in the last section on ported-box enclosures. They are said by some audiophiles to have superior bass response and clarity, but they are very complicated, esoteric, and difficult to build. You might have a blast experimenting with building transmission-line enclosures, but I feel as though I would be wasting my time experimenting for any slight advantage in sound quality that would be gained.

As just stated, the transmission-line enclosure is a box that requires a long passage for the sound pressure to travel through. If you have considered using a transmission-line enclosure, think about the potential specifications of a system of this sort. These enclosures are almost always large—usually very long. Some transmission-line enclosures might not even fit into your car widthwise! Also, the transmission lines in these systems are normally filled with acoustic damping material. Large amounts of damping material have a problem with settling to the bottom in a stationary box, let alone in a mobile speaker enclosure. As a result, these enclosures are much less practical for auto audio applications than either closed-box or even ported-box enclosures. One commercial exception to this is the Power Mowse line of enclosed speakers from Harrison Labs (Fig. 7-14).

Fig. 7-14 *Harrison Lab's Power Mowse is an amplifier and speakers built into a miniature transmission-line enclosure.*

SPEAKER ENCLOSURE CONCLUSION

This section just skims the surface of the topic because its breadth and complexity. What is included here is intended to help you gain some understanding of speaker enclosures and to be able to build simple, solid, high-quality boxes for your vehicle. For additional information on designing speaker systems, enclosures, and crossovers, read *Designing, Building, and Testing Your Own Speaker System with Projects (3rd Edition)* and *Great Sound Stereo Speaker Manual With Projects* by David B. Weems. Although these books both cover home audio and not auto audio, they are an excellent resource and they should give you a number of ideas if you are an audiophile and experimenter. A great periodic source of information for the audiophile is *Speaker Builder* magazine, which features numerous designs that are mainly tailored for the home audio market, but it does feature designs that can be used or modified for auto audio use.

CONCLUSION

Speaker enclosures are just as important as the speakers you buy. Shapes and cabinet styles aren't the only factors. Just as important are the materials and how they are used. For more information on the building materials, see Chapter 9.

8

FILTERS & CROSSOVERS

Filters and crossovers are two often-misunderstood pieces of audio equipment. Although the various computations and applications for crossovers can be very difficult and complicated, the basic concept of what crossovers do is quite simple. A crossover is an electronic circuit that channels audio frequencies to the speakers where the sound can be best reproduced. This system of high-pass and low-pass (and possibly also of bandpass) filters is used to direct low-frequency audio to the woofers, mid-frequency audio to the midrange drivers, and high-frequency audio to the tweeters.

Most people who start working on an auto audio system know nothing about crossovers even though they might have set up a very nice, good-sounding home audio system. Because few hi-fi enthusiasts are electronics buffs who design and build their own equipment, nearly all auto speakers are commercial models, which have built-in crossover circuitry. However, many car speakers are inserted sans cabinet into a hole somewhere in the auto interior—kick panels, doors, dashboard, etc. These might be for systems with either full-range or multiple-driver speakers, which don't require crossovers unless subwoofers are also used. As a result, crossovers are only included in enclosed speakers and they are very conspicuous—you must make a deliberate choice to use them.

CROSSOVER USES

As mentioned earlier, a crossover consists of high-pass, low-pass, and possibly bandpass filters. The two primary practical purposes of crossover networks are to prevent the high-frequency speakers (i.e., the tweeters) from being destroyed and to make the audio system sound better.

FILTERS & CROSSOVERS

Tweeters are built to handle high-frequency audio, which consists of much smaller, faster vibrations. Whenever these smaller speakers, which often have stiff speaker cones, are subjected to the large, powerful low-frequency waves, the voice coils will often quickly overheat and blowout. On the downside, you have two (or more) dead tweeters. On the upside, you've now got a pair of powerful refrigerator magnets. The only way to protect the tweeters is to use a crossover network to prevent the lower frequencies from reaching them.

Another problem with not using a crossover is that the audio simply doesn't sound as good. Speakers just can't reproduce audio across the entire human-hearing frequency range as well as several speakers that are each assigned to a different part of the frequency range. Without the crossover network, each speaker will attempt to reproduce across the entire range. Although this system will sound better than just one speaker of comparable quality, it won't sound nearly as good because the speakers will be playing frequencies beyond their particular ranges, where distortion becomes noticeable. By cutting out the areas where the audio is rough and "assembling the pieces," you can produce a sound that is much better.

That sounds easy enough: just pick up a high-pass filter for the tweeters, a low-pass filter for the woofers or subwoofers, and a bandpass filter for the midranges. Then, you're all set. The problem is that there are a number of variables with crossovers. For example, what frequency should each filter cut off at? Also, the cutoff rate (also known as a *skirt* because of its image when graphed) of each type of filter is somewhat gradual. How steep you want the skirts to be will change the type of crossover that you plan to purchase or build. And, where should the crossover points be and how should they overlap?

As was previously stated, the use of crossover networks causes other problems, yet they are almost essential to attain good audio and safe speaker operation. These are the scientific anomalies that books are made of and companies survive upon. In all, crossovers can be a real pain to deal with, and it's a whole lot easier to pick up a commercial crossover (either one that is built into a head unit, into a speaker cabinet, or one that is separate) that was engineered for those specific speakers than it is to buy parts, guesstimate the values, and experiment (Fig. 8-1). Crossovers are one of those things that are best left to people with about intermediate-level (or above) electronic experience (i.e., typical electronics hobbyists) and a great deal of patience.

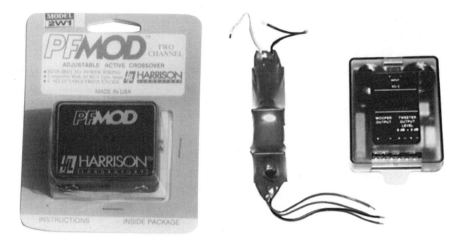

Fig. 8-1 *Three small, self-contained crossovers.*

BUILDING AND BUYING CROSSOVERS

Now that car audio systems have become an art, a science, and big business, you can find just about any sort of crossover or crossover assembly on the market. In addition to crossovers that are built into speakers, preamplifiers, dedicated amplifiers, and equalizers, many types of separate crossovers are available. Companies such as Parts Express, Scosche, Sound Quest, Crutchfield, etc., offer several types of capacitors, power resistors, inductor coils, and even PC boards so that you can build your own crossovers. If these don't quite suit your needs, some of these companies have tiny in-line units (with or without tiny enclosures) and larger assembled crossovers that are open, carefree, and enclosureless (Fig. 8-2). The crossovers that you choose could run

Fig. 8-2 *Several different passive crossovers.* Stillwater Designs KICKER car audio systems

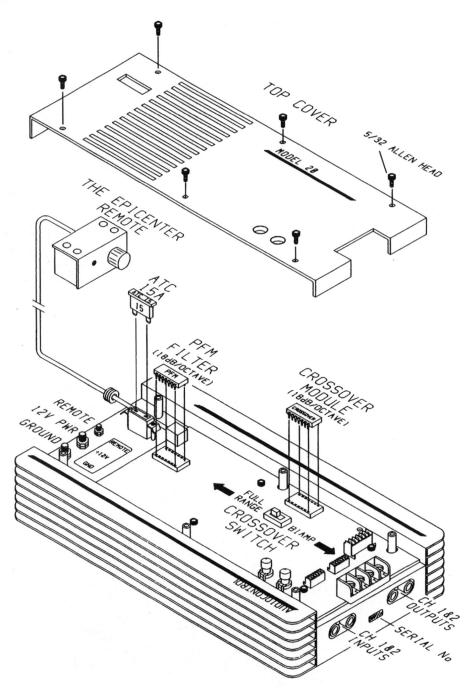

Fig. 8-3 *An exploded view of the AudioControl System 90 Model 20 Crossover.*

anywhere from close to $5 to approximately $1400. In general, the differences in performance aren't nearly as wide as the price gap. The major difference between the two (other than the obvious) is that the expensive crossovers have a number of different inputs and outputs: they might have phase controls or switches, digital delay, various settings for different networks (Fig. 8-3), equalizers, continuously variable crossover points (Fig. 8-4), etc.

Fig. 8-4 *Front and back of the Altec Lansing ALC 10 electronic crossover.* Altec Lansing

The problem is trying to match up a crossover system with the audio source and the speaker arrangement. A crossover system that totals out at over $175 could be much less effective than a $10 crossover system, depending on the way that it has been matched.

Fig. 8-5 *The AudioControl EQQ filter/equalizer.* AudioControl

BASIC CROSSOVER THEORY

As stated in the last section, the goal of any crossover system is to transmit different chunks of the audio frequency range to the proper speakers. For the end result, the unattainable optimum is for all of the signals and speakers to fit together perfectly, as if it was one perfect speaker that was receiving audio directly from the head unit. This isn't easy and it's been known to make some audio tough guys scream for their mommies.

ACTIVE VERSUS PASSIVE CROSSOVERS

The qualifying difference between active and passive crossovers is simple: active crossovers require external power via a battery and passive crossovers require no extras; they passively filter the audio. Active crossovers are typically only used in commercial products, such as in amplifiers, equalizers, or as separate crossover devices. On the other hand, passive crossovers (Figs. 8-5 and. 8-6) are quite simple, inexpensive, and are commonly used in both commercial applications (such as built into speaker enclosures) and hobby projects. Because of the complications of the active crossovers, they are not covered in this book, but the basic passive crossover systems are covered in the following sections. If you decide that an active crossover would best suit your system, you should probably pick up a commercial unit that is either separate or built in with other equipment. Otherwise, keep reading.

BASIC CROSSOVER COMPONENTS

Crossovers seem to have built up a large mystique among many audio enthusiasts—particularly among the newcomers to the hobby. To some degree, at least, the aura of crossovers seems to rival waxing audio cables for a "slicker" sound or building a "flux capacitor" to power your system. In reality, passive crossovers are quite simple, as far as assemblies and parts are concerned. It is the effects of the crossovers and the crossover points that are difficult to control. Most crossovers consist just of inductors or capacitors in series or in parallel, depending on the speaker arrangement.

ORDERS OF CROSSOVERS

The different orders of crossovers have nothing to do with secret societies, although somewhere in the world there is probably a group of guys

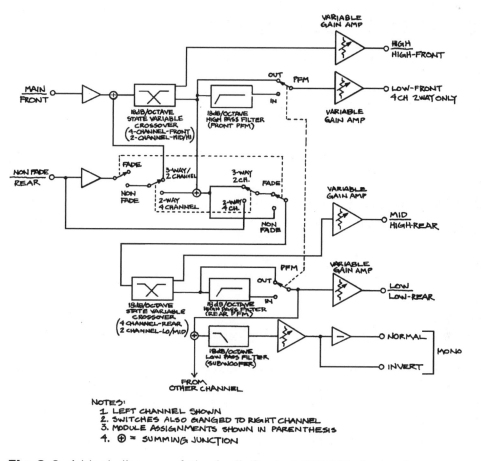

Fig. 8-6 *A block diagram of the AudioControl 4XS-110 electronic crossover.*
AudioControl

who have a secret chant and handshake, and a silly hat, who get together to drink beer and talk about crossovers. They might even go bowling together and sell raffle tickets for crossover networks. Even if these guys aren't so noticeable in your community for you to have heard them talking, they have surely discussed the merits of the *first-order crossover*. The first-order crossover was evidently so named because it is the simplest of all passive crossovers. For a set of two speakers (a woofer and a tweeter), only a single capacitor and an inductor are used (Fig. 8-7). The capacitor is used as a high-pass filter to prevent damage to the tweeter, and an inductor is used as a low-pass filter so that the woofer won't sound poor in its attempts to reproduce the higher frequencies.

In a system such as this, just half of the first-order crossover, a high-pass filter (a capacitor) could have been used to protect the tweeter (Fig. 8-8),

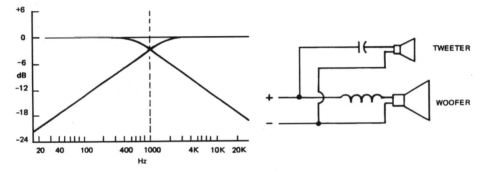

Fig. 8-7 *A first-order crossover network.* AudioControl

but then again, this would be just a low-pass filter and not a crossover. Even so, you might feel that your woofer/tweeter combination sounds fine without any crossovers. In this case (and for the sake of saving some money), you could just insert a single capacitor as a high-pass filter to protect the tweeter.

Nearly all crossovers produce a cutoff slope that is a multiple of 6 dB per octave. The orders of crossovers are all very exact, and as a result, you can multiply the number of the order times the 6-dB per octave figure to find the cutoff slope for any of the basic crossover designs. So, the cutoff slope for the first-order crossover is 6 dB per octave (1 × 6 = 6). This is a very light, gradual cutoff rate and it is either praised or degraded by audio enthusiasts. Supporters of first-order networks praise the simplicity and low-cost of the system, and also the easy-to-control phase characteristics and the natural-sounding frequency division. Skeptics see the very gradual cutoff slope as being slightly better than not using any crossovers at all, and they would probably also say that you get what you pay for.

As you now know from the previous descriptions, the *second-order*

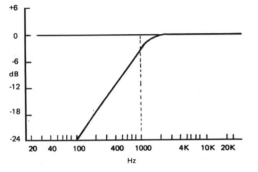

Fig. 8-8 *A 1000-Hz high-pass filter.*
AudioControl

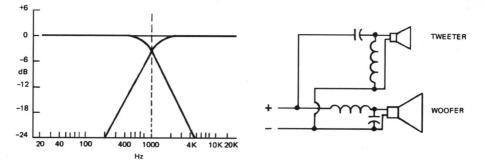

Fig. 8-9 *A second-order Butterworth crossover network.* AudioControl

crossover is more complicated than the first-order type, and it has a cutoff slope of 12 dB per octave. As far as the actual parts count goes, the second-order network doubles the number of parts that were used before—the high-pass and low-pass filters each consist of a capacitor and an inductor (Fig. 8-9). The 12-dB-per-octave cutoff rate tightens up the frequency division, and it also provides more protection for the tweeters than the first-order systems. The three well-known types of second-order crossovers consist of the Butterworth filter, the Bessel filter, and the Linkwitz-Riley filter.

Unfortunately, the increased complications of the second-order crossovers create a few esoteric electrical problems. The major problem is that the signals to each speaker in the crossover network arrive 180° out of phase. When the same signals arrive in opposite phase (180°), they will tend to cancel out. In this case, the best that you can hope for is a "hole" in the sound between the two speakers. In the worst case, the frequencies will cancel out and the frequency response of the system will be hindered (probably sounding "thin" or "tinny"). If you have installed a second-order crossover system and you don't like the sound (or even if you just like to experiment), try connecting one of the speakers out of phase and see if the sound improves.

Of course, the increasing complexity of crossovers also increases the complexity of the problems that result from using these systems. Now that the phase has been corrected, the frequency response is distorted and there is a peak in the response at the crossover frequency of the Butterworth version. Take your pick: either a null or a peak at the crossover frequency. This is where the Linkwitz-Riley filter fits in. Instead of producing a peak in the frequency response, the Linkwitz-Riley filter has a dip in its overall total power response. As a result of these complex problems, the Linkwitz-Riley filter is probably a better pick for a home or an auto audio system. The second-order Butterworth filters are commonly used in public address and auditorium audio systems because the audio peak is usually in the midrange. Because most of the sounds for voice recognition is in the midrange, this system is perfect for maximum intelligibility, where pure high-fidelity audio is not a concern. Bessel filters also peak at the crossover frequency and dip in the power. Bessel filters are not as commonly used, although some high-end companies, such as Audison, exclusively design their crossovers around this design of second-order crossover.

When you page through the auto audio catalogs, you will rarely see what type of network is being utilized in any particular system. I suppose that most of these companies feel that knowing the filter types won't be particularly useful. Some companies, such as Parts Express, don't list the orders of the crossovers in the component descriptions, but they do list the cutoff slopes of each (which is the most important information anyway).

The very steep skirts of the third- and fourth-order networks are rarely used for crossover applications (Figs. 8-10 and 8-11). The cutoff slopes are 18 and 24 dB per octave (respectively), and in most cases they are much steeper than is necessary. After all, the goal of audio and crossover design is to reproduce the source audio as closely as possible and blend the sounds together, not perform laser surgery.

Third- and fourth-order crossovers are sometimes used with subwoofers to prevent the upper bass range from being audible. One of the great assets of subwoofers (as described in previous chapters) is that because the low-frequency sound waves are so long, subwoofers can be placed anywhere in the car and the bass audio will not sound as if it is coming from one particular direction. However, if the upper end of the bass frequencies is allowed to pass through the speaker, these frequencies will "give away" the location of the subwoofer. One possible solution to the problem without using third- or fourth-order crossovers is to mount the subwoofer in the trunk and hope that the upper bass frequencies will be filtered out by the back seat.

Another application for third- and fourth-order crossovers is to reduce "boomy" bass. Like the problem with hearing where the subwoofers are (in the previous paragraph), the problem with boominess also can be traced to having too much upper bass being output by the subwoofers. If

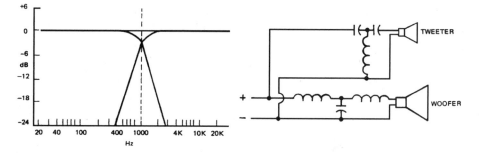

Fig. 8-10 *A third-order Butterworth crossover network.* AudioControl

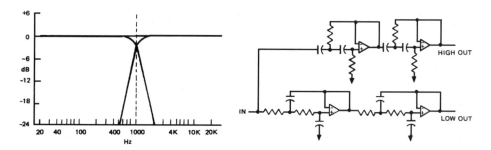

Fig. 8-11 *A fourth-order Butterworth crossover network.* AudioControl

you try to lower the frequency of the first- or second-order crossover, you might cut out some of the important low-bass frequencies. The best solution in these cases might be to slice off the upper-bass range with a third- or fourth-order crossover. Or, as in the previous paragraph, you can try mounting the subwoofer in the trunk with the hopes that it will filter out the upper-bass frequencies, and as a result, eliminate the boomy sound.

In the third-order crossovers, two capacitors and one inductor form the high-pass filter and two inductors and one capacitor form the low-pass filter. In fourth-order crossovers, two capacitors and two inductors are used in both the high-pass and the low-pass filters. Both of these crossovers can become very complicated when using them in a three- or four-way system. Also, the phase issue reappears. The problem of phase with these crossovers is that the signals do not arrive in phase (as with first-order crossovers) or completely out of phase (as in the second-order crossovers). Instead, the signals arrive at two different points along the waveform. The only way to solve the phase problem is to modify the electronic circuit and probably cause even more negative side effects.

If you want to play it safe, avoid the third- and fourth-order crossover network designs. They are much more complicated, expensive, and frustrating than they are worth.

DETERMINING THE CROSSOVER VALUES

Determining the crossover frequencies for your speakers and the values for the parts of your subsequent crossover might seem like difficult tasks—especially if you have no electronics background. But, it really isn't so bad; there's even a table to help you find the values after you determine the crossover points.

DETERMINING THE SPEAKER CROSSOVER POINTS

If you have the frequency specifications or a frequency response chart for your speakers, determining the crossover points shouldn't be an overly difficult task. If you want to protect your tweeters and want a decent-sounding system, but you don't want to waste your time, try the pin-the-tail-on-the-donkey approach. Most of the crossover points in commercial systems are at between 3,000 and 5,000 Hz (to define the border of the tweeters' range), approximately 800 and 1000 Hz (to define the bottom edge of the midrange and the top edge of the woofers' range), and at 100 and 300 Hz (to define the bottom edge of the woofers' range and the top edge of the subwoofers' range).

If you are taking the simple random route with two speakers per corner and a first-order crossover, you would probably want the crossover frequency to be closer to 3,000 Hz for better tweeter protection. The slope of the first-order network is so gradual that dropping the crossover frequency below 4,000 Hz could still allow enough low-frequency audio through to damage the tweeter. If you feel that some of the sound in the midrange would be lacking with such a high crossover rate, use a second-order network (with a much steeper cutoff skirt) instead and drop the crossover lower (to about 5,000 Hz). In either case, it's still a good idea to use a solid-quality midbass or midrange speaker to fill out the rest of the sound. With a good midbass, an average (or better) tweeter, and an appropriate crossover network, you can have a great, natural-sounding installation. Some people even prefer this arrangement because it is simpler and fewer sound-debilitating complications can arise. Also, for the cost of six average speakers, you can buy two really good midbass speakers and two tweeters instead.

The alternative is to dig out the frequency specifications of the speakers that you are using for your system. Normally, good speakers will produce a fairly flat line of response for the range that they are built for. Then, toward either edge of the flat response, the response line will either drop or will begin to spike. Flat response is the key. Spikes, peaks, and sudden dropoffs will alter the overall quality and destroy the realistic sound of the audio. As a result, you can locate potential crossover points by finding where the response begins to get flakey and divert from the smooth line of response. You need to trim off these rough edges, so whenever possible, configure the high-pass or low-pass (depending on which needs to be used) appropriately. The problems crop up when your speakers are basically mismatched and the response lines get flakey at overlapping frequency regions. If you tried to cut out the areas that aren't flat in a system such as this, you would be left with a gap in frequency response. Depending on the size of the gap and the steepness of the skirt, a gapped-out system can sound really bad—in part because the gap will often occur toward the middle of the hearing range (i.e., where most crossovers are set).

Shown in Fig. 8-12 is the graphed response for the Audax HM 130Z0 midrange speaker. The response is very flat and it drops off almost as if it already had a crossover installed. However, its frequency response does carry well into the bass frequencies. The manufacturer recommended parts for a first-order high-pass filter at either 500 or 800 Hz, depending on your preference.

Another problem with rolling up your sleeves and digging into the frequency ratings and graphs is this: What if your speakers don't have any sections of relatively flat response across the graph? If the frequency response of a speaker looks as though it had been chewed up by a Doberman, you should probably reconsider purchasing the speakers. If you already own the speakers and still want to use them in your system, try to place the crossover frequencies in such a way that you can make the most of what response is there and still cut off some the more extreme response fluctuations. Just try to follow the general guidelines for commercial crossovers that were listed several paragraphs ago. Otherwise, you could wind up with a system that requires eight speakers in each channel. Even if you had all of this stuff on hand, the performance would still be lacking because of the electronic complications involved.

DETERMINING THE PARTS AND VALUES TO USE IN YOUR CROSSOVERS

Any technophobic Spice Girls fan can pull out a few graphs of speaker

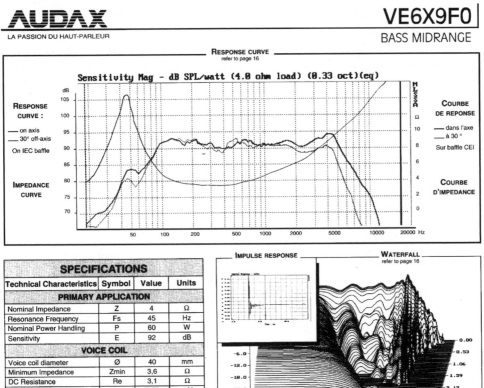

AUDAX
LA PASSION DU HAUT-PARLEUR

VE6X9FO
BASS MIDRANGE

RESPONSE CURVE refer to page 16

Sensitivity Mag - dB SPL/watt (4.0 ohm load) (0.33 oct)(eq)

RESPONSE CURVE :
— on axis
— 30° off-axis
On IEC baffle

IMPEDANCE CURVE

COURBE DE REPONSE
— dans l'axe
— à 30 °
Sur baffle CEI

COURBE D'IMPEDANCE

SPECIFICATIONS

Technical Characteristics	Symbol	Value	Units
PRIMARY APPLICATION			
Nominal Impedance	Z	4	Ω
Resonance Frequency	Fs	45	Hz
Nominal Power Handling	P	60	W
Sensitivity	E	92	dB
VOICE COIL			
Voice coil diameter	Ø	40	mm
Minimum Impedance	Zmin	3,6	Ω
DC Resistance	Re	3,1	Ω
Voice Coil Inductance	Lbm	0,26	mH
Voice coil Length	h	11	mm
Former	-	Aluminium	-
Number of layers	n	2	-
MAGNET			
Magnet dimensions	Ø x h	100 X 18	mm
Magnet weight	m	0,55	kg
Flux density	B	1	T
Force factor	BL	6,2	NA⁻¹
Height of magnetic gap	He	6	mm
Stray flux	Fmag	-	Am⁻¹
Linear excursion	Xmax	±2,5	mm
PARAMETERS			
Suspension Compliance	Cms	0,57.10⁻³	mN⁻¹
Mechanical Q Factor	Qms	2,61	-
Electrical Q Factor	Qes	0,51	-
Total Q Factor	Qts	0,43	-
Mechanical Resistance	Rms	2,35	kg s⁻¹
Moving Mass	Mms	21,7.10⁻³	kg
Effective Piston Area	S	2,06.10⁻²	m²
Volume Equivalent of Air at Cas	Vas	33,6.10⁻³	m³
Mass of speaker	M	1,7	kg

APPLICATION PARAMETERS

Vb	Box volume	dm³
Fb	Tuning frequency	Hz
Dp	Port diameter	cm
Lp	Port length	cm

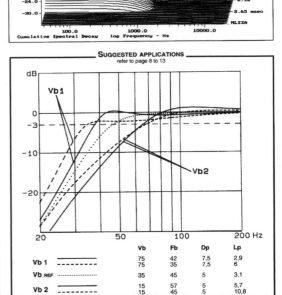

IMPULSE RESPONSE

WATERFALL refer to page 16

Cumulative Spectral Decay   log Frequency - Hz

SUGGESTED APPLICATIONS refer to page 8 to 13

		Vb	Fb	Dp	Lp
Vb 1		75	42	7,5	2,9
		75	35	7,5	6
Vb REF		35	45	5	3,1
Vb 2		15	57	5	5,7
		15	45	5	10,8

Please refer to method of measurement and measurement conditions pages 15 to 19.
Audax may, without prior notification modify the specifications on its products further to research and development requirements.

249

Fig. 8-12 *Speaker-response curves for the Audax VE6X9FO speaker.* Polydax

specifications, draw a few lines, and say "I want the crossover points to be here and here." Actually implementing these changes is another story altogether. You need to determine what parts values to punch in for each component. This task might sound like another "this is beyond the scope of this book" topic or you might be groaning "Oh no, he's going to bring out an arsenal of equations." Nah. Thanks to some good mathematicians and stereo enthusiasts, the inductor and capacitor component value charts for crossovers have been available for a number of years (Fig. 8-13).

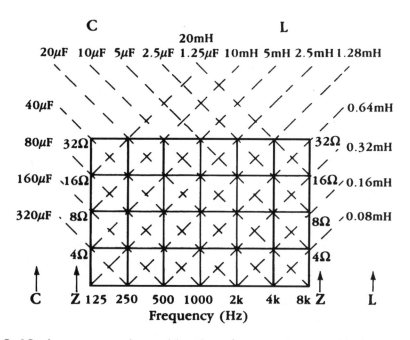

Fig. 8-13 *A crossover chart with values for capacitors and inductors.*

At first, the crossover value charts look more like an aerial bombardier's street map of Grand Forks, North Dakota than a useful electronic chart. The impedance (in ohms) lines are those that are the horizontal lines on the graph. The frequency range (in hertz and kilohertz) is across the bottom. The capacitance values (in microfarads) are the diagonal lines that run from the upper left corner toward the lower right. The inductance values (in millihenries) run from the upper right corner toward the lower left corner. To read the chart, first find the impedance of the speaker(s) that you are using. Then, find the crossover point that you intend to use on the appropriate horizontal line. Follow the lines from that point toward the inductance and capacitance values. If your intended crossover point falls between two lines, use a little math to guesstimate the appropriate values for each component. The main values in this chart are for first-order crossovers. The italicized values that are listed beside each main value are for second-order crossovers. In case you are scientifically curious, the second-order values were found by multiplying each first-order capacitance value by 0.7 and each first-order inductance value by 1.414. A chart of values is also included to make the value-hunting process even easier (see Table 8-1).

For example, to create a simple first-order crossover for two 4-ohm speakers at 4,000 Hz, the value of the high-pass capacitor would be 10 uF and the value of the low-pass inductor would be 0.15 mH. For a second-order crossover at 4,000 Hz, the value of both of the capacitors would be 7 uF and the value for both of the inductors would be 0.212 mH. The difference between the high-pass and the low-pass filters for the second-order network is that for the high-pass filter, the inductor should be wired in parallel and the capacitor should be wired in series; for the low-pass filter, the inductor should be wired in series and the capacitor should be wired in parallel.

Sure, most any electronics components could be used in your crossovers, but the parts that are used in audio crossovers are strange because the values aren't standard. For capacitors, the voltages are much higher and the capacitance ratings are much lower than those used in modern electronics. The typical capacitors used in crossovers are nonpolarized electrolytics and Mylar types. The inductors (also known as *crossover chokes* in some company catalogs) are peculiar little coils of wire. Unlike capacitors, the crossover chokes have strange enough values that they

Table 8-1 *Values for components in various crossovers.*M&M Electronics

Crossover point desired	This is a 6-dB/octave crossover				This is a 12-dB/octave crossover			
	4-ohm speaker		8-ohm speaker		4-ohm speaker		8-ohm speaker	
	MFD	MH	MFD	MH	MFD	MH	MFD	MH
50 Hz	796.7	12.7	398.1	25.5	998.0	32.0	499.0	64.0
75 Hz	530.8	8.5	265.4	17.0	665.3	21.3	332.7	42.7
100 Hz	398.1	6.4	199.0	12.7	499.0	16.0	249.5	32.0
125 Hz	318.5	5.1	159.2	10.2	399.2	12.8	199.6	25.6
150 Hz	258.4	4.2	132.7	8.5	332.7	10.7	166.3	21.3
175 Hz	227.5	3.6	113.7	7.3	285.1	9.1	142.6	18.3
200 Hz	199.0	3.2	99.5	6.4	249.5	8.0	124.8	16.0

(Continued) **Table 8-1** *Values for components in various crossovers.* M&M Electronics

| Crossover point desired | This is a 6-dB/octave crossover | | | | This is a 12-dB/octave crossover | | | |
| | 4-ohm speaker | | 8-ohm speaker | | 4-ohm speaker | | 8-ohm speaker | |
	MFD	MH	MFD	MH	MFD	MH	MFD	MH
225 Hz	176.9	2.8	88.5	5.7	221.8	7.1	110.9	14.2
250 Hz	159.2	2.5	79.6	5.1	199.6	6.4	99.8	12.8
275 Hz	144.8	2.3	72.4	4.6	181.5	5.8	90.7	11.6
300 Hz	132.7	2.1	66.3	4.2	166.3	5.3	83.2	10.7
400 Hz	99.5	1.6	49.8	3.2	124.8	4.0	62.8	8.0
500 Hz	79.6	1.3	39.8	2.5	99.8	3.2	49.9	6.4
600 Hz	66.3	1.1	33.2	2.1	83.2	2.7	41.6	5.3
700 Hz	56.9	0.9	28.4	1.8	71.3	2.3	35.6	4.6
800 Hz	49.8	0.8	24.9	1.6	62.4	2.0	31.2	4.0
900 Hz	44.2	0.7	22.1	1.4	55.4	1.8	27.7	3.6
1000 Hz	39.8	0.6	19.9	1.3	49.9	1.6	25.0	3.2
1100 Hz	36.2	0.6	18.1	1.2	45.4	1.5	22.7	2.9
1200 Hz	33.2	0.5	16.6	1.1	41.6	1.3	20.8	2.7
1300 Hz	30.6	0.5	15.3	1.0	38.4	1.2	19.2	2.5
1400 Hz	28.4	0.5	14.2	0.9	35.6	1.1	17.8	2.3
1500 Hz	26.5	0.4	13.3	0.8	33.3	1.1	16.6	2.1
1600 Hz	24.9	0.4	12.4	0.8	31.2	1.0	15.6	2.0
1700 Hz	23.4	0.4	11.7	0.7	29.4	0.9	14.7	1.9
1800 Hz	22.1	0.4	11.1	0.7	27.7	0.9	13.9	1.8
1900 Hz	21.0	0.3	10.5	0.7	26.3	0.8	13.1	1.7
2000 Hz	19.9	0.3	6.6	0.4	25.0	0.8	12.5	1.6
3000 Hz	13.3	0.2	6.6	0.4	16.6	0.5	8.3	1.1
4000 Hz	10.0	0.2	5.0	0.3	12.5	0.4	6.2	0.8
5000 Hz	8.0	0.1	4.0	0.3	10.0	0.3	5.0	0.6
6000 Hz	6.6	0.1	3.3	0.2	8.3	0.3	4.2	0.5
7000 Hz	5.7	0.1	2.8	0.2	7.1	0.2	3.6	0.5
8000 Hz	5.0	0.1	2.5	0.2	6.2	0.2	3.1	0.4
9000 Hz	4.4	0.1	2.2	0.1	5.5	0.2	2.8	0.4
10000 Hz	4.0	0.1	2.0	0.1	5.0	0.2	2.5	0.3

are typically made by domestic audio supply companies, specifically for crossover applications.

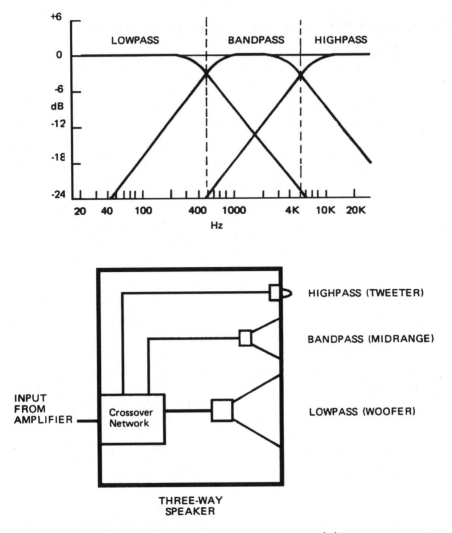

Fig. 8-14 *Response rate for a three-way crossover and the crossover arrangement for the system.* AudioControl

Capacitors with appropriate crossover values are very difficult to find in most electronics supply houses. Also, most inductors for crossover applications are made by audio supply companies, so your best bet when ordering these parts is to check first with an mail-order audio component supplier, such as Parts Express. With a company such as this, the parts are labeled specifically for crossovers, so you know that the components are appropriate.

CROSSOVERS FOR THREE-WAY SPEAKER SYSTEMS

For the sake of simplicity, the systems described in the book thus far have been for two-way speaker systems. Also, because of the extra cost, space, and work involved, you might just be better off sticking with a set of tweeters and midranges, rather than throwing in woofers, or possibly a subwoofer, too. Or, even if you want to mount a subwoofer in the trunk, the higher frequencies would already be filtered out by the back seat, and one of these beasts certainly won't be damaged by some higher frequency audio! Still, if you are truly into auto audio, you might choose a set of separates (as opposed to three-way multiple-driver speakers) that requires a three-way crossover (Fig. 8-14).

The common crossover points for two-way and three-way crossover networks were covered in the first paragraph of the section titled "Determining the speaker crossover points" earlier in this chapter. Combine this information with the tips for determining the crossover point in a two-way speaker system and you're all set. The only peculiarity of the three-way crossover is that you have to lump both a high-pass and a low-pass filter on the midrange speaker (Fig. 8-15). One strange problem that you could have if you don't really think about what you're doing is getting the values reversed. For example, if you set the crossover rates

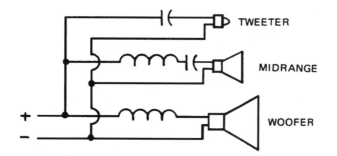

Fig. 8-15 *The three-way crossover schematic.* AudioControl

at 500 and 4,000 Hz, the necessary values for the high-pass and low-pass filters are 80 uF, 1.28 mH, 10 uF, and 0.16 mH. If these are reversed, then none of the audio will reach the proper speakers and everything will be cut out from the midrange. If you install a crossover network and think that you might have blown the speakers out because the audio is low and unbalanced, check your crossover values to make sure that they aren't reversed.

MIXING AND MATCHING DIFFERENT CROSSOVER ORDERS

There's no rule that says that "You must use the same crossover networks in a system or everyone in Wisconsin will turn into slabs of Monterey Jack and the Montreal Expos will win the World Series." Of course, you would only be able to use dissimilar crossovers in three-way or four-way separate speaker systems because the two-way systems only have one crossover.

Really, there's nothing special about using different crossovers in the same network. A number of different commercial crossover networks use a first-order crossover at the lower frequency (bass/midrange) and a second-order crossover at the higher frequency (midrange/treble). This system allows the audio to be smooth and natural across the important lower frequencies, and it still can quickly crossover the high frequencies to the tweeter to prevent it from being damaged (Fig. 8-16).

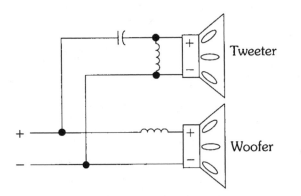

Fig. 8-16 *A combination crossover with a first-order low-pass filter and a second-order high-pass filter.*

RESISTANCE AND L PADS

I have heard some stories about how a few do-it yourselfers upgraded to some really hot, expensive speaker systems. They were really excited about the great sound that would soon be pouring from their cars. Instead, they found that although the audio was clean, it was very shrill and high-pitched. What to do? This looks like a job for Resistance

Man—a masked superhero, who installs carbon and wire-wound electronic resistors during the day and who protests the government at night (maybe that was a dumb, cheap joke, but at least I didn't make any jokes about Crossover Man!).

Resistors and L pads are not part of the crossover network, but they can do plenty to control the individual speakers. Also, they are simple electronics that are built into the same physical areas that the crossover networks are constructed, so L pads and crossovers are often mentioned in the same breath. A *resistor* is an electronic component that limits the flow of a signal through a wire.

If you are a daring, experimenting-type person, you can use resistors to reduce the volume from one particular type of speaker (e.g., the tweeters) in a multispeaker system. Just wire a resistor with a low-value (such as 10 ohms) in parallel across the terminals of the overpowering speaker.

The problem with wiring a resistor in parallel across the inputs of a speaker is that the value of the resistor will change the value of the crossover point. With some work and experimentation, you can tame the overpowering speakers and tune the crossover frequency, but it would probably require a large effort, which might not be worthwhile.

If you decide to go ahead with the experimentation, the second major obstacle is that you don't really know what value will work properly. There is no standardized method for determining these resistor values, like there are for determining crossover values. Part of the trouble is that speakers vary in efficiency, so unless you check the efficiency of each speaker to make sure that they match, one of the speakers will overpower the others. Matching efficiencies usually isn't a great idea anyway because chances are that you will not get the best quality or the best prices that you would find if you just got the best speakers that you could afford and matched them later. That is where the resistances are helpful in balancing out the system. The fixed-value resistors are very inexpensive (usually only a few cents apiece), but you will need to experiment with plugging in a number of different values so that you can pick the one that is most suitable for the system and your ears (Fig. 8-17).

Another possible solution might depend on the type of capacitor that you used in your crossover. Although a capacitor is obviously built to add capacitance at a specific point in the circuit, it also has other values,

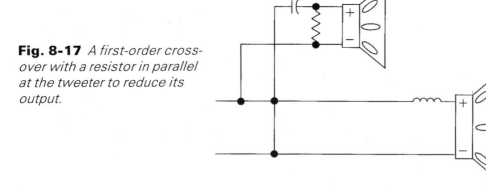

Fig. 8-17 *A first-order cross-over with a resistor in parallel at the tweeter to reduce its output.*

such as resistance and inductance. Different types of capacitors have different ratings of resistance, inductance, etc., even if their values of voltage and capacitance are the same. Depending on the type of capacitors you are using, you might be able clear up your problems with overly "bright" tweeters by using a different type of capacitor (one with more inherent resistance). This solution might border on "snake-oil" remedies, but if you already have the components, it might be worth a try just to see what happens.

The L pad is handy because it is not virtually permanent, like soldering in the resistors, and it can be tuned to the proper resistance to limit the audio of the speakers. The *L pad* is a component with two separate sources of variable resistance. When it is installed, one resistance element is connected in parallel to the speaker and the other is connected in series. When the L pad is tuned, it can reduce the output to the driver while maintaining a steady impedance. In all, the L pad is a variable resistor (potentiometer) that is able to maintain a steady impedance.

For some reason, perhaps because of the door-panel and rear-deck installations, I have rarely seen or heard of anyone who used L pads in their auto audio systems. The normal car stereo technique for correcting a mismatch in the output of the speakers is to tone down those frequencies with an equalizer. This might be a workable solution, but I'd rather correct the problem immediately and toy around with the minor tweaking later—especially if I felt as though the audio was good enough that I could avoid purchasing an equalizer.

Most L pads are configured to control tweeters or midrange speakers, and some even have both types built into the same front panel. So, if you want to control the speakers with an L pad, you will need to either build special speaker cabinets for the tweeters and the midrange speakers or find a nearby position to mount the L pad, then wire the speakers to it from their separate mounting locations.

You should never try to use an L pad in conjunction with woofers and subwoofers. The system would require massive power resistors, and the effective Q of the system would be increased, which would make the sound "boomy."

CONCLUSION

Crossovers are essential for any system with speaker separates, both to improve the audio quality and to protect the tweeters. Signal-limiting resistors and L pads are very handy audio-balancing components, although they aren't necessary in all systems. Although a great amount of mystery and alchemy surrounds all of these components, they are all fairly simple to construct and use, so long as you keep it simple and follow some of the recommendations, such as using the crossover values component chart.

9

FIBERGLASS & MORE

For years, the little car stereo guides and magazines have stuck to guidelines of technical importance (such as specifications) and design (what to ask your installer to create for you). For the most part, the structural materials for your auto audio system are ignored. People just don't say much about plywood, MDF, fiberglass resin, and fiberglass compound. Maybe its because these materials aren't actually part of the audio system (although they do affect the sound) or maybe because the solutions vary from car to car and person to person.

WORKING WITH PLYWOOD

Plywood is any type of building material consisting of thin, complete sheets of wood, glued and pressed together. Typically, the grain of each sheet (ply) runs opposite to that of the grain of the ply under it. Thus, plywood is very strong in all directions and is very resistant to splitting completely through. General home construction-grade plywood ranges in thickness from approximately 1/4 to 1 in. and in number of plys from three to seven. Thick plywood with more plys is stronger and more resistant to warpage (Fig. 9-1).

Flakeboard is a form of very inexpensive composition wood sheeting. It consists of chunks of wood that have been pressed together. Flakeboard is much weaker and susceptible to damage than plywood. Never use it in your car.

Plywood also varies in grade, from low-grade house sheathing to finish-quality material and subflooring. The differences in the quality lie in the

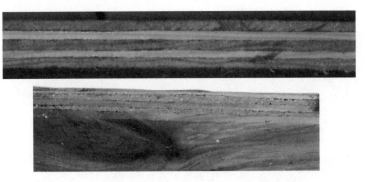

Fig. 9-1 *An end-view of 5-ply plywood (top) and a medium-grade plywood with an unfinished surface and a large knot (bottom).*

density and type of wood used. For example, low-grade plywood is very rough and is a softwood, such as pine or hemlock, typically with large knots (that are sometimes missing). High-grade material is very smooth, with virtually no splinters, cracks, or holes. Because it can be made smoother easier, a harder wood is used, such as birch. Some of the high-grade plywoods are dense enough that they suitable for building speaker enclosures, but they can't compare in either cost or performance to using MDF (see the MDF/particle board section later in this chapter).

In car stereo systems, plywood is unnecessary, except for heavy-duty systems. For serious installations, plywood is excellent for building amplifier racks, dashboard equipment-mounting consoles, video consoles, recrafted trunks, and redesigned rear decks.

Aside from avoiding getting plywood wet (you don't want water in your car anyway), there are no real concerns about working with plywood, as opposed to some other materials.

WORKING WITH MDF

MDF (medium-density fiberboard) or *particleboard* is sometimes confused with flakeboard because both consist of pieces of wood that have been pressed into sheets or boards. The difference is that flakeboard is composed of large chunks of wood, often inches in diameter, whereas MDF is basically wood powder that has been pressed into a solid mass, hence the name *particleboard*. When buying MDF, look it over and don't just buy it blindly. The *particleboard, flakeboard,* and *fiberboard* names are often used incorrectly, and companies make different densities of this material (Fig. 9-2). If it's labeled *MDF*, you can assume that it really is MDF, but MDF is often labeled by one of the other names instead. And if you ask for MDF by name at a hardware store, chances are, they won't have the faintest idea what you're talking about. So, get to know MDF by sight.

Fig. 9-2 *Different grades of flakeboard: particleboard (top) and MDF shelving with dyed "grain" (bottom).*

Although flakeboard is absolutely useless in car audio applications, MDF is almost essential. MDF is the perfect material for speaker enclosures because it is incredibly dense and heavy, and because the pieces of wood are so tiny, it has no dead spots. It's also very firm, so it doesn't flex and cancel out the sound waves. See Chapter 7 for more information concerning speaker enclosures.

Unlike plywood, there are some serious concerns when building with MDF. Although it's heavy, it is not strong. When it is drilled or chiseled, it behaves somewhat like very heavy, thick cardboard (Fig. 9-3). It's especially difficult to build joints because of the cutting involved and because MDF is susceptible to splitting. I've discovered the hard way that all screw holes in MDF must be countersunk or the board will split. The countersinking must be as wide as the shaft of the screw (not including the height of the threads). Also, the head of the screw must be countersunk.

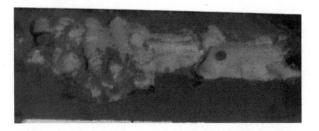

Fig. 9-3 *A piece of MDF that has been drilled out and chiseled. In these applications, it is worked much like very dense cardboard.*

Because of its weight and physical weakness, it should never be used in applications where plywood is best suited, such as building amplifier racks, dashboard equipment-mounting consoles, video consoles, recrafted trunks, and redesigned rear decks. Use it only for speaker enclosures.

Finally, never let MDF become wet or very damp for any length of time. It will decompose quickly and become squishy, like soaked cardboard, if allowed to absorb too much water.

FIBERGLASS

Fiberglass is a mixture of glass strands in a plastic base, which was first used during World War II because of its low weight, easy workability, high strength, and resistance to corrosion. Since the war, it has become commonly used in boat hulls, car bodies, swimming pools, bath tubs, etc. Often, fiberglass is applied over a woven mat of glass strands. *Fiberglass* is really a misnomer because the name refers only to the woven glass strands, not to the plastic. In fact, "fiberglass resin" contains no fiberglass; it is 100% polyester or epoxy.

The two main types of fiberglass liquids are compound and resin (Fig. 9-4). Fiberglass compound is a thick, grey paste, sometimes called *car putty* or *Bondo*, after the most famous brandname of compound. The other is fiberglass resin, which is a clear plastic liquid.

Both fiberglass compound and resin are liquids that require a catalyst or hardener to transform the stuff into a hard, sandable surface. The compound or resin is poured into a container; then the hardener is added and stirred in at a certain ratio (such as six parts fiberglass to one part hardener). The mixture is then applied to the surface and within

Fig. 9-4 *Fiberglass resin.*

minutes it begins to become warm from the chemical reaction and harden. Any fiberglass leftover from the mixture will harden and quickly become unusable.

Be careful when working with all fiberglass-related materials. All are extremely flammable, including the fumes, so smoking or working around sparks or flames are out of the question. The fumes themselves are not only flammable, they are dangerous to breathe. So, the fiberglassing work area must be adequately ventilated—a real plus for applying fiberglass outside in the summer! The fumes can cause numerous long-term health problems and immediate skin and eye irritations. And even the fiberglass fibers themselves can cause skin and respiratory inflammations. Follow the directions on the can of fiberglass resin or compound to determine what precautions you should take.

WORKING WITH FIBERGLASS RESIN

Fiberglass resin is really just clear plastic that requires a hardener. It pours out of the can a little thicker than motor oil, and depending on how much hardener you add to the mix, can become solid in as little as 10 minutes.

The most important issue when working with fiberglass resin is the mold. Because the resin is such a thin liquid, it must be either brushed on a mold in separate coats and allowed to dry or it must be poured into a mold. Unlike building an MDF box enclosure, making an enclosure with fiberglass resin requires some planning, creativity, and skill.

First, you must be sure that the enclosure you're about to make can fit into the location where you want it. This sounds easy, but it can be particularly difficult—especially when fitting it into a nonflat area, such as a kick panel (Fig. 9-5). In these instances, it can be handy to pull out

Fig. 9-5 *A commercially manufactured subwoofer box that was made specifically for the VW Golf.* JL Audio

the spray-on foam insulation. Build a little section of walls to contain the foam to the area where you want it to be applied. After it dries, pull it out and either apply a layer of fiberglass mold release to the bottom or tightly tape a layer of plastic to the bottom with two-sided tape. Then paint several thick coats of fiberglass resin to the bottom. When the fiberglass layer is thick enough, you can pull it off, use it as the bottom of the kick panel, and build up the top side of the enclosure from there.

The outsides of enclosures can be created using a variety of materials, both preformed and those that you have shaped yourself. For example, plastic and styrofoam containers are excellent examples of preformed materials. Even a light cardboard bowl coated with layers of fiberglass resin could make a decent enclosure for a small circular speaker (Fig. 9-6).

MOLD TYPES

The two different types of molds are *male* and *female* (Fig. 9-7). The male mold is an exact replica of the enclosure and it is also the most common type in the do-it-yourself world because it doesn't require extra planning or mold making. Because the mold is a replica of the enclo-

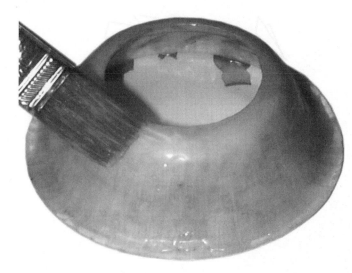

Fig. 9-6 *A cardboard bowl with fiberglass resin being brushed on. The hole in the top is cut for a 3.5" circular speaker.*

sure, the resin is brushed on in numerous coats over the mold. When it is finished, the mold is popped out and the enclosure is sanded.

If the enclosure doesn't have so many steep valleys and sharp peaks, a female mold might be easier to use. With a female mold, the fiberglass resin is placed in the inside of the mold and the enclosure is pulled out after it is dry and of sufficient thickness. The female molds are excellent because sometimes the resin can be poured into the mold, saving you the trouble of those seemingly endless repetitions of brushing, drying, brushing, drying, etc. Mold-release agent is generally necessary with female molds, although I've had good luck with resin popping out of plastic.

It's also handy to mold in a tabs so that you have something to grab to pull the fiberglass out of the mold. If you try this, it's best to lay down a few coats of resin before adding the string, binder twine, etc., that you might want to place in the fiberglass to pull it out.

Whether using a male or female mold, make the enclosure as close to finished as possible at this point in the process. For example, mold out

Fig. 9-7 *A female (pour-in) mold (left) and a male (brush-on) mold (right).*

Fig. 9-8 *It's difficult to see in the photo, but the speaker box sitting on the styrofoam platter is actually covered with pantyhose and ready to have resin applied to the surface.*

the hole for the speaker right away so that you don't have to go back and try to cut a perfect hole through the fiberglass.

INTERIOR FORMS

To fabricate your own enclosure, you can cut wood or MDF or even make your own mold out of clay. Probably the easiest way to make an enclosure with fiberglass resin is to build a structure that actually becomes part of the enclosure. An example of this technique is the cardboard bowl that was mentioned earlier.

An example that's more useful in a variety of circumstances is to build the enclosure up with some material, then to stretch nylon pantyhose overtop and coat the pantyhose with resin. This is an excellent method because it is very difficult to cut and sand wood or to shape clay with perfect curves. But pantyhose will smoothly contour around any shape. The only concern is to cut the shapes that fit under the edges smoothly.

One of the easiest types of interior-form speaker enclosures is to loosely place a sheet of pantyhose over a round, oval, square, or rectangular form. Then another object that's approximately the same size as the speaker can be pushed up through pantyhose (Fig. 9-8). If you search around for containers, you can make some professional-looking enclosures with this method. When everything is fixed in place, the pantyhose can be brushed over with several coats of fiberglass resin. It's best to start with a fairly light coat because the resin will bleed right through the pantyhose, potentially causing a big mess.

Unlike the examples with the molds, it's better to let the inside of the hole for the speaker to remain and to just cut it out with an X-Acto knife after a few coats of resin have dried. Then, you can continue to coat it numerous times until the enclosure is solid.

WORKING WITH FIBERGLASS COMPOUND

For the most part, working with fiberglass compound is unnecessary. It's cruder to work with than resin, which is a serious disadvantage for these applications. However, it can be used effectively in nonvisible areas, such as the inside of enclosures that were made with fiberglass resin. Ever notice how many coats it takes to make a thick resin enclosure...and how many paint brushes you go through? It's much easier to coat the pantyhose a few times, then to add a good, thick coat of fiberglass compound to the inside of the enclosure so that you can finish off the fiberglassing in one quick step.

BUILDING SPEAKER ENCLOSURES

Building a speaker for good sound is not overly difficult: just follow solid construction practices and tighten everything up a bit more from that. In order to build most of these boxes, you will need to have at least a few tools, but a full-blown workshop isn't a must. The only tools that you must have to construct a simple closed-box enclosure are these: a saw (either a hand saw or an electric table saw), a screwdriver, a tight-fit hand saw, a caulking gun, an inexpensive soldering iron, and a hand drill. If you use a hand saw, you will probably also need to use a miter box. Depending on the techniques that you plan to use, you might need more tools, but these are the only must-haves.

First, you must determine the box volume that your speaker (assuming that the enclosure is intended to be used for a single woofer or subwoofer) requires. Then, determine the height x width x depth specifications that you plan to use. Particleboard is available in a number of different sizes, shapes, and styles, but my favorite type is that which is used for inexpensive shelving. This type has harder finish, so it is less likely to flake apart while you are building the cabinet. Also, if you can design the cabinet's sides to be either 8 in. (20.32 cm), 10 in. (25.4 cm), or 12 in. (30.48 cm) wide, you will only have to cut the ends of the boards, not the lengths.

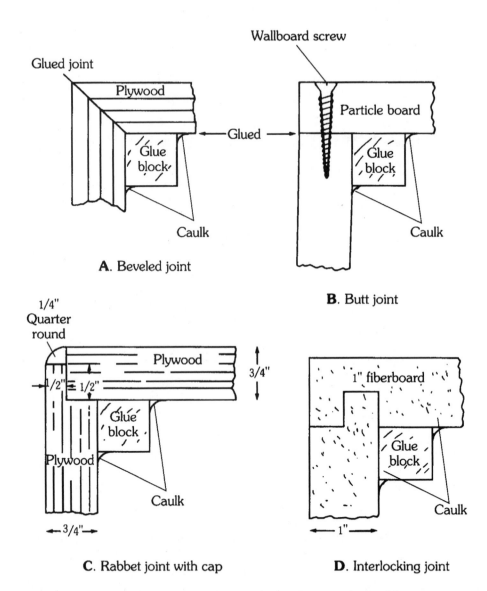

Fig. 9-9 *A variety of different cabinetry joints for speaker cabinets.*

Wood corners can be made in a number of different ways, but not all of the styles are appropriate for speaker enclosures. For example, the very popular dovetail joint is not effective because the particleboard is not strong enough to hold together at the dovetails. Also, a pretty joint is not particularly useful when you plan to cover it with carpet anyway. The most useful joints are the butt joint, the rabbet joint, and the beveled joint.

The *beveled joint* is one in which the edges have been cut at 45° angles and then are glued and sealed. The joints must be sealed, so you must use a table saw or a hand saw with a mitre box so that the joints are tight (Fig. 9-9A).

The *rabbet joint* has the edge of one board butted into a grooved board. You should also use two or three wood screws in each corner for extra strength. You can easily remove the rectangular-shaped groove from the corner with two passes on a table saw. However, the rabbet joint requires more work and tools if you only have hand tools. You can make the cut that is perpendicular to the board with the hand saw. Then, use a finer toothed saw, such as a hack saw, to cut through the board edge and meet the perpendicular cut. You should avoid removing the corner piece with a chisel because the edge will be rough and the joint won't provide a tight fit (Fig. 9-9B).

The *butt joint* is the simplest and one of the most common joints in carpentry work. It is simply two boards that have been butted, glued, and screwed together. Unfortunately, the butt joint is also one of the weakest joints, and the edges must match almost perfectly in order to achieve a strong and airtight joint. If you don't cut the edges perfectly straight, you might need to use a disc sander to get a tight fit (Fig. 9-9C).

When you build any box enclosure, you should screw the corners together so that they hold solidly and don't pull apart when you drive across some lousy pothole-riddled road (which is more often than not the case if you live in Pennsylvania or New York).

For the sake of having both a sealed enclosure and structural integrity, you should build a small wooden frame inside of the enclosure (Fig. 9-10). Glue and screw in small, square or rectangular lengths of wood that are approximately 1 x 1 in. (2.54 cm x 2.54 cm) around the entire inside front and rear edges of the speaker enclosure. To prevent the particle board from splitting or cracking, be sure to drill countersink holes that are approximately two sizes smaller in diameter than the screws that you will be using (Fig. 9-11). Then, another strip of wood should be glued into each corner. After the glue dries on the entire

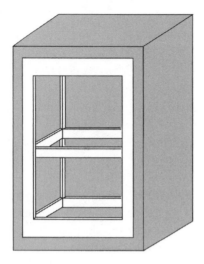

Fig. 9-10 *A speaker cabinet frame built from MDF (grey) and wood (white).*

speaker cabinet, use a tube of all-purpose caulking to seal all of the edges of the wooden frame to prevent air leaks and vibrations within each of the pieces. Be especially careful to make sure that the corner joints are sealed tight. You could probably get away with skipping the inside frame (except for the corner pieces) and screwing the front and rear panels directly to the sides of the enclosure. However, although the particleboard is strong, it is also brittle. By screwing through the front panel and into the particleboard edge, you will risk having the edges chip apart and strip out the edges where the screws would fit in. So, the wooden frame is, for all intensive purposes, a must if you want your box to last any length of time.

The front and rear panels are a bit easier to build and assemble to the frame of the enclosure. The worst problem with the front and back pieces are cutting the holes for the speaker and for the terminal block. You have several options for cutting the speaker hole in the front panel. You can use a special drill bit that is used to cut large-diameter holes, you can cut it out with a jig saw, or you can improvise. Of course, the drill bits can only be used to cut circular holes, so if you are working on a noncircular size, such as a standard 6" x 9" (15.24 cm x 22.86 cm) oval multidriver speaker, you are stuck with either the improvised method or using a jigsaw.

If you have a jigsaw, you should already know how to use it. Most of us aren't lucky enough to own a wood shop, so the improvised method is described next. Draw an outline of the planned speaker hole. Make sure that you use the proper size that is required for the actual speaker and that you don't just trace the outside of the speaker or you will have nothing to mount the speaker onto. Then, drill small-diameter holes (about 1/8-in. or 3.18-mm in diameter) along the speaker outline. Drill enough holes together that the blade of a jeweler's saw or a tight-fit hand saw will fit through. Use the saw to cut the speaker hole out (Fig. 9-12). Using this method will make the outside edge of the hole a bit rough, but you won't see this edge anyway. Then, insert the speaker in the hole and be sure that it fits well. Draw an outline around the outside of the speaker and measure the thickness of the speaker gasket. If you want to have a perfect fit, drill this wood as deep as the gasket is thick with a drill press. You will have tough time drilling out the gasket depth with a hand drill, so if you don't have a drill press, you might just be better off skipping this process and having the speaker slightly raised off from the front panel. Once the hole is cut properly and the speaker fits in just right, apply a light coat of strong adhesive (such as Liquid Nails) to the bottom of the gasket, which will rest on the drilled-out front panel of the enclosure. After the adhesive has dried, seal the edge of the speaker to the front panel with caulking.

Next, the front panel can be attached to the enclosure. Be sure to drill countersink holes before inserting the screws. You will probably need to insert one screw for approximately every 2 in. around the perimeter of

Fig. 9-11 *The joints of a commercially manufactured speaker cabinet might develop cracks that are wide enough to see the cabinet's interior, which obviously thwarts the idea of an airtight chamber.*

the front panel. That might seem like a lot of screws, but they are necessary to prevent the front panel from vibrating and either buzzing or just leaking and altering the sound of the enclosure.

A number of different types of speaker terminal panels are available from distributors, such as Parts Express. Nearly all of these terminals are panels that require you to cut out a hole in the back of the enclosure. However, a few only require you to drill two small holes to pass the wires through. Then, the terminal block can be screwed onto the back of the cabinet (Fig. 9-12). Some other speaker terminal panels include

Fig. 9-12 *Cutting a hole with a close-quarters hacksaw in the back of the speaker enclosure so that the speaker terminal blocks can be added afterward.*

extras, such as fuses, spring-loaded or screw-on terminals, gold plating on the terminals, and multiple terminals for multispeaker enclosures. Choose a speaker terminal panel that best suits your needs: fused blocks for high power, multiterminals for multispeaker enclosures, gold-plated terminals for high power or audiophile quality, and inexpensive spring-loaded terminals for inexpensive applications.

To complete the speaker enclosure, cut the hole for the speaker terminal panel using the same improvised method that was used to cut out the hole for the speaker. The only difference is that this hole will probably need to be shaped like a square or a rectangle. To achieve the squared corners, drill the holes in the middle of the sides so that you can cut to the edge of each corner with the saw. If you are using a round terminal panel, you will need to cut the hole out with either a wide-diameter drill bit or a jeweler's saw—the close-quarter hacksaw has too wide of a blade to cut out an approximately 3 to 4-in. (7.62- to 10.16-cm) diameter hole.

To attach the speaker terminal panel (Fig. 9-13), use a strong construction adhesive and screws. Then, seal the edges of the panel with caulking.

Fig. 9-13 *A terminal block screwed into the back of a speaker enclosure.*

If you are building an aperiodic enclosure, cut another hole in the back panel that is approximately 2 to 3 in. (5.08 cm to 7.62 cm) in diameter, although it can be most any shape that you want. Attach a piece of strong (but fine) plastic mesh over this hole with either staples or with wood, small screws, and a strong construction adhesive (Fig. 9-14). Then, cover the hole with about a 1-in. thick sheet of acoustic damping material and attach it with a strong adhesive.

After the caulking and glue have dried, wire the speaker to the speaker terminal panel. To wire between the speaker and the speaker terminal panel, use the same gauge of wire that you are using for the speaker wire between the amplifier and the speaker. If this is a competition or audiophile installation, be sure to use a type of wire with the same

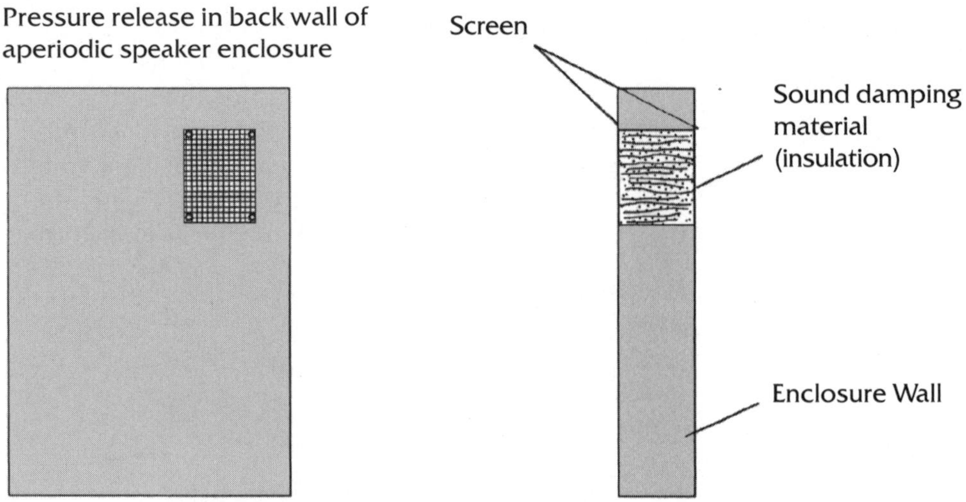

Pressure release in back wall of
aperiodic speaker enclosure

Screen

Sound damping
material
(insulation)

Enclosure Wall

Fig. 9-14 *The aperiodic hole.*

quality (if not the same brand of wire) as you're using throughout the rest of the car. Chances are that your speaker will require standard female slide-on connectors. Make sure that you purchase terminals that are made to be soldered onto the same gauge of wire that your system is using. Measure out enough wire so that you can easily pull the back off of the cabinet if you need to get inside to fix a problem. Then, solder the connectors onto the wire and attach them. Line the inside of the cabinet with a bit more acoustic-damping material than you thought was necessary.

Drill the sink holes for the screws and install the corner screws in the back of the cabinet. Do not use a strong construction adhesive on the back panel of the enclosure or you will never be able to pull the box apart without wrecking it. Connect the speaker to your system and listen to the sound. Then experiment with removing and adding more acoustic-damping material. Listen for any rattles or hums in the speaker cabinet and also listen to the decay of the bass frequencies. If the cabinet is loose and vibrating, tighten it. If the decay is not clean, add more acoustic-damping material; if the bass sounds weak, try removing some of the material or try a thinner sheet of acoustic-damping material.

Of course, other designs will require other, more specific, construction methods. However, these basic methods will help you to build some of the simpler designs, and if you care to build a monster ported masterpiece at a later time, this example will help prepare you.

MAKING SPEAKER BAFFLES AND ODD-SHAPED ENCLOSURES

From the chapter about speaker enclosures, you know that closed-box subwoofers work much more efficiently than speakers placed in a free-air environment. For this reason, very few people use free-air subs. But fewer people think about their component or multiway speakers. Think about it: any time that you place these speakers in a standard dash, door, or rear deck location, they are essentially running as free-air speakers. To hear the difference, try connecting a boxless speaker to your home stereo system, then try it with an enclosure. Without the enclosure, the sound will be thin and weak.

The problem with speaker baffles is that the areas behind the speaker-mounting locations are typically odd shaped. You can't simply cut some MDF and expect it to fit. Commercially manufactured baffles are available for some of the standard sizes of speakers, but these are soft foam and are intended to keep the speakers dry, not to improve their performance.

Probably the easiest way to make custom speaker baffles is to place spray foam insulation into the speaker-mounting location. It's also helpful to place in a handle, as you fill up the hole, so that it's easier to pull out the chunk of foam when you're finished.

If the area inside of the hole is larger than the opening, you've got a problem because you won't be able to put the insulation chunk back out. If this is the case, you'll want to fill some of the hole so that the foam can be pulled back out (Fig. 9-15). Another consideration is that the insulating foam is made to stick firmly to whatever it contacts. You will need to line the area of the hole with plastic (such as garbage bag plastic) so that the insulation will not stick to the inside of the hole.

Fill the hole so that it is level, but fill it no further. The foam expands after you squirt it in and it takes a few hours to harden (Fig. 9-16). After it hardens, you can grab the handle and start to gently pull out the foam. If it sticks in places, have a putty knife ready so that you can cut the foam loose around the edges. Now, you have a mold for the baffle.

Another possibility that is a little less expensive is to fill the hole with newspapers and to tape the edges with masking tape. The biggest problem here is that the newspaper can expand to fit the hole. If you aren't careful, you could wind up with a baffle that won't fit into the hole.

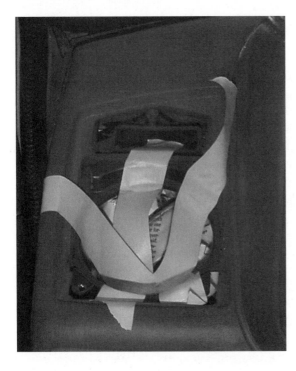

Fig. 9-15 *The first step of making the mold. The outer edges of the hole are filled with newspaper and masking tape so that the lump of insulation can be pulled back out. The black bolted-on speaker frame could be removed to provide extra space in the enclosure.*

If you can find a container of fiberglass mold-release (available from some specialty boat stores), spread it on the outside of the foam. Let it

Fig. 9-16 *The insulation is sprayed into the hole, where it begins to expand. Notice that much more tape has been added so that the insulation can't leak out through the holes while in the liquid state and then freeze fast to the inside of the dashboard. Instead, the tape can be used like a handle to pop out the insulation chunk after it has dried.*

dry, then brush coats of fiberglass resin over the outside of the foam. Coat it until it's about 1/4 to 1/2 in. thick. Allow it to dry for at least 24 hours in a relatively open environment (so that you won't have to inhale the fumes), such as a garage.

Here's an area where Bondo body putty works well. To save time on brushing resin all over the mold, you might want to just coat the mold with fiberglass body putty. It doesn't have to look pretty, so it works fine in this application.

When it feels hard to the touch, pop the baffle off of the mold and set it in place in the car. If possible, seal the baffles into place with caulking. Now, you can screw the speaker in place (provided that it's a standard mounting location) or mount the speaker and its panel (if adding a custom enclosure).

COATINGS

For extra protection from moisture, for increased stiffness, and for a finish that's easier to paint, some people coat their MDF speaker enclosures with fiberglass resin (Fig. 9-17). Fiberglass compound is too thick;

Fig. 9-17 *A close-up view of a resin-coated MDF joint. Obviously, the surface will then need to be sanded.*

although it could be used, plenty of sanding would be necessary to smooth the surface lumps and streaks. It would also require much more time to apply the coating.

A coating of fiberglass resin would simply be painted on and allowed to dry. Then, it can be sanded until it's smooth.

GRILLE CLOTH AND METAL GRILLES

In simple speaker replacement upgrades, you don't need to worry about grille cloth or metal grilles. You buy a set of standard-sized speakers, open the box, and there are the grilles, ready to be installed over the speakers (Fig. 9-18). No muss, no fuss.

Fig. 9-18 *A speaker grille that was manufactured specifically to fit on a 6-in. by 9-in. Infinity speaker.*

But when you start doing custom work, it seems that every aspect of the installations become difficult, right down to the grilles. Many speakers are sold with grilles, but some aren't, apparently assuming that your car will have a plastic grille plate to screw in over the speaker. If you are building your own enclosure, you will need to be very careful that the grille for your speaker will match up properly with the enclosure that you're building. If not, you could be in for quite a few headaches. Another case is with subwoofers. Subs aren't sold with grilles because most people want them either to be completely visible or totally hidden. If you want to use grilles over your subs, you are going against the mainstream (unless you are building a bass tube or pull-out bass boxes).

One problem with grilles and grille cloth is that they aren't 100% transparent, meaning that they will muffle or deflect the sound at least a tiny bit. Fine grille cloth is the most audibly transparent, but it offers almost zero protection for the speaker cone (Fig. 9-19). Metal grilles are the strongest, but they cover up more area than grille cloth and they have a tendency to either rattle or vibrate (Fig. 9-20). For the most part, grille

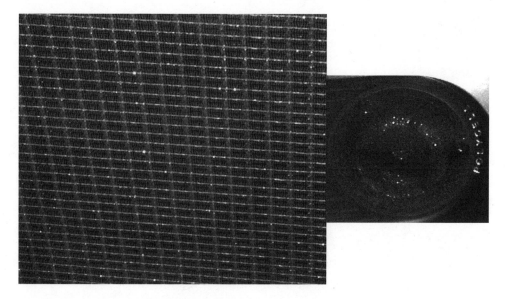

Fig. 9-19 *Strong and decorative grille cloth (left) and very fine, delicate cloth (right).*

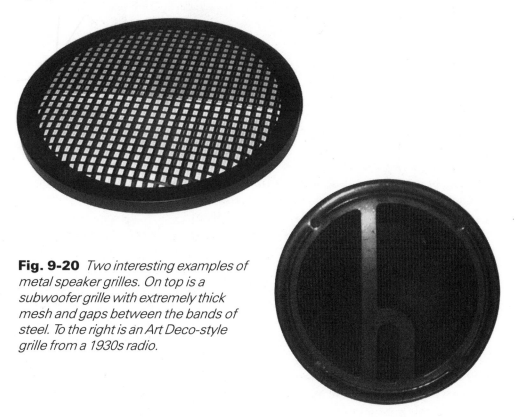

Fig. 9-20 *Two interesting examples of metal speaker grilles. On top is a subwoofer grille with extremely thick mesh and gaps between the bands of steel. To the right is an Art Deco-style grille from a 1930s radio.*

cloth isn't used in auto audio applications, although you could find some creative ways to both protect the speakers and use it attractively.

Grilles are sometimes specified in sales literature by both thickness and coverage area. This way, you can see both how strong they are and how much area is covered between you and the speaker. The problem with this high-grade grille screen is that it is often extremely expensive. It is often less expensive to modify grilles from old or blown speakers, such as those that can be found at flea markets or hamfests.

LEXAN (POLYCARBONATE) AND PLEXIGLASS (ACRYLIC) SHEETS

Mechanical and electronic components are fun to look at. That's why people stop to watch trains and why some telephones use see-through plastic. And sometimes people like to have an inside peek at their audio equipment. I've never seen anyone use Plexiglass on their dashboards because behind the dashboard is a mess of wires and hoses—and I think that most people would feel a little exposed with having the dashboards exposed.

Instead, the favorite locations for viewing are amplifiers and subwoofers. With a few sheets of Plexiglass, you can see the fancy amplifiers, the thump of the subs (from behind), and all of those shiny gold connectors. Some people even have Plexiglass panels so that some of the wiring is exposed.

First, take a look at the materials involved. Plexiglass is the tradename for sheets of clear or tinted transparent acrylic. When most people think "plastic window-like material," they think "Plexiglass." But Plexiglass isn't the only material of this type. Lexan is the tradename for a certain type of polycarbonate, which also features these characteristics. Lexan (polycarbonate) is much harder and, as a result, is more scratch resistant, than Plexiglass. Polycarbonate is often used in greenhouses and it is the plastic coating on CDs and DVDs. The disadvantage of Lexan is that it is much more expensive and difficult to purchase.

Although Lexan is harder to scratch, it is still easy enough to leave scratches or dull the finish. So, it's best to only use Plexiglass or Lexan in areas where it will face very little wear. For example, even the amplifier and wiring panels are often covered with carpeted doors or pop-out panels that match the car's interior. Years back, it was recommended that people rub toothpaste on plexiglass to remove scratches. It worked, but not very well and the job was certainly tedious. Today, special Plexiglass scratch removers are available, but it's still best to avoid using Plexiglass or Lexan in high-wear areas.

PANELS

When Lexan or Plexiglass is used in a panel-type application, it is typically placed in behind the structural wall (Fig. 9-21). If several

Fig. 9-21 *A commercially manufactured enclosure with a clear plastic window.* JL Audio

amplifiers were to be placed behind the seat in the trunk, for example, a strong plywood enclosure would be built. The inside wall would be carpeted and the amplifiers would be screwed onto it. The outside wall would have a hole cutout, where the Plexiglass will be placed.

First, the hole is cut out with a jigsaw, then the plywood is sprayed with adhesive and covered with carpet. A few inches of carpet are left along all edges so that they can be tightly stapled to the plywood on the inside. The carpet that is over the hole should be cut in a star (like a pie) pattern from the center. Then, these pieces can be pulled to the inside and stapled tightly to the plywood. Try to get the tension about even on all of these pieces so that ripples don't appear in the fabric.

The Plexiglass or Lexan should overlap the hole on the inside by about 1 in. You can mark the corners of the Plexiglass and then drill out the pilot holes and the countersink holes in it. Using screws that are no longer than the combined thicknesses of the Plexiglass and plywood sheets, tighten the Plexiglass in place. It's best to make these panels hinged so that they can easily be raised the next time you need to access the amplifiers.

Attaching the Plexiglass sheets in this way is easier, holds it in place stronger, and because the Plexiglass isn't flush with the plywood, it is better protected against scratches. However, the Plexiglass can be installed closer to flush, such as with "window-style" mountings.

SUBWOOFER BOXES

Although Plexiglass or Lexan is fine for use in panels, Plexiglass is too flexible to be used for subwoofer enclosures, even in large thicknesses. As the walls flex, some of the sound waves will be absorbed, deadening the punch of the bass. Lexan is the only option, but even in this case, the panes must be very thick—at least 3/4 in. for best results.

Commonly, a single sheet of Lexan will be screwed onto the back of a sub enclosure, either as an entire side or as a window in the back of a sheet of MDF (similar to the procedure in the previous section). The only difference in the latter construction is that the Lexan would have to also be sealed to the plywood using some heavy-duty adhesive and it would be best to run a bead of caulking around the outside of the edge where the Lexan meets the plywood. Also, to strengthen the window-cut MDF wall, it would be a good idea to strengthen it with a coat or two of fiberglass resin.

Few people use a full, single sheet of Lexan as a side on a subwoofer box because the joints where the MDF and Lexan meet will look messy and it would be very difficult to strongly and neatly cover them.

However, some hobbyists with a penchant for the clear stuff have built entire boxes from Lexan. In a sense, this is a little easier than constructing a mixed MDF/Lexan enclosure because you can buy the Lexan from a glass/window company and have them cut each piece to your specifications. Another advantage is that you can buy special transparent adhesive to chemically bond the Lexan together, without leaving a blur of glue at each joint. If you don't use screws to anchor the joints, the toughest part of building this way (aside from the high cost) would be to anchor the pieces until the adhesive bonds solidly. Corner box clamps are the best option. They're uncommon, but it's worth spending the extra money for them if you're already going to the expense of using Lexan. Speaking of expense, to save a little money on an "all Lexan" enclosure, you could use a sheet of MDF on the bottom, which wouldn't need to be clear.

Another option is to make an MDF enclosure with a bent top/back piece of Lexan. The first problem is how to bend a piece of thick Lexan. Some specialty car stereo companies sell Lexan heaters so that you can bend pieces. These "benders" consist of a long, adjustable metal rod and a thin heater element on the other side. You just attach the "bender" around the Lexan, plug it in, and let it heat for a while (of course, away from children and any flammable materials). Then you can bend it to the appropriate angle. Because the heater is so narrow, you can get smooth, straight bends. Rather than waste the extra expense on a Lexan bender that you might never use again (and without ever trying it), you should check around at car stereo installation shops to see if any of these companies are able to bend Lexan for you.

The easiest way to build a "bent-back" Lexan cabinet is to make the sides a little larger than the center. Once you get the bent Lexan back from the installation shop, you can trace the inside edge of each of the side boards. Then, you can cut two 1-in. boards with a jigsaw so that they exactly follow the shape of the lines on the sides. These boards can then be glued to the sides, and the sides, front, and bottom can be glued and screwed together. After the pilot holes have been drilled, the Lexan can be screwed in place on each of the long sides. Finally, a 1-in. wide piece of plywood can be warped with water to fit along each edge of the Lexan. Then, speaker carpet can be stapled on the inside of the warped piece and each piece can be screwed down to hold the Lexan and the carpet in place. The other side can be finished in the same way and stapled to the bottom of the enclosure.

It's expected, but still worth noting, that the insides of the speaker enclosure must look presentable if you're using Lexan. For example, the inside of the enclosures should be either painted or carpeted (vinyl or veneer would be acceptable, too), damping material would probably be out of the question, and high-grade connectors and display-quality speaker cables should be used.

VENEER

Wood veneer, although almost a unanimous selection in the home audio world, is essentially unused in car stereo systems. One reason is that wood doesn't stand up to the beating sun and moisture as well as carpeting, vinyl, or plastic. But, perhaps the most important reason is that wood doesn't match car interiors. Part of this problem is because it's too expensive for most car companies to include wood (Fig. 9-22).

But that doesn't mean that you can't use wood on your speaker enclosures or in the interior of your car. The only problem is that it will

Fig. 9-22 *An excellent example of beautiful veneer work: A small view of a 1938 black walnut radio case.*

require some extensive work if you want the enclosures to match the rest of the interior of the car.

Several companies manufacture and sell wood veneers in a wide variety of types and wood types. Because veneers are rarely used in auto audio, they aren't included in this section. For more information, see *Home Audio* by Andrew Yoder.

VINYL AND CARPETING

Finally! After all of the work with MDF, plywood, Lexan, and fiberglass, you can finish up the project with a covering of vinyl or carpet. Both are relatively similar to work with because both materials are thin, stretch over a form, and need to be anchored firmly along the edges.

The best vinyl and carpeting to use in auto audio applications are those that are manufactured specifically for these purposes. Maybe that's just common sense, but it's easy enough to use old car vinyl. The difference is that car stereo vinyl is extremely flexible and is capable of stretching. And car audio carpeting isn't regular carpet. It's a thin fibrous material with no backing. It's somewhat like felt, but several times thicker and with thick fibers. It is also very stretchable; with some good upholstery work, the rough fibers will cover edges and look almost seamless. Because of this and because carpet wears and hides dirt well, it is much more popular than vinyl.

The last part of the covering equation is spray-on adhesive. Once again, you should use adhesives that are intended for auto audio applications. In the case of carpet, for example, most glues or adhesives would simply soak into the carpet and fail to bond with the wood. Don't opt for cheap spray-on adhesives or you might soon be faced with peeling carpet or vinyl.

No matter what you're covering, it's necessary to keep the visible seams at a minimum. That means running seams at the back or bottom of enclosures. If possible, it's best to run the seams on the insides of enclosures so that they can't be seen and can be firmly held in place.

First, you should place the vinyl or carpet over the enclosure and pull the loose areas fairly tight so that you can determine exactly how much you need and what size a piece you should cut. In the case of kick panels and other "open bottomed" enclosures, be sure to allow extra material to wrap on the inside and fix in place. In other cases, I think its still best to leave a little extra (approximately one extra inch) around the seams, just to be safe. I'd prefer to lose a few extra square inches of material in overlap that will be trimmed off at the end than to waste a few hundred square inches of carpet or vinyl because I measured everything 1/2 in. too short.

When covering over openings, it's best to cut a pie or star-shaped pattern, starting from a point in the center of the hole. If the hole is round, be sure to cut the pieces the same size. If the hole is a square or rectangle, cut the "pie" in four pieces so that each cut meets a corner in the inside. Then, the "pieces of pie" can be tightly folded inside and held with a stronger adhesive or even stapled in place (if the enclosure is MDF).

OTHER FINISH MATERIALS

Other materials can be used to finish off your speaker enclosures. Really, for styles of enclosures and types of coverings, the possibilities are restricted only by your imagination. Although carpeting is very professional looking, it just doesn't have any personality. Vinyl is a bit of a change, but it's still not a huge change of pace.

Leather is rarely used for speaker enclosures and other places in the car, not because it's a bizarre look, but because it's too expensive! About the only time that leather is used is in the expensive cars that aren't advertised on TV: Jaguars, Mazaratis, Rolls Royces, etc. But there's not law that says you can't redo the interior of your AMC Gremlin with black walnut wood and leather. And there's no economic rule against it, either. Small amounts of black walnut are inexpensive from rural saw mills and beautiful deer leather is free if you're a suc-

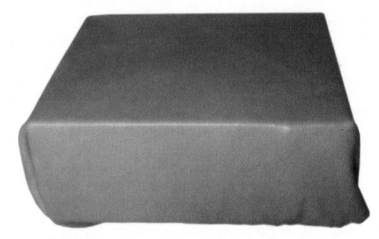

Fig. 9-23 *Wrapping an enclosure with leather for the initial fitting , before making the finish cuts and gluing everything down.*

cessful hunter. Leather (Fig. 9-23) can be somewhat similar to vinyl to work with—or it can be much different. It all depends on the type of leather and the way that it was cured. For example, deer and rabbit hide are known for being soft and thin, but cow hide is heavier and stronger. If leather is your thing, be sure to pick a type that is relatively thin and soft, as opposed to the type of cow hide that's used to make belts!

I think that paint is the most underutilized finish for speaker enclosures and car interiors. Oh sure, there's a little paint inside, but not much. You could make your speaker enclosures more fun by making different colors, designs, and textures. The first step would be to apply a coating of fiberglass resin to any MDF that you're going to paint. This coating will soak in, harden, and fill in the surface. Then you can sand off any imperfections, runs, or drips. Give it a coat of primer, then get to work, Rembrandt, and paint something interesting. To help preserve your masterpiece, apply a clear coat of enamel (anything from high gloss to satin) or use several coats for a stronger finish and a "deeper" look.

Or what about a mixed media? For example, painting a sub box black, wrapping it in a few pieces of police tape, and coating it all with a few layers of clear coat? Another possibility, which has probably already been done, is to cover every possible surface with vinyl stickers. If some of these finishes seem a little too fragile, you could even cover an enclosure with sheets of tire rubber, for that rough'n'ready look.

CONCLUSION

In auto audio applications, because of the tight and restricted locations, the installation materials are just as important as putting the equipment in place. It's not like home audio, where you pick out the speakers that you want and move them around to get the best imaging, and you're done. It requires some work to put together a highly customized system that is well integrated into the interior of your car. This requires working with a number of different materials.

10

AUTO VIDEO

After I wrote the first edition of this book, I wrote books titled Home Audio *and then* Home Video. *This isn't a plug for those books; it's a lead-in story for the chapter. At the time, we made some jokes with friends that the next book in the series would have to be* Auto Video. *It seemed absurd: setting up video systems in the car? My thoughts were running along the lines of the recent car insurance ads where people are driving recklessly while doing attention-consuming tasks (such as putting in contacts).*

Well, it happened, and now a small number of video screens, decoding boards, and head units are manufactured specifically for mobile video. For the most part, video systems in vehicles are best suited for minivans, large sport-utility vehicles, and Winnebagos, where long trips with many passengers are common. Typically, a VCR and video screen are mounted in a location between the two front seats so that those in the back can watch something while riding.

Auto video systems are fairly easy to configure and install in a large vehicle. The only major concern is that the video screen must be out of sight from the driver's seat. If it's not, the distraction could cause an accident; even if this worst-case scenario doesn't occur, a policeman could (and probably would) write up a hefty fine for the safety violation.

Because this book is about car stereo systems, not primarily video systems, I'm not getting into the specifics of how monitors display information, how DVD encoding works, how VCRs operate, the future possibilities of HDTV, etc. Instead, this is simply a little romp through adding a video system to your vehicle, with some information concerning available equipment and installing some of that equipment.

VIDEO SOURCES

The most common approach to a video source unit would be to use a VCR, "the people's video machine." Like its audio brother, the cassette deck, VCR technology has become so widespread that the prices have become almost dirt cheap, considering the complexity. Even many of the stereo (hi-fi) VCRs have dropped below $200.

Of course, for a mobile video system, you can't use a standard home VCR, which is operated from 110-VAC power (wall outlet power). And most inverters (except the very expensive ones) produce "clipped" waveforms that will distort the audio and the video. So, the only real solution is to buy a specialty mobile, 12-VDC unit. These units are manufactured by a few companies, such as Alpine and Clarion (Fig. 10-1). They are significantly more expensive than home VCRs, often running more than $300. Aside from the power, they are standard VCRs,

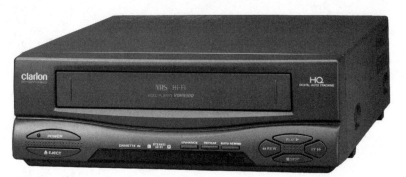

Fig. 10-1 *A 12-V VCR, made specifically for auto video applications.* Clarion

with the exception of the VCPs. About 15 years ago, VCPs were common, but they've become so unusual that I'll define the term here. *VCRs* are *video cassette recorders* (they can play and record) and *VCPs* are *video cassette players* (they can only play). Most people traveling wouldn't need to have the recording capabilities, but it could be handy if you wanted to record a copy of your aunt's home video of your cousin's birthday party, the time when he tried to blow out the candles and he caught his hair on fire.

Aside from recording, the only other truly important feature is hi-fi stereo audio. It's a must for the car stereo fiend. A number of the commercially manufactured video consoles offer a small speaker (usually about 4 in.) built into the unit. You wouldn't tolerate mono audio through a tiny speaker in your car stereo system, so don't suffer through poor video with your car video system either. Simply connect an FM modulator to the audio outputs on the VCR and you can tune in to the audio from the video program on the FM band in the head unit in your car. I've seen FM modulators for as little as $15 new at hamfests, so if you look around a little, you can find a great price (they list for more than $50). Also, some companies are currently manufacturing wireless headphone systems so that those watching the video don't disturb the people in the rest of the car (Fig. 10-2)

Fig. 10-2 *A pair of wireless headphones.* Clarion

Currently, one bit of technology could enable you to avoid videotapes and large between-seats consoles altogether: the DVD head unit. Alpine currently manufactures the DVA-5200 DVD head unit, designed for both audio and video systems (Fig. 10-3). For video systems, the unit will play back video DVDs so that the video can be fed to a separate monitor and the audio will play through the car's audio system. When you don't have any passengers or if everyone feels more like listening to music, then you can play standard audio CDs through the same drive in the head unit. With a price tag of more than $1000, don't expect many to go right out and buy the DVA-5200. Still, it won't be long before many more DVD head units follow and drive the prices down.

DVD is especially touted for its vastly superior video quality. However, because of the drawbacks of the vehicle, the constant motion, the tiny

Fig. 10-3 *An Alpine DVA-5200, which can playback both DVDs and audio CDs.* Alpine

monitor of the player, and the bright sunlight entering the vehicle, mobile viewing isn't a medium for those demanding perfect performance. For these purposes, any increase in performance from the DVD will not be especially noticeable over the VHS format.

MONITORS AND TVS

Depending on space, convenience, and price, there are a few options when choosing a monitor for the car (although the large-screen projection TVs are out of the question).

The first possibility is the CRT monitor. It's basically just a standard TV, except with no TV tuner section. CRT is specially noted here because the CRT is the standard large glass cathode-ray tube, which requires extra space. The idea is that if you're just watching videotapes in the minivan, then why spend extra money for the TV tuner? Unfortunately, the monitors are usually comparable in price with TVs anyway, so unless you find a deal, the point is moot. One bother with mini CRT monitors is that they need to be mounted in an enclosure or solidly bolted down so that they won't fly, and subsequently smash, in case of an accident or an unusually hard application of the brakes. The problem is that this will require some space and either money or extra work. CRT monitors are available with anywhere from about 5 in. to 9 in. (diagonally measured) for mobile video applications.

The mobile CRT TV is essentially a monitor, except that it also has a receiver built in. The advantage is, of course, that TV reception is possible. But it's not that easy to tune in to stations while being shielded inside of a metal vehicle. The metal of the vehicle works like the shielding around coaxial cable and prevents the broadcast signals from reaching the TV. The only alternative is an outside antenna. A typical home outdoor TV antenna would be unwieldy, so several companies manufacture window-mount TV antennas, which help to pull in a few more stations (Fig. 10-4). A free alternative is to just connect some extra wire to the antenna terminals of the TV and run the wire out to the edge of the window. That will pull in a few stations in urban or nearby suburban locations. Or solder an alligator clip to the end of the wire and clip it to the radio's whip antenna.

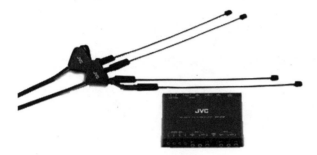

Fig. 10-4 *A set of antennas made specifically for mobile reception. In the foreground is a mobile TV tuner.* JVC

For best reception, the antenna must be mounted outside of the vehicle, otherwise the television signals will be partially shielded from the antenna. The best mounting locations are on the flat surface between the trunk and the back window and on the roof. On tall vehicles, the antenna should be mounted either flat or with the antenna elements pointed at very low angles so that they don't catch on low-hanging branches or overpasses.

The final monitor possibility is a flat LCD panel. This is the hot solution that garners media attention because it's new technology (as opposed to seeing a common VCR and a cheap TV in a vehicle). The LCD panel (Fig. 10-5) is notebook-thin, and can be mounted on the back of a seat, near sun visors, etc. Presently, the main drawback is cost, with 9-in. flat-panel monitors selling in the $800 to $1000 range. Also, LCD displays are more susceptible to temporary "washout" from sunlight and heat. The screens need to be in dark areas out of direct sunlight, so dark window tinting is almost a necessity if watching videos will take a priority.

COMBINATION VCR/MONITORS

Some companies manufacture combination VCR/TVs for mobile use. These combinations have been popular for institutional use (for convenience sake) for the past decade. My personal feeling about these units are negative. Both VCRs and TVs are susceptible to failures. Combining the two greatly increases the chance that everything will need to be either replaced or repaired (and repairs are often more expensive than

Fig. 10-5 *A 10" LCD monitor.* Clarion

replacements). And if you decide to upgrade the screen size, switch to an LCD screen, or opt for a DVD head unit, you're stuck. Also, the combination units that I've had experience with aren't of the best quality and haven't offered stereo audio. Unless you find a great deal somewhere, avoid the combination VCR/monitors.

TV BOXES

Mobile TV boxes or tuners are simply plug-in units so that you can receive TV stations when using monitors (as opposed to TVs). This equipment is only useful if you are using LCD monitors to view programming (Fig. 10-6). There's no point in buying a CRT monitor and a

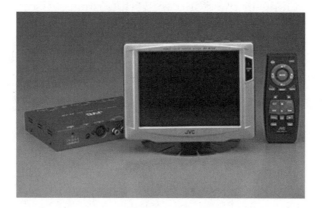

Fig. 10-6 *A mobile video set: TV tuner (left), monitor (center) and remote (left).* JVC

separate mobile TV tuner when you could just buy a TV—especially when the TV tuners come with a price tag that matches the LCD monitors.

A PORTABLE COMPUTER SOLUTION

For the most part, there are two equally viable possibilities for mobile video: either go with a large console containing a TV (or CRT monitor) and a VCR or buy a DVD head unit and a flat-screen LCD monitor. However, there's another option that's easier to use and install, offers better performance than the former system, and is less expensive than the latter system. Best of all, you can use it for many other applications. Look no further than the good old laptop computer.

Laptops are beginning to include DVD drives; at this writing, the prices for a DVD-laden laptop computer (Fig. 10-7) are going for as low as $2000, which is quite pricey, but is almost a bargain compared to buying a DVD head unit for $1000 and an LCD monitor for $900. Best of all, DVD laptop prices are bound to drop significantly over the next year. The same case could be made for the audio equipment, but it's a fact

Fig. 10-7 *Instead of building a complete video system in your car, maybe you would find it more cost-effective to use a laptop with a DVD drive.* ©2000 Gateway, Inc. All rights reserved

that computer technology is developing and dropping in price faster than audio or video equipment. If you don't believe me, compare the price of a new computer and a MiniDisc player from 1995. Expect to pay $400 or more for a new MiniDisc player that is essentially the same as one from 1995. On the other hand, a laptop that's twice as fast as 1995's $3000 machine will only cost about $700.

Just like the VCR solution, the audio output from the laptop can be connected to an FM modulator and received through the FM radio portion of the head unit. With the unit, high-quality stereo audio will be available.

One problem with the computer DVD concept is that laptops are more fragile than the other options, which could be a real concern if the system is intended to entertain kids in the back seats. Just one drink spilled in the keyboard and it's lights out. And even if you ban drinks in the back, how do you know that they haven't gone into Windows and started dumping files into the Trash Bin.

Otherwise, my personal belief is that the laptop computer with a DVD drive is the hands-down winner for the supplying mobile video conveniently at a competitive price.

INSTALLATION

In the case of the DVD head unit, the installation would be essentially the same as for a typical head unit. The only difference would be that you have to run a video output cable from the head unit to the monitor and then mount the monitor somewhere. Any company that sells mobile video equipment also offers accessories, such as mounting pads for flat-panel monitors. Just screw in the mount, connect the video cable, and it's ready to roll.

The VHS and CRT monitor (or CRT TV) system can be a lot more complicated structurally, but is very simple technically. From a simplicity perspective, it's easiest to purchase a loaded system console, such as the EZCPG from Audiovox, which is a mounting rack that contains a monitor, VCR, and a speaker. Just mount the whole unit in your vehicle, connect it to power, and it's ready to go. The complications occur if you decide to build your own console or if you decide to custom build some other parts of the car. For example, the console could be built from pieces of plywood or MDF, then covered with carpet, vinyl, or leather.

Any installation of this type would be specific to each vehicle, and also to your own tastes, available materials, skills, and money. See Chapter 9 for more information on building with these materials.

As mentioned earlier, the electrical and audio/video wiring systems are simple, much easier to deal with than running the cabling for an amplifier. The audio path is taken care of with the FM modulator, and the equipment in a console can be run directly from the cigarette lighter power.

CONCLUSION

Currently, mobile video is essentially a "cutting-edge technology," with only a handful of companies experimenting in the field. However, with Clarion's AutoPC, Panasonic's DVD head unit, and Alpine's declaration to increase multimedia-related car stereo equipment, you can bet that more companies will get in the act. And if the DVD format becomes popular in head units, they should be automatically capable of video output as well (unless no video outputs are included).

In addition to the purely entertaining aspect of mobile video, other safety and maintenance features are being integrated into car video systems. For example, one of the new hybrid gas/electric cars features a video display panel that shows various aspects of the car's performance. Another prototype car features video cameras and monitors, rather than mirrors. If these safety displays become standard in cars, then little extra money will be required for the car companies to include built-in video entertainment systems.

11

WIRE & CABLING

The most forgotten part of any audio system is what actually trans-mits the power and audio signal from one part of your car to an-other. Wire and cabling are often forgotten because they are about as boring as a Paul Anka record. Why would you waste your time and money working on wires when you could purchase and spend your time with a really cool head unit? I have no idea. I would much rather play with all of the buttons and displays on the head unit!

When you get right down to it, the subject of wire and cabling is very important. With a bad choice in wire, you could decrease the quality of the sound, pick up interference, or even start a car fire. However, the dangers of a poor wire choice is an extreme. As long as you follow the manufacturer's specifications for the gauge of the wire that handles the power to and the audio from any particular piece of equipment, your system should be safe. After that point, the only difference will be in efficiency and overall sound quality.

SHOULD I PURCHASE HIGH-END AUDIO CABLES?

The science of cabling audio is quite esoteric and it is one of the most-argued over topics of auto audio (and home audio, for that matter). Claims about the cabling run from being an audio cure-all to being an absurd case of snake oil advertising. I won't tell you to spend a large sum of money on high-end cables, but I would say that these cables could help in some specific applications.

The problem is that when the cables use precious metals, for example, they are bound to be hugely expensive. And if you can't afford a thousand dollars for your stereo system, why would you blow several thousand on the audio and power cables? However, many of the high-quality commercial cable companies (such as those made by Scosche, AudioQuest, Streetwires, and Straight Wires) make cable that is much less expensive. These companies all sell cabling that runs from the very high end to that which is affordable for anyone who can purchase a new auto audio system.

Like everything with high-end audio, if it is important for you to have the best and you have the money, then buy it. Otherwise, if the different grades of audio cables are a concern to you, then do some comparison shopping. Check the cables in different systems if you have a chance. Or, talk to some salesperson at different local stereo installation shops and see if you can do some comparative listening. If you are lucky, you might be able to test the same system using different audio cables. Of course, beware of some of the sales tricks, such as turning the volume up higher on the one head unit so that the system will "sound better." If you have some friends that have trustworthy opinions on car audio, you should talk with them if you can't find any reference audio cabling.

After these tests, choose the cabling that sounds the best for the lowest price. Even if you can notice a difference, the better cabling might not be worth extra cost. If you are running cables in a competition vehicle or want a car that is impressively meticulous, then you might want to purchase cables that look as good or better than they sound. Some of the wires that are protected with clear insulation are excellent for this purpose.

Another option, rather than to either buy expensive or cheap cables, is to experiment with making them yourself. I'm not suggesting that you extrude your own wire, but rather that it's possible to assemble your own cabling runs. And if it's possible to "roll your own" for only a fraction of the cost of commercially manufactured cables, then you can spend all of that leftover money on something fun!

WIRE

Other than one peculiar exception, wire is always used to transfer audio and electricity between the various components. Few people think about the different qualities of wire and the efficiency as a signal travels from one component to another. However, wire is made from several different materials (of many different qualities) using different drawing methods.

Also, wire can be made with one single wire, with many strands, or with bundles of strands; it can be shielded to prevent other signals from causing interference; and multiple wires can be either encased within a round or a flat cable (Fig. 11-1).

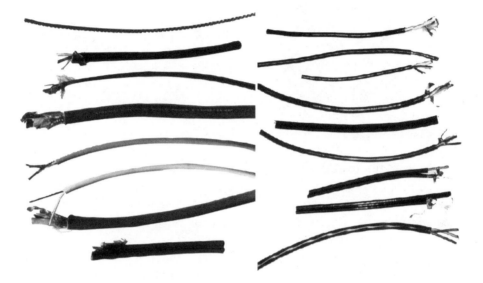

Fig. 11-1 *A number of different types of speaker, interconnect, and power cables.*

Most audio and power cables are made from copper. But if you use wire that was intended for some other electrical application, it might be made from another element or elemental combination, such as aluminum or copper-coated steel. Generally, copper is the only element to use to transmit audio and power signals through your car. Aluminum is fine for use in electric fences or in long radio antennas, where low cost is more important than high efficiency.

As stated in the previous paragraph, copper is an excellent conductor of electricity. Several other elements, such as silver and gold, conduct better. However, their costs are obviously prohibitive for most electrical applications. Silver is occasionally used, though, for very high-end wiring applications; gold is commonly plated over wiring connectors (such as the audio inputs to amplifiers, speakers, etc.).

WIRE SHAPES AND STYLES

A number of problems can occur when different components are connected together via wire. Two major problems are resistance and skin effect. *Skin effect* is the scientific property by which electricity travels on the outside (the "skin") of a conductor (Fig. 11-2). Skin effect causes

Fig. 11-2 *A visual representation of skin effect.* AudioQuest

different problems in different applications. For example, when transmitting at radio frequencies, if a station is outputting too much power into too small of a conductor (one that has too little surface area per watt of power), the resulting heat could cause the radio antenna to burn up. However, at audio frequencies, skin effect is a completely different monster. Instead of the "bigger is better" maxim that rules for radio conductors, larger diameter wires can cause other problems that result in high-frequency distortion. This distortion problem occurs in both solid and multistrand conductors.

Resistance is another problem that plagues electrical circuits. As stated previously, *resistance* is the opposition to an electrical signal flow. Although the resistance through a wire will cause a slight decrease in the signal strength, it will also cause some distortion.

Solid (single-strand) wire has a much higher resistance than stranded wire. You can see that problems occur with this type. If the diameter of solid wire is too large, the signals will distort slightly as a result of skin effect. Yet, if the diameter is too small, the resistance of the wire will cause slight distortion. Worse yet, the two boundaries overlap and you can be stuck with some sort of distortion, no matter what the wire gauge is. Probably the worst problem with solid-conductor wire is that it's prone to breaking.

Now that your dreams of using solid-conductor house wiring for your auto audio system have been dashed, it's time to move onto the different types of stranded wires. The typical speaker wire is usually something along the line of "zipcord," which consists of two insulated parallel conductors of stranded wire. Unlike parallel twisted hookup wire, the two independent zipcord wires are connected along a seam that runs the length of the wire.

Returning to the problem of skin effect in speaker cables, some companies try to reduce this dilemma by gradually twisting the wires throughout the length of the cable (Fig. 11-3). By doing so, wires that are in the

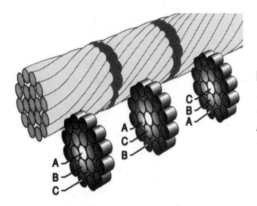

Fig. 11-3 *Separate wire strands running throughout a cable length. Notice how they shift position in the cable to reduce skin effect.* AudioQuest

center at one point are later shifted to the outside, where most of the current is being transmitted. This technique greatly reduces the negative results of skin effect. To further eliminate the negative effects, sometimes either stranded bundles or solid wires are gradually twisted around an insulating core. As a result, each of the wire strands within the bundles or surfaces of the single stand wires is being slowly turned, so the anti-skin effect is doubled. Sometimes, these solid wires or bundles are insulated and kept a certain distance apart to prevent them from interacting (Fig. 11-4).

Another type of audio cable uses several parallel or twisted solid conductors or stranded wire bundles. The purpose is much the same as the

Fig. 11-4 *Insulated wire bundles.* AudioQuest

theory behind the bundled wires from the last paragraph (Fig. 11-5).
Like the other types of wire, the parallel multiconductor ribbons are
made with a variety of wire types, spacing distances, and jacket and
insulating materials.

Fig. 11-5 *Parallel flat cable.*
AudioQuest

The last general category of audio wire is that of shielded cable.
Shielded cable is any cable that shields the wires inside and prevents
various types of electrical interference from entering the lines. Shielded
cable is especially important if the car's electrical system is noisy or if
the speaker cables will be running parallel to power cables. Likewise,
some power cabling is also shielded to prevent electrical impulses from
emanating out from the cables.

One of the most common forms of shielded cable is *coaxial cable*, which
consists of a center conductor that is surrounded by an insulating dielectric material; then a layer of braided copper wire shielding wraps around
the dielectric (it makes a sort of cylindrical copper plaid pattern), and it
is covered with an outer insulating jacket (Fig. 11-6). One of the most
visible applications of standard coaxial cable is for cable television.
Coaxial cable is always used to route the television signals from the
source to the home (at least in all of the television cable runs that I've
seen). A number of different types of coaxial cable have also been designed for audio-specific purposes (Fig. 11-7).

So which cable is best for listening in the car? In general, the aforemen-
tioned cables are all of much better quality than what you would typically
find packed along with your speakers or at a local electronics store.
Most of the specialty cable companies specifically produce their cabling
for audiophiles (such as Scosche, AudioQuest, StreetWires, Straight
Wire, etc.), so their products won't be low grade. The differences between the specialty cables probably won't be important to anyone except
audiophiles.

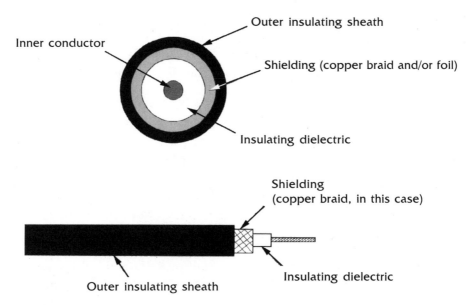

Fig. 11-6 markers:
Outer insulating sheath
Inner conductor
Shielding (copper braid and/or foil)
Insulating dielectric

Shielding
(copper braid, in this case)
Outer insulating sheath
Insulating dielectric

Fig. 11-6 *A breakdown of coaxial cable, showing the separate parts.*

FM TRANSMITTERS FOR COMPACT DISC PLAYERS

The one peculiar exception to using wire for transporting signals from one location to another is in the case of compact disc players. Because of the cost of compact disc head units, it is common for people to use a portable compact disc player in the car. This method is relatively inexpensive and the player can be used at various places outside of the car.

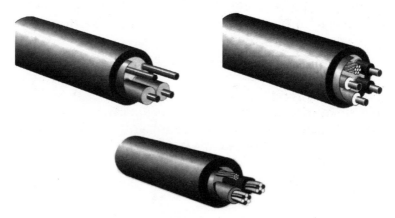

Fig. 11-7 *Several different types of coaxial cable that are intended for audio purposes.* AudioQuest

Normally, the portable is connected to a cassette head unit via a wire and an audio adapter that resembles a cassette. The cassette adapter loads into the cassette player, just as a standard cassette would. The audio from the portable compact disc player then travels through the wire, into the cassette adapter, and through the heads of the cassette player. The adapters normally sell for about $20 to $30, so they really are a cost-effective means of bringing digital sound into your car.

However, the loose wires do bother some people, and if you don't have a mount for the portable compact disc player, there is a chance that it could get kicked over or stepped on. As a result, some people would rather connect their portable to a small FM stereo transmitter. After the connection is complete, you tune the transmitter to operate on a clear frequency. Then, you turn it on and tune to that frequency on the FM (VHF) portion of your radio. This method is especially handy for anyone who wants to listen to compact discs in a rental car—without tearing into its wiring.

In the first edition of *Auto Audio*, the wireless way to transport CD changer audio to the head unit was via a little hobbyist FM kit transmitter. Sure, a few of the car stereo companies offered FM transmitters, but some of these units were selling for several hundreds of dollars. If you had a budget, your only choice was to dig into the world of soldering and kit building. Unfortunately, many of these kits were also very drifty (slowly changing in frequency) and many had mediocre stereo separation. That kit that originally seemed like a good deal for about $25, suddenly became a waste of time and money.

Today, many car audio companies are offering small, self-contained FM transmitters (sometimes called *FM modulators*) at an inexpensive price. I've seen bins full of the new surplus CD changer transmitters for $15 apiece. For that price, you couldn't even buy the parts individually and build it yourself for less money.

These days, the commercially built FM modulators are definitely the top choice, and you shouldn't even consider building the kits unless you really enjoy kit building or want to learn more about electronics (Fig. 11-8).

MAKING CONNECTIONS

Making good connections is quite important if you want your system to sound as clean as possible. High-end audio connections are made in a bit

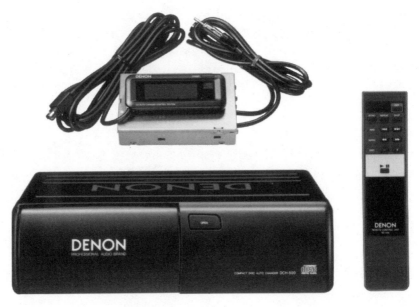

Fig. 11-8 *A compact disc changer with a matching FM transmitter.* Denon

different manner than for nearly any other electronics application. Normally, either the wires are "tied off" together or they are soldered and possibly weatherproofed. Some solder and a few wire nuts would be all that you would need to install the wiring on an electrical system of some sort.

However, this is a far cry from connections in the audio world. If you want to see some looks of terror and/or absolute disgust, talk to a professional installer about how you connected your system of JL and a/d/s speakers and Rockford Fosgate amplifiers using only 18 wire nuts! That's almost on par with ordering caviar from an exclusive French restaurant and dousing it with cheap ketchup.

The standard method of connecting audio and power cables together is to crimp them into terminal blocks or plug-in assemblies. The terminal blocks consist of a plastic block with an even number of small open cylinders running through them (Fig. 11-9). Two screws run into the top side of each little cylinder. Once you find the two wires that you want to connect, place the end of each one into the opposite ends of one of the cylinders, then screw the screws down from above and (as a result) crimp the wires together. Speaker and power terminal blocks are normally different—power terminal blocks are very heavy-duty units that often have thick "windows" (so that you can see inside), large screws, solid

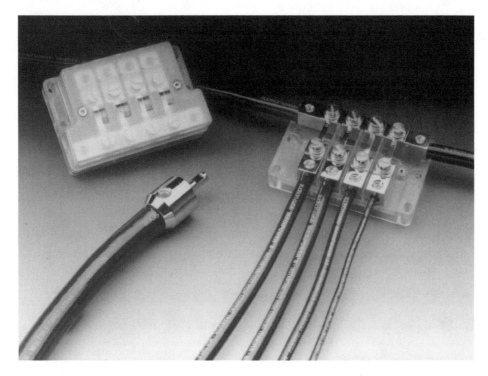

Fig. 11-9 *Connecting wires together in terminal blocks.* Audison USA, Floral Pk., NY

cylinders, etc. In short, they are built to handle the amps. Speaker terminal blocks are much smaller and less stout because they don't need to be any tougher.

One method that is even neater than using terminal blocks is to use wiring harness plugs. These plugs are similar to those that are often used in the backs of head units to input the power cables and to output the line and speaker audio levels. Although they are often only used at the head unit, these plugs can be used in other locations, such as at each of the speakers to form a sort of "quick disconnect" speaker arrangement. The problem with these plugs is that although they are easy to plug and unplug, they are difficult to remove for rearranging wires. This isn't normally a problem, but it is if you like to experiment with your system and frequently need to rearrange the wires.

Another method is to skip the terminal blocks altogether, put a piece of heat-shrink tubing on the wire, and crimp the wires together using a crimping tool or a multipurpose wire stripper. Then, solder the wires together and slide the tube in place over the connection. If the wires weren't hot enough to shrink the tubing, heat it until it shrinks tight against the wires.

Remember: solder should only be used as an electrical connection, not a mechanical one. Although solder will strengthen any joint, it does not handle physical stress very well. Some audiophiles will say that solder is not much of an electrical connection either. In my opinion, that's a mostly bogus argument. The antisolder folks claim that because solder is a mixture of lead and tin (neither of which conduct electricity nearly as well as copper), the signal loss and distortion will be severe at these joints. If the installer took his or her time and solidly crimped the wires together before soldering, then the wires would still be making very close contact with each other. The solder would then serve to make the joint a bit stronger (both electrically and physically) and it would also help to waterproof the joint.

Wire nuts are a poor method to connect the wires together because the joints are not especially reliable. A few years of road vibrations will cause these connections to become even less reliable. It would be terrible to hit a pothole and have one or more wire nuts pop loose and short out. Depending on what wires shorted together, you could damage or destroy your head unit, speakers, amplifier(s), or power system.

My favorite method for connecting wires is to use terminal blocks because everything can be connected simply and easily, the blocks are usually only a couple of dollars apiece, and it allows the easiest disconnection process. To make the wire runs even neater (such as in locations where the wires will be visible), screw the terminal blocks onto a hard, flat surface and secure the wires so they won't get pulled out of place.

SOLDERING PROBLEMS AND DANGERS

Soldering isn't difficult, but it seems as though many people with interests in auto audio have never soldered before. To make a solder joint, have the connection (wires, terminals, etc.) in the position that you want them to be in. Then, preheat the soldering iron until it reaches a very hot temperature and can melt solder easily. If you try to solder as the iron is still warming up, there is a much better chance that you will make a cold solder joint or that you will overheat the wires and melt the insulation. Next, heat the joint from underneath and place the tip of the solder against the joint from above. The solder will flow into the connection (Fig. 8-10).

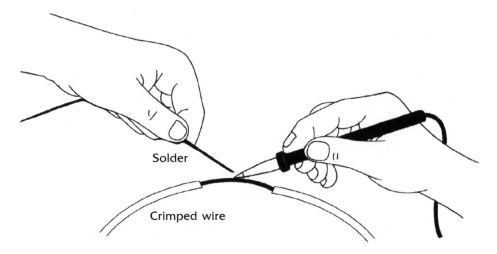

Solder

Crimped wire

Fig. 11-10 *Making a solder joint.*

Some people try to solder by melting the solder against the tip of the iron, but solder is always attracted to the heat, so the solder will stick to the iron and it won't flow into the joint. By using this method, you will almost surely get a cold solder joint.

The last two paragraphs covered the problems, now here is the danger. Be very careful when soldering so that you don't overheat a component that is in the circuit. For example, never solder a connection in a speaker line while the speaker is still connected. It probably won't be a problem if you are soldering at the other end of the wire because the heat will dissipate along the way, but if you are anywhere near the end of that line, you could quickly zap out the speaker. If your refrigerator already has its fill of powerful magnets, you now have a handy cassette eraser!

This soldering situation can also be dangerous to parts other than speakers. Heat is especially damaging to transistors and integrated circuits, but chances are that you won't be soldering around those parts anyway. However, you could basically end up doing this if you solder the wires in a wiring harness while it is attached to the head unit. The heat will conduct through the wires and into the power inputs or the speaker outputs and you could severely damage your head unit.

MAKING TWISTED PAIR AUDIO CABLES

The most direct way to prevent signal loss from or noise reception by a pair of wires is to shield them, as in coaxial cable. It's kind of the brute-force method. But you can also accomplish these goals through electrical, rather than physical, solutions.

The easiest way to electrically "shield" signal-carrying cables is to twist the wires together. This method is called *the twisted pair.* Because the wire is twisted, the impedance is lower, which makes it more resistant to receiving signals from outside sources (whether electrical noise or signal crosstalk).

Twisted-pair technology can be traced back to the beginning of radio (about half a century before the advent of hi-fi audio). Back then, twisted pair was used as transmission line (cabling that carries the signals from a radio to an antenna). Before long, it was mostly replaced by the more stable, balanced ladder line. And finally, by the 1950s and 1960s, coaxial cable was manufactured commercially, where it has dominated ever since. Outside of radio applications, twisted pair has been used for decades in telephone cables to prevent *crosstalk* (signal bleed-over between parallel cables) and it has become common in computer applications.

Many of the audio cables on the market are shielded twisted pair, which would be very difficult to make yourself. Some people say that the shielding in cable reduces the punch of the low end and the crispness of the high frequencies. I doubt that my ears could notice a difference between a "clean" (interference-free) run of unshielded twisted pair cable and shielded cable, but that's not the point. Unshielded twisted pair cable runs are simple and really inexpensive to make. And if it sounds as good as other cable, you can save some money.

For each balanced stereo audio cable, you need to have two sets of two wires and four high-quality RCA plugs. The wire should be insulated and stranded, anywhere from #12 to #16. To identifying the wires a little easier, be sure to buy two different spools of wire, each with a different insulation color. Measure the length of the cable run, as necessary to fit along the contours of the car, then add about 6 to 10 in. extra, just to be sure that it's long enough. Pull the lengths of wire from the two spools and you're ready to twist the wire.

The cumbersome wire-twisting method is to twist the wires by hand. The easy method is an old-time amateur radio trick: use a hand drill to twist the wires in a few seconds. To do so, put a large wood bit in the drill (1/

2 in. diameter, for example). Then fit the ends of the two wires into the opposing grooves of the bit and wrap everything in place with a piece of electrical or duct tape (masking tape is too weak). Turning the drill slowly, the wire will all be twisted in a few seconds (Fig. 11-11).

Fig. 11-11 *Twisting wires together with a small hand drill.*

To finish the cables, cut the wire and slip one piece of heat shrink tubing (optional) down each end. Then the RCA plugs can all be soldered in place. Be sure that the shield side of each plug is connected to the same wire and that the center of each plug is soldered to the other wire. Now, either the heat-shrink tubing can be heated to shrink it over the wires to hold it in place or you could just opt to tightly wrap a piece of electrical tape at each end, where the wires begin to twist together. Either the heat-shrink tubing or the electrical tape will prevent the wires from untwisting.

PLANNING AND ASSEMBLING THE SYSTEM

As has been stated earlier in this chapter, the wiring in an audio system is one of the most forgotten aspects of an installation. In terms of being overlooked, wire rates with the spider in a speaker.

Likewise, as people are thinking about whether or not the head unit will look handsome in the dashboard, how to mount the amplifier in a convenient location, or whether the holes in the speaker plates will match the factory mounting locations, the wiring goes unnoticed. But when the need to rewire occurs, then it's time to scratch your head and wonder why you didn't think about this earlier.

Before you start working on the wiring in an auto audio system, be sure to disconnect the negative terminal of the battery. There's no reason to endanger yourself and the components in your system.

The wiring in your car runs throughout the dashboard of your car. Everyone knows that. However, it also runs from the front to the back for the rear speakers and for the tail lights, turn signals, etc. Because it is out of sight, this wiring is often quickly forgotten. The standard cable routes are either along the bottom side of the transmission or by the edges of the door, in the corner where the floor panels reach the door frame (Fig. 11-12).

Fig. 11-12 *A bundle of wires routed underneath the carpeting.*

Replacing the speaker wiring or running the wiring for a new dedicated amplifier can be a major task. Before you start to install the system, you should determine what type of cable you will be using and how much you should purchase. To find the lengths, determine where the speakers, amplifier(s), head unit, equalizer, compact disc changer (and whatever else might be in the system) will be laid out. Then, use lengths of string or wire to find the exact lengths. Be sure to account for any extra bends or corners that the wire will be making. Allow an extra 6 in. to 1 ft. (15.24 to 30.48 cm) for every long cable run and about an extra 3 to 6 in. (7.62 to 15.24 cm) to be safe. It might seem like a lot of extra work just to measure the wires, but when you deal with custom wiring, that extra foot or two here and there could add up to quite a bit of money. Then, note any specific connectors that you might need, such as terminal blocks, RCA plugs (Fig. 11-13), slide-on speaker clips, etc. (Fig. 11-14).

Fig. 11-13 *StreetWires cables with specialty RCA plugs at the ends.* StreetWires by Esoteric Audio USA

When you plan out the wiring for your vehicle, try to either run the audio cables and the power cables on opposite sides of the car or use shielded cables to prevent noise from entering the audio cables (Fig. 11-15). Even if you can't place the power and the audio cables on opposite sides, at least try to space them a few inches apart. This distance alone will decrease the noise pickup, compared to having the wires bundled together. Before you start running the wires, make sure that you have made any solder joints that are necessary; the exception is if you have a 12-V soldering iron and plan to make the solder connections while you are in the car installing the wiring. After you have run these wires, tape them in place with a few pieces of duct tape in the areas that will be under the carpeting.

POWER CABLES AND FUSES

Wiring is a relatively boring subject and power wiring is the most boring aspect of this topic. Power wires and fuses don't do anything, and although you might notice a difference in audio quality between using light-duty and heavy-duty cables, chances are that you probably won't. But you will notice the difference with fuses if there is a problem, such as a line spike or a general overvoltage condition (Fig. 11-16).

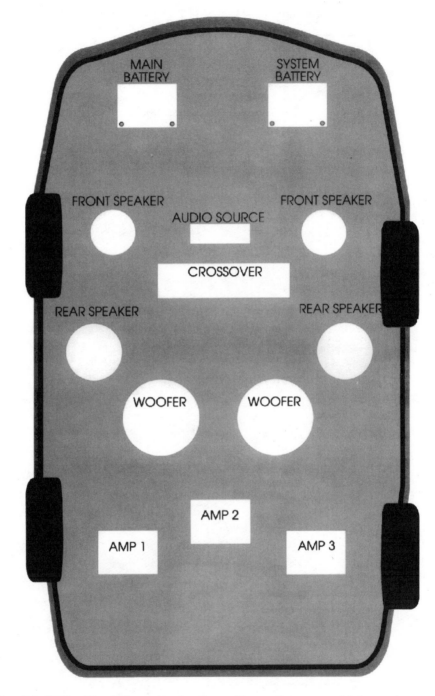

Fig. 11-14A *The "Blueprint for Sound" car diagram, which can be used to plan your system's wiring with much more ease and exactness.* StreetWires by Esoteric Audio USA

BLUEPRINT FOR SOUND

VEHICLE INFORMATION

CAR_____

POWER

WIRE

RED	BLACK
10ga_____	10ga_____
8 ga _____	8 ga _____
4 ga _____	4 ga _____
2 ga _____	2 ga _____
1/0 ga_____	1/0 ga_____

CONNECTORS

10 ga___ 8 ga___ 4 ga___ 2ga___ 1/0ga___

distribution block $_____
fuse/distribution $_____
ring terminals $_____
battery terminals $_____
barrier spades $_____
fusing $_____

AUDIO

RCA CABLES

AUDIO SOURCE TO EQ/CROSSOVER
_____ X _____ $ (each) $_____

EQ/CROSSOVER TO AMPS
_____ X _____ $ (each) $_____

SPEAKER WIRE

( )g _____

FRONT AMPS TO FRONT SPEAKERS
_____ ft X _____ $/ft $_____

( )g _____

REAR AMP TO REAR SPEAKERS
_____ ft X _____ $/ft $_____

( )g _____

SUB AMP TO SUB WOOFERS
_____ ft X _____ $/ft $_____

SPEAKER CONNECTORS

_____
_____ X _____ $ (each) $_____

TOTAL CONNECTOLOGY® _____

SYSTEM INFORMATION:

HEAD UNIT _____
EQ/CROSSOVER _____
FRONT AMP _____
REAR AMP _____
SUB AMP _____
ALTERNATOR, CAPACITORS, ECT... _____

_____

INSTALLATION COMMENTS _____

_____
_____
_____
_____
_____
_____

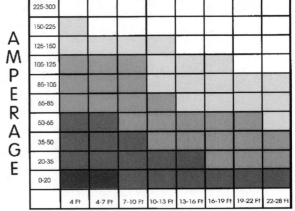

1/0 Gauge   2 Gauge

4 Gauge   8 Gauge   10 Gauge

Power Cable Calculator

AMPERAGE	4 Ft	4-7 Ft	7-10 Ft	10-13 Ft	13-16 Ft	16-19 Ft	19-22 Ft	22-28 Ft
225-300								
150-225								
125-150								
105-125								
85-105								
65-85								
50-65								
35-50								
20-35								
0-20								

Fig. 11-14B *Page two of The "Blueprint for Sound" car diagram.* StreetWires by Esoteric Audio USA

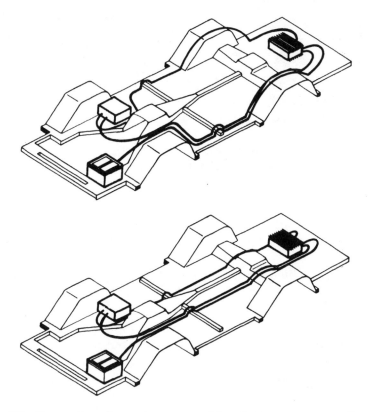

Fig. 11-15 *Runs of audio and power cables that are on opposite sides of the car to reduce noise pickup.* Scosche

With wiring gauges, the problem is just as great, if not even greater. If you fail to follow the manufacturer's recommendations for correct wire gauges (particularly in the case of high-powered systems), you could overheat the wires and start a car fire. But that's an extreme; chances are that if you choose too small of a gauge of power cable, you will underpower your amplifier.

Always play it safe and stick to the recommended wire gauge. And just what is the best gauge of wire to use? You can't go wrong with larger-than-necessary wire diameters, so pick a larger cable if you're not sure. Generally, safe amplifier gauges are #8, #6, and #4. Use #8 for smaller amplifiers drawing "normal" currents, such as 4 ohms. #4 is a must if you're bridging the amplifiers and running the speakers at less than 4 ohms. #6 is good for higher-power amplifiers. Many amplifiers are sold with power cable, so you might not even have to worry about buying new cabling unless you're running the amplifier at less than 4 ohms.

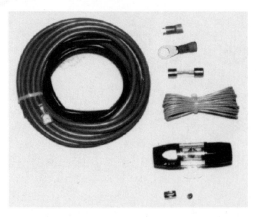

Fig. 11-16 *The heavy-duty cables, screws, fuses, etc. that are supplied with the Rockford Fosgate Punch 200ix amplifier.*

Likewise, be sure to use heavy-duty power terminal blocks and power splitters on the initial power wires. Otherwise, these blocks could overheat and melt, which could cause a fire or a short-circuit that would be dangerous to the audio system.

Many of the power-connecting devices on the market are primarily for competition vehicles that output a literally deafening amount of decibels. This book isn't aimed at competitors or at people whose main goal is to vibrate all windows within 150 yards (137.16 m). As a result, this material is succinct.

The foundation of a superpowered system is the alternator. Without a huge amount of current, you can't have a huge audio signal. Several companies offer high-power replacement alternators. Scosche even offers optional gold plating on some of its alternators. That would surely be one of the only cases where a car thief would pass by the car stereo to steal the alternator!

Quite often, people try to boost the power to the audio system by installing a larger battery. Actually, a larger battery will do nothing but allow the car to be started with more ease in the wintertime and produce a few extra minutes of stereo operating time when the car is turned off. Massive batteries seem to be big sellers via the specialty audio companies. This feature is especially important for car audio competitors (Fig. 11-17).

Another hot item is the brass or gold-plated battery terminal post. The theory behind these items is this: The better the connection, the more power can reach and the head unit and the amplifiers. This is true, but it won't make a difference unless you are pushing your car's power system to its limits. If you are pushing the system to that point, you should probably buy a new, higher-powered alternator or turn back the volume to give your ears and your neighbors a break.

When running power cabling, particularly for amplifiers, you will have to run the cable through the firewall and to the battery. This is downright annoying because you need to find a hole in the firewall that can accommodate the large-diameter power cable. If you can't find it, you will have to drill another hole. This is tricky because you need to be sure that you don't drill into any wires or objects on the other side of the firewall. So, if the power cable won't fit in any existing holes and you don't feel comfortable about drilling your car apart, take it to an auto body shop to have the work done. If the firewall must be drilled, the hole should be as small as possible and it should be primered and repainted to prevent rust.

When you are about to run the cable through the hole, you will need to get under the dash and remove one or so of the access panels so that you can see where the cable will be coming through. Then, you should tape the end of the wire to a straightened-out clothes hanger and try to feed it through the hole and to the place under the dash where you can grab the end and pull it out. This part might take some time fishing around! Once you get it, you can run it under the carpet and to the amplifier(s).

GROUNDS

The ease of grounding an auto audio system is often on par with trying to pin a tail on a cat. The process of debugging ground noise problems is so complicated that Scosche's *Autosound Encyclopedia* dedicates over 60 pages to grounds and noise problems! The *ground* is the point in a circuit that is used as a zero-voltage reference and which is connected to the Earth or to a circuit that is filling in as a substitute for Earth. It is impossible for an auto audio system to be connected to a true ground (the Earth) unless you listened to music in an immobile car. So, the car requires an artificial ground. Because a car consists of a large mass of steel, it (the chassis or frame) can be successfully used as an artificial ground.

In order to complete a sufficient electronic ground, the ground wire must be electrically and physically connected to the ground. This means that although the ground wire must be physically against the chassis, that steel must be clean and bare. Any surface dirt, dust, or grease will

Fig. 11-16 *A heavy-duty competition gel cell battery that can output 50 amps for 50 minutes.* StreetWires by Esoteric Audio USA

insulate the wire from the chassis and it will, at the least, cause audio problems (noise, hums, alternator whine, etc.).

To install a ground, find one of the ground bolts (behind the dashboard) and loosen it. Then, scrape the metal edge around the screw or (better yet) use a metal brush to shine the steel. Then, connect the ground wire and tighten the bolt or nut. To prevent the connection from taking in some water and rusting, lightly cover it with caulking or silicone grease. At that point, you should have no ground problems unless you add more components to the system. If you can't find a close ground terminal, don't add more wire and hunt for another already-established terminal. Long ground wires are generally ineffective even if the ground connection is good. Instead, drill a hole in a solid piece of steel in the car, add a screw or bolt, and follow the procedure outlined earlier in this paragraph. Just be careful, make sure that the spot the you plan to drill is free of any wires, and be sure that it is in a structurally sound area.

If the ground is sufficient, everything will work properly and you shouldn't have any major problems with noise or interference in the audio. That's fine and dandy, but what happens when the system doesn't work? One of the complications of ground systems in a car is having a number of components connected to the same ground. When this happens, the chances of getting ground loops are multiplied. So, anyone with an amplifier in the system will have to pay attention. *Ground loops* are differences in the ground reference voltage, between two (or more) different components in the same system. Ground loops often result in hums on the audio (Fig. 11-18).

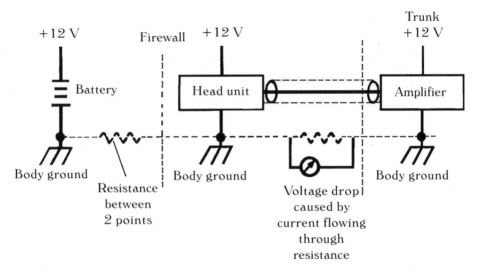

Fig. 11-18 *The anatomy of a ground loop.* AudioControl

The primary solution to the ground loop problem is the "star ground;" connect everything to the same ground point (Fig. 11-19). This is a fine system if you don't have a compact disc changer in the trunk or an amplifier (or several) in the trunk or under the seats.

As was stated earlier, grounds are a complicated matter and they vary from car to car—sometimes even between cars of the same make. You can "sniff out" ground loops and noise problems with electronic test equipment, but that is an extensive process—beyond the scope of this book (Fig. 11-20). My advice for grounding problems is to try grounds at different positions and experiment with noise-limiting capacitors. If you are an installer, try checking out the Scosche *Autosound Encyclopedia*. The high price (into the hundreds of dollars) will prevent any layperson from purchasing it, but it is an invaluable resource for the professional or shadetree installer.

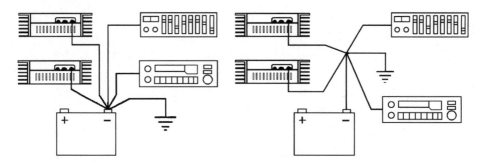

Fig. 11-19 *A star ground, where all audio components are connected to the same ground.* AudioControl

TRACING GROUND PROBLEMS

If your system has a ground problem, you'll hear a hum in the audio. Before trying to isolate the problem, be sure that your ground is connected properly and be sure that the ground wires are connected to a true ground and not just to an isolated piece of metal. The easiest way to find ground problems is to strip the system down to its bare minimum. Disconnect everything and connect only the head unit to the speakers. At this point, the system should lose the hum. If not, it's a very basic ground problem and you should try connecting the head unit to a different ground.

After the system checks out at the most basic level, connect any sound processing equipment (equalizers, DSPs, etc.) that you might have in the system. Next, reconnect an amplifier, one at a time (and reconnect their loads, whether subwoofers or standard speakers, as you go), until you have finished. When the noise returns, you've found the source of the noise.

INTERMITTENT NOISE

If the noise is intermittent, the problem could be either a loose ground or an intermittent wire connection. First, check the ground connection to be sure that it is solid. If so, check the audio cables to see if they are solid. If you wiggle the wires while the system is turned on and the noise changes or disappears, you've probably found the problem. Tighten the wires or replace the audio cables.

For information on solving more problems, see Chapter 13, which covers troubleshooting and repair.

CONCLUSION

Wire, cabling, connectors, and transmission systems are not the most interesting aspects of audio systems, but they certainly are important. They require some extra work to estimate lengths, plan, and install, so it is important to take your time and think about the arrangement. Grounds are not as difficult to plan out, but they are often much more contrary to install. Fix-it jobs, therefore, are often quite complicated.

A

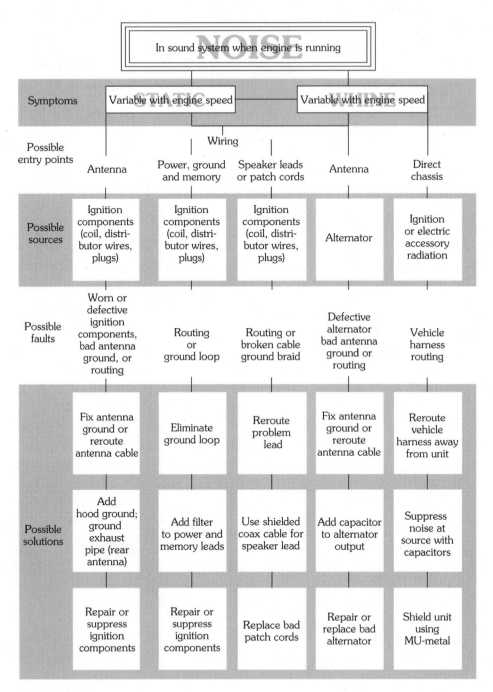

Fig. 11-20A *Troubleshooting charts for eliminating noise in the system with the engine running.* Sanyo

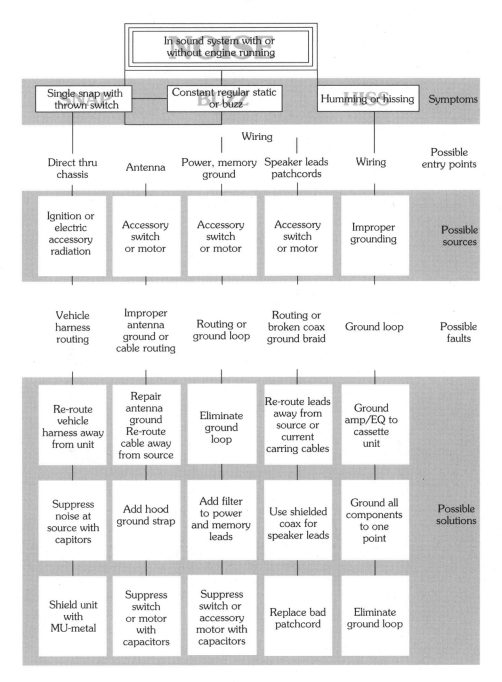

Fig. 11-20B *Troubleshooting charts for eliminating noise in the system with or without the engine running.* Sanyo

12

INSTALLATION

Aside from the decisions that you need to make when purchasing equipment for your system, the most important work involved in having a great-sound car audio system is the actual installation. The planning and methods that you use to install your system could make a great difference in its performance. Or you could cause great damage to one or more components if you install something wrong.

The first installation matter is to read the manual and installation directions for each piece of equipment that you are planning to install. Read over the information and get a good grasp for the task. Then, when you start, make sure that you have the tools that the manual recommends. Even if you are familiar with the techniques of installing audio systems in cars, make sure that you have a copy of each manual with you; the specific wiring diagrams and other information could be handy.

Unfortunately, every auto audio installation is a bit different. A huge number of different audio components are available, and every different car has a different set of acoustics, installation, ground, and wiring problems. Every new installation will involve different problems. Because of the "if-then" nature of the work, it is difficult to cover everything in a chapter without utterly confusing the issues. As a result, this chapter covers one specific installation thoroughly and several others are described and many photos are shown.

The only time that methods are skipped are where they would otherwise be repeating from previous sections. In these cases, references are made back to the previous sections, rather than make this chapter totally redundant. Because I am a firm believer in the learn-by-your-mistakes method of education, all of my stupid errors are also recorded here. So, be sure when reading about my installations that you read each section to the end before following the steps that I took! In some cases, I originally made some decisions, then found that they were creating problems by the end.

The first two installations are in-depth looks at installations in my own two cars. Next are three completed systems that all include some clever design twists. Essentially, the first two installations show the hurdles, compromises, and planning that occurs when assembling a system, and the last three show the possibilities that you can achieve with some hard work, thought, and creativity.

For those of you who are on the Internet, URLs are included so you can see the progress of these systems. Over the coming years, these systems might be altered, replaced, and the cars will be sold and, eventually, scrapped. Car audio is far from permanent and even a masterpiece system only has an average lifespan of a few years.

1981 VW Rabbit

A RELATIVELY INEXPENSIVE, BUT COMPLETE, INSTALLATION

When I decided to go ahead with installing a good sound system into our workhorse car, I ran into a few nonstandard problems, but this, too, requires some background. This car is interesting, too, because we've owned it for nearly 10 years, far longer than most cars are kept by a single owner.

Flashback to 1991: because I am somewhat of a spendthrift, I wanted a no-frills utilitarian car with great gas mileage—something that was cheap, but solid and dependable. The only car that met this criteria was the diesel Volkswagen Rabbit. The days of Fahrvergnuegen have long since swept away the Rabbit, so I sought a used one.

After months of waiting and searching, I found a 1981 model on one of those lots that has everything from rusted out 1970s-era station wagons to rusted out 1950s-era flatbed trucks. The common denominator was rust. However, my Rabbit looked clean, and even with 120,000 miles, it was still one of the nicest-looking cars on the rather homely lot. The catch for this car was that it was in a front-end accident and the hood and fenders were either puttied or replaced, then the whole car was repainted. A few days after I bought the car, the battery went dead and later the alternator died (the case was cracked in the collision).

The stereo system was also interesting; there was none. Whatever had been in the car was evidently salvaged by the previous owner before scrapping it. Considering that the car was not modified anywhere else and that it was strictly an economy car, it seems as though the stock audio system stayed in until the accident. Why anyone would ever want to strip stock 10-year old 3.5-in. (8.89-cm) speakers out of a car is beyond me. Nevertheless, the 3.5-in. (8.89-cm) round speakers were removed from the dash, the 6- x 9-in. (15.24- x 22.86-cm) speakers were removed from the rear deck, and the head unit was gone. In addition, the wiring harness was sliced in the dash, revealing only three wires, and all speaker wires seem to have been stripped out with the speakers.

After only driving to the sounds of a rattling diesel for several years, it was time for a change! A lack of time, money, and courage had prevented me from taking on the stereo challenge. When I decided that I *had* to put in a new system, I considered what would suit my needs. The bottom line was that I wanted to be able to play music that I liked in the car. Next, I wanted a system with enough power to override the sound of the diesel engine for under $500. I decided to splurge; I also went with a head unit that also had the option of shortwave reception.

The fact that I didn't have a show car (and didn't want one) helped as well. I didn't want to fill the trunk with speakers or amplifiers or concrete. And I didn't want a pounding set of subwoofers that could stop a pacemaker or shatter windows at 30 ft. I went with a Philips DC-777 (the only AM/FM cassette deck with shortwave), a pair of two-way 3.5-in. (8.89-cm) speakers for the dash, and a Harrison Labs Power Mowse system for the rear deck. All of the wiring in the sound system are aftermarket cables from Audioquest.

This system didn't last long. Fundamentally, almost everything was wrong with the initial installation, as you will soon see.

SPEAKER SYSTEM

I wanted to put the speakers in the stock locations, except for the subwoofer, and thus save a great deal of time and demolition. When I received the speakers, however, I realized that I screwed up and the

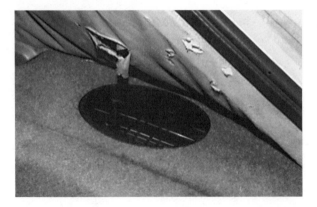

Fig. 12-1 *One of the standard 4-in. by 6-in speaker-mounting locations in the side of the rear deck.*

speaker-mounting positions at each side of the rear deck were made for 4-in. × 6-in. (10.16- × 15.24-cm) speakers (Fig. 12-1). I bought 6 × 9 in.'s (15.24 × 22.86 cm) that were wider than each of the speaker positions, so I couldn't even consider cutting larger holes for the new speakers. I could have returned the 6 × 9 in.'s (15.24 × 22.86 cm) for speakers to match the holes, but I wanted a beefier sound from the back and I didn't want the 12″ woofer to drown out the coaxials.

After staring dumbfoundedly into the trunk for some time and considering the possibility of building new speaker decks, the "easy," practical solution hit me. Removable speaker cabinets. I wanted to keep the ugly, but functional, easy-lift rear deck, so the cabinets had to sit on either side of the deck to hold it up. They also needed to be solid in construction and be able to be easily disconnected and pulled out of a slot from the inside wall of each rear fender.

I picked particleboard for the box material and decided to line the inside with insulation for maximum damping and reflection reduction. Particle board is strong, very dense, and it doesn't have large flaws, like most plywood. Fiberglass insulation or cotton/polyester batting are very common types of speaker damping materials. I based my material choices in part on what materials were the best for the job and in part on what was already on hand. I had leftover particleboard shelving and a roll of fiberglass insulation in the basement and this made the decisions much easier.

Temporarily, I used a Harrison Labs Power Mowse 3-Way system in the back. This system is a stereo pair of midrange and tweeters, a transmission line subwoofer, and a 100-W amplifier, all built into a relatively small, carpeted box. It's convenient because the only installation involved is running the wiring, and the box can be removed at any time, but I felt that it was too bulky for the rear deck, so I moved it to fill in a sub in my home system.

Afterwards, the 6- x 9-in. box speakers were mounted "loose" to the rear deck. This was temporary and not advisable because in an accident, the carpeted MDF projectiles could fly with enough force to injure...or worse.

The front speakers offered little power and midrange/bass response. They sounded harsh and generally tinny. These were finally just scrapped from the system and went unreplaced for quite some time while other work projects took precedence.

THE ACTUAL INSTALLATION WORK

After looking through the manual a few times for specifics, I embarked upon the mind-expanding ritual of installing the auto audio system. First on the checklist was the head unit. The Rabbit's dashboard radio hole is for one of the old two-knob head units and the DC-777 is a standard DIN size (Fig. 12-2). So, I removed the metal mounting sleeve from around the head unit and held it up to the original radio's mounting hole. Then, I used a pencil and traced around the outside of the mounting sleeve onto the black plastic. After I had the tracing visible, I cut

Fig. 12-2 *The dash of the Rabbit, showing the installed head unit.*

inside of the pencil lines with a tight-fit hand saw. The plastic was thin enough that the cutting was easy. By making a few diagonal cuts from the knob holes, I had no problem cutting out the corners without mangling them. I tried to draw and cut along the lines so that they were relatively straight and accurate, but I was a bit off. This was no big deal because the lip of the mounting sleeve covers nearly all of the rough plastic edge. The tiny bit that wasn't covered was overshadowed by the overhang of the front of the head unit, and these rough spots were not noticeable in the solid black plastic anyway.

One major question that I had with the system was the identification of the wires. The Rabbit's wires were cut, so I had three snipped wires: blue/white striped, green, and red. I assumed that the blue/white striped wire was for the lights, the red wire was connected to the battery, and the green wire was ground. The head unit had a spade lug on the end for a chassis connection, but I couldn't find a good close chassis ground on the car. So, I pulled out a multimeter and switched it to the continuity mode. Then, I touched one probe to the green wire and the other probe to the ground shield of the cigarette lighter. The tone sounded and everything was go. I stripped the insulation back about 1/4 in. (6.35 mm) from the ends of the wires with a knife. This isn't a very safe practice and you should use a wire stripper, both to be safe and to keep from breaking the individual wire strands. Then, I placed each wire from the head unit inside of the terminal block and screwed each shut with a tiny screwdriver. Afterwards, I matched up the wires from the car and screwed each one into the appropriate hole of the terminal block.

Next came the speaker assemblies. The wires were missing from the car, so I had to feed new ones from the head unit to the speaker locations. The area behind the dashboard was packed with wire harnesses, heating vents, and plastic deadends of various sorts. There was no way that I could feed the wire through by itself or run it through with my hands; the space was too complicated and too small for my hands to fit through. So, I dismantled a coat hanger and straightened it. Then, I taped the end of one of the speaker wires to the end of the coat hanger. I worked the end of the coat hanger through the dashboard and into the hole for the head unit. After this was completed, I did the same maneuver with the other side.

I attached the front speakers and screwed the other ends of the speaker wires to another terminal block. Then, I tested the system before pushing everything into a more permanent position. Voila! It worked on the first try. So, I stuffed all of the cables back into the DIN hole, then fed and snapped the head unit in place for the time being. By the time that the head unit was mounted in the dash, it looked like it was meant to be installed there—a nice feeling from a quickie hack'n'slash operation.

Everything sounded relatively good, considering that I only had a pair of 3.5-in. (8.89-cm) two-way speakers mounted in either side of the dashboard. Unfortunately, the speaker grille covers couldn't be put back in until after I had cut off the metal screw installation flange off the one side of the speaker. As I was driving to work, the speaker on the passenger side began to short out. I thought that one of my co-workers had stepped on the wire and shorted it out. Instead, I discovered that the speaker hole was entirely metal and it was difficult to prevent the speaker connections from shorting against this obstacle. As a temporary fix, I moved the speaker in its hole and tightened the screws. Later, I taped the leads with electrical tape to shield them from contacting the hole.

The drive to work brought up a few more problems that I hadn't initially noticed. The shortwave radio had a "whump, whump" noise whenever the engine was started; this interference sped up in proportion to the speed of the engine. I guessed that this interference was coming from the alternator. Also, I noticed that the heavy engine noise and the deep rattles throughout the car canceled out the lower audio frequencies. As a result, the system's sound was even harsher and tinnier than I had expected from just the front pair of speakers. The last major problem that I encountered was that I only seemed to be hearing one of the audio channels through both speakers.

I took the car home that night and pulled the head unit out. The first thing that I checked was the speaker connections. Rather than check the connections on the head unit when I initially hooked them up, I just connected the two speakers sequentially on the wires and didn't notice that they were both for the right channel. I reconnected this wiring.

When I got tired of having the loose audio cables pulled out of the speakers in the rear deck, I decided to actually run cables under the carpet of the interior. The carpet was easy to pull back from the interior of the car: just unclip the strips around the edges of the door frame and pull the carpet away from the adhesive strips. I made the connections at the other ends of the wires and moved the carpet and the door frame edges back into place. Easy. The most difficult part was keeping the wires from being readily noticeable. But, by having them come out in the trunk, behind the back seat, this was not a difficult task.

CAR NOISE REDUCTION

The worst problem with the audio system is not with the system itself, it is that the car is so loud. As described previously, it is difficult to compensate for, and the engine noise cancels out much of the lower frequencies. To eliminate some of this noise, I started to use sound-deadening material in the car. A number of different brands of sound-deadening material are currently available; I went with Accumat from Scosche. Most types of sound-deadening material are available in different forms (such as that for doors, floors, and hood headliners, and that which spreads on for difficult mounting locations), so be sure to choose the proper type for your specific application.

My first target was the doors. To access these cavities, I removed the door handle and the window crank with a screwdriver. Then, I wedged a screwdriver behind the decorative door panel padding. This padding is connected to the door with a series of plastic connectors that can be popped out of their holes. Unfortunately, I also discovered that they can also easily be popped out of the padding and I lost one. One method to remove the padding that worked well for me was to wedge my hand in behind the padding and find where it was connected. Then, I wedged a flat-head screwdriver in behind each connector so that it wouldn't pop out of the padding.

After I popped off the door panel, I noticed that it was just painted steel (with speaker holes) covered with plastic. I peeled back the plastic and was careful not to rip it, then I cut the Accumat into pieces that were large enough to cover the holes in the door (Fig. 12-3).

To install sound-deadening material into the inside of the car, you must carefully peel back the interior carpeting and clean the surface if it is a bit dusty, dirty, or fuzzy (from the carpet backing). Then, simply cut the sheets into appropriate shapes and sizes, peel the backing, and move it into place. Rub it down with your hand or with a roller to remove and air pockets under the material. Then, place the carpeting back over the material and reattach it.

THE FUTURE OF THIS SYSTEM

This system is in transition. I plan to use this car until it finally disinte-

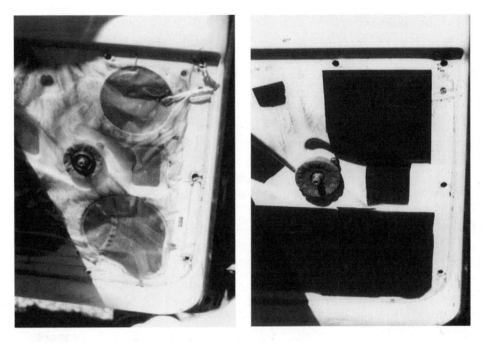

Fig. 12-3 *The front door panel before (left) and after (right Accumat sound-deadening material was installed.*

grates, like my 10th-grade gym socks. The car is now 19 years old and has well over 220,000 miles, but I'm still planning to keep driving it for at least five more years. So, despite appearances, the sound system is going to be relatively permanent.

The old head unit has some mechanical problems, so I'm in the process of getting a new one and replacing the old. I bought a new head unit, but I'm not satisfied with its quality and I want to replace it with another cassette head unit. I might even move the Blaupunkt head unit from our minivan to the Rabbit and go with a CD deck there instead.

The front area is so small that there aren't many places to mount speakers (as mentioned previously). The in-dash locations can only handle 3.5-in. speakers, mounting in the possible door locations means not being able to roll down the windows, and I'm afraid that the speakers and enclosures will get kicked out in the kick panels. So, as I write this, I am about halfway through building dash-mounted enclosures to handle a pair of Altec Lansing 4- x 6-in. plate speakers. I'm not sure that these speakers will have enough "oomph" to overpower the rumble of the Rabbit, but they do have much better low-frequency response than the old 3.5-in. units that I had. It's worth a shot.

The rear deck is also in the process of a makeover. I'm removing the old rear deck and installing a slab of MDF that's hinged for easier access to the trunk space. The rear deck is cut with a jigsaw so that the old 6- x 9- in. box speakers can be dropped in and screwed in place. I had been planning to sink a 10-in. subwoofer in the middle of the rear deck (as a free-air mounting). I think that it would just make the hatch too heavy and probably quickly warp the hatch. Instead, I'm going to build one or two 8-in. sub boxes to fit in the back wheel well spaces. They should be small and fairly efficient so that the tiny trunk space won't get eaten up.

I considered carpeting everything, but I think that I might just coat it with fiberglass resin and paint it with some dizzying pattern.

Finally, I plan to use more sound-deadening material inside (especially inside of the trunk) so that the Rabbit will hopefully be as loud inside as a jeep, not a Sherman tank. Also, I'm considering replacing the front speakers with better units that don't distort audio in the lower treble frequencies. While I'm at it, I might also do a little cosmetic work to the interior of the Rabbit to make it a more hospitable place. With any luck, the new front speakers and the quieter Rabbit will vastly improve the sound of this system.

1988 Plymouth Grand Voyager

The mini van installation

Have you ever noticed that you never see standard minivans with after-market stereos? Competition vehicles are nearly always 16- to 24-year-olds with sporty cars or low-rider pickups. Although I don't plan to ever enter my Voyager into any competitions, it is worth noting that you don't have to give up on good audio after the age of 30.

The audio in the Voyager was pretty good to start with. Unlike most vehicles of the time, it contained a specialty system with decent specs. It's an Infinity system with a cassette deck, 5-in. round front dash speakers, and 6- x 9-in. speakers mounted in the bottom of the hatch. From the beginning, the sound wasn't bad, although it could have been improved some everywhere. I probably would have been happy to just let the system go "as-is" with the factory equipment and not even mention it in this book, but the cassette deck failed, so it was time to get to work.

HEAD UNIT

After about a year of using the van, the head unit suddenly failed with a cassette inside. It was still on and hiss was audible, but all of the cassette functions stopped working, including Eject. Because I was busy with other projects, I let it go for a while. Miraculously, it came back to life a few months later. It then worked consistently for a few more weeks, but it then failed again. I removed the front plate from the dash, which only required unscrewing about six or seven screws. It was downright simple, compared to removing the dash panel from a Chevy Celebrity (from the first edition of *Auto Audio*).

The folks who designed this head unit made it so that it couldn't be repaired without great difficulty. All of the screws in the case were drilled out in the centers so that they couldn't be removed without completely drilling out the screws (and getting metal tailings all through the guts of the head unit in the process). Thus, it's essentially disposable; one problem and it finds a new home in the trashcan.

Rather than try to figure out which wire was which, I simply bought a new head unit from Crutchfield so that I could get the wiring harnesses thrown in for free. The stock head unit was 1.5 DIN size, so I bought a Scosche adapter to match the opening. Unfortunately, the system is an oddball. It uses negative grounding for the speakers and a hidden external amplifier. So, it requires an adapter to bring the speaker-level outputs to attenuate the levels down to line levels (Fig. 12-4). These are kind of pricey, and now, I wonder, if I would have been better off buying a line-level output head unit or rewiring everything to bypass the system amplifier. In terms of time and cost, the line-level unit would have been the way to go. But I bought a closeout head unit, so the cost probably worked out even in the end anyway.

Overall, the installation was really simple. I used a wire stripper to remove about 1/4 in. of insulation from the ends of the wires. All of the positive speaker outputs from the head unit were screwed into the appropriate terminals in the level adapter. The harness adapter was plugged into the wiring harness, and all of the speaker wires were connected to the appropriate output terminals in the level adapter. All of the negative wires were twisted together with the ground strap and taped tightly with electrical tape. I bought strip terminals from Radio Shack so that I could screw the power terminals from the head unit together with those from the car.

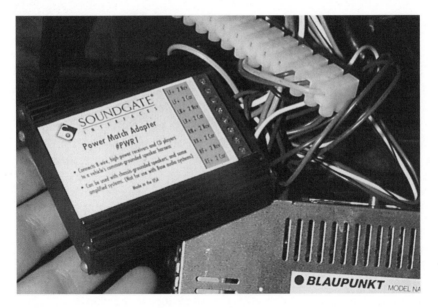

Fig. 12-4 *A power-matching adapter which is used so that the outputs from high-power head units can be attenuated to line levels.*

I cleaned up some of my mess in the car and placed some of the equipment in a functional location. I fired it up and voila! Nothing. It turned on, played cassettes, tuned the radio, but no audio could be heard. Well, almost. I tried turning it up really loud and I could just barely hear some tinny audio. Now, that's progress! Now, I knew that the problem was that the amplifier wasn't amplifying the audio to the speakers. I looked through the extensive Crutchfield info pack to see the problem, but I couldn't find it. So, I called their tech support line and discovered that the remote turn-on line for the amplifier was turned on by connecting the power antenna wire from the head unit to the power antenna wire of the wiring harness adapter.

Then, it worked fine…well, almost. The deck sounded terrible when playing cassettes: very bassy and muffled, but good when set to the radio. I tried cleaning the heads and playing different tapes, but nothing worked. It was still under warranty, so I sent it back and received a head unit (Fig. 12-5) that worked fine this time (I also chose a model from a different company).

SPEAKERS

The sound from the speakers is decent in this vehicle, but the speakers

Fig. 12-5 *The second replacement cassette deck installed in the Voyager.*

could be improved. One problem is that they start to distort the bass frequencies just as the audio is getting fairly loud. Replacement speakers would help to blast a little better.

I think that the greatest problem might be speaker locations, not speaker quality. The Grand Voyager is a very long minivan and the only speakers are mounted on the top of the dash (Fig. 12-6) and in the hatch. Thus, the front speakers are only about 3 to 5 ft. from your ears,

Fig. 12-6 *One of the stock front dash speakers pulled out of the Voyager, with the grille popped out.*

but the rear speakers are approximately 10 to 12 feet from the front seats. To make matters worse, the rear speakers are mounted low on the lid, so they fire directly into the lower portion of the back seat. As a result, the rear speakers are not only a long distance from the front, they are muffled by the back seat and whatever is stuffed behind it.

To get decent imaging, you really need to blast the rear speakers, which will still sound too bassy; anyone sitting in the back will have an unpleasant listening experience. Aside from replacing the rear speakers and removing the back seat as often as possible, the best solution for those in the front seats would be to mount speakers a few feet behind and to keep these on a small remote amplifier so that they can be turned on or off, depending on who's in the van. It's a nice idea, but there are some problems. First, "a few feet behind the front seats" is right into the next seat, which would probably be an annoyance in terms of both audio and physical location. Also, one of the speakers would fall into the sliding door space, so it would be out of the question, too. And these speakers couldn't be mounted on the back or sides of the front seats because they would be too close and you'd get a strong left channel and weak right (or vice versa). Finally, if they were mounted on the ceiling, everyone would be smacking their heads on the pods. I'm going to have to think about this problem some more.

The next problem is the imaging in the front. In the stock positions, the front speakers fire off of the windshield and the sound is reflected down...and it sounds like it, too. When listening to the head unit, the audio is "empty" at the bottom, giving the impression that you're in an empty orchestra pit, listening to music coming down from above. Kick panel speakers, pointed properly, would eliminate this problem.

Finally, it would be nice to improve the low-bass frequency response of the system. It should be fairly easy to design a small subwoofer box to either fit in between the front seats or under the middle seat. The worst part of adding the subwoofer would be adding another amplifier and running the power and audio cabling to mount it.

FUTURE

The future of this system is undecided. I don't have enough time to do everything that I'd like to do in the near future, and I don't know how long we'll have it. I'd like to replace the rear speakers with better co-axial 6 x 9 in.'s, replace the front speakers with kick panel component speakers, and add a small enclosed subwoofer.

1998 VW GOLF

STEVE HUNTER
http://www.sounddesign.com/installation/
search_details.cgi?id=2608
shunter@lclark.edu

I have started competing this season in the novice 151-300 class and have done reasonably well. My very first competition yielded a first place victory. Since then I have gotten a second place at a key event and most recently fourth place at the Oregon state championship (Fig. 12-7). I

Fig. 12-7 *Here she is on a beautiful sunny day in Portland (pretty rare occasion).*
SoundDesign

have done every bit of the installation myself, which really adds to the excitement whenever I beat out a professional install in competition.

Well, it all starts here at the Sony Mobile ES CDX-C910 (Fig. 12-8). I just got this about a week before my first competition. The display on it is really dim even with the contrast maxed out. Anybody have this and the same problem? This setup allows me to use a fiber optic cable back to my equalizer which really made everything sound a lot better; I lost some hiss and it made my music a lot more dynamic/lively. A definite suggestion to anyone using the Sony ES digital eq without the fiber-optic.

Fig. 12-8 *The Sony Mobile ES CDX-C910 head unit installed.* SoundDomain

Here is the 6 1/2-in. part of the Diamond Audio Hex series separates (Fig. 12-9). They sound EXCELLENT! I have the soft dome tweeters, which sound extremely natural and not harsh at all. You can get them with a titanium tweeter, too, but I appreciate a natural sound in my tunes. I would definitely recommend tracking a set of these down to listen too if you are thinking at all about a set of high-end separates. I

Fig. 12-9 *The 6 1/2-in. part of the Diamond Audio Hex series separates.*
SoundDomain

Fig. 12-10 *The small tweeter component of the Diamond Audio component set mounted in the stock speaker hole on the top of the dash with the grille removed.*

SoundDomain

compared them to the mighty MB Quarts back to back and there was literally no comparison. I also considered the Oz, but while their 5 1/4 in. sounded good the 6 1/2 in. had muddy midbass and I wanted a 6 1/2 in. so that I could get as much bass up front as possible.

Here is the tweeter on the right side of my dash underneath the stock grille (Fig. 12-10). I am still playing around with the angle a little in hopes of getting a perfect image. So far, they work pretty good where they are. When I get it just right I'll put a pin of some kind through the near side to secure it.

This is the headquarters for my stereo (Fig. 12-11). The amplifiers are Precision Power PC250 rated at 50 x 2 into 4 ohms, which runs all my highs and mids, including my stock rear speakers. Also a PC2100 rated at 100 x 2 at 4 ohms which is bridged to run both of my PC12 12" subs with 200 W each. The enclosure measures 1.75 ft.^{3} per side and is tuned to about 55 Hz. I've had these in a 1.25-ft.^{3} sealed box and I liked it a lot. So far with this setup I've hit a high SPL of 136.2 off the dash. The box was built with 18-mm Trupan, which is extremely light and dense. I could easily lift the entire enclosure, without subs or amps, with just one hand.

Here is a pretty good picture of the Diamond Audio crossovers (Fig. 12-12). They allow me to attenuate as well as change the phase of my tweeters from my midranges. I can also wire my rear fill off of the same channel and attenuate them up to 8 dB, allowing me to reap the full potential of my amplifier.

Fig. 12-11 *The trunk mounting box, which contains two 12-in. subwoofers and two Precision Power amplifiers.* SoundDomain

Behind the panel holding my Diamond Audio crossover on the left (Fig. 12-12) is my Mobile ES 210 equalizer (Fig. 12-13), which gives me 21

Fig. 12-12 *The side panel in the trunk, which houses the Diamond Audio crossovers.* SoundDomain

bands of adjustment and doubles as my hi/low pass crossover between my subs and midranges. This has a great low-pass slope of 36 dB/

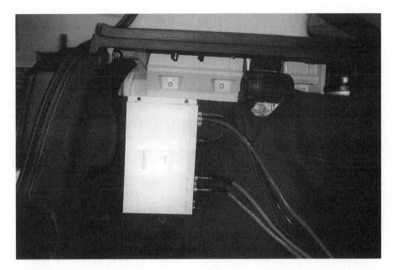

Fig. 12-13 *Behind the side panel in the trunk that holds the crossover is the Mobile ES210 equalizer.* SoundDomain

octave, and allows me to cross the subs over at a fairly low 62 Hz, which really improves my staging.

Here's what you see when my back seats are down looking back at the hatch. It looks a lot better in full size (Fig. 12-14).

Fig. 12-14 *Looking toward the back from the inside.* SoundDomain

Did I mention that I have all this in the hatch and I can STILL use my spare tire (Fig. 12-15)? The box is hinged in front where the rear seat

Fig. 12-15 *The trunk box, which can easily be lifted up for easy access.*
SoundDomain

belts attach and bolts to the rear of the car via the angle iron visible on the back of the box. These two pieces of angle iron mate to a matching set which are bolted to the car. A bolt then goes through both pieces and is tightened by a nut welded to the bottom of the angle iron attached to the car. This is very tight and I get absolutely no squeaks or rattles from my trunk. Oh, and as added security the bolts in the back can only be reached and removed with a tool that I hand made.

Like I said, I did all the work myself except for some help from my dad. I also received a lot of tips from Audio Synergy of Naples, Florida (where I used to live). If you have any questions, comments, tips, or even criticism, please e-mail me at shunter@lclark.edu.

1998 HONDA ACURA

Sarah Galloway, Regina, SK Canada

http://www.net1fx.com/~sound/acura.html
nygacr@cableregina.com

Fig. 12-16 *The stock Acura head unit that has been modified to include a digital output.* SoundDomain

Unlike other people who just drop off the checkbook or the credit card and come back when it's done, we built this car ourselves! The car competes in IASCA in Novice 1 to 150 and is currently undefeated. We will be attending the IASCA World Finals. One of the top priorities was a stealth install because the vehicle is a daily driver. The other priority was, of course, great sound! If you want to see more about the construction of the stereo system, visit our Webpage. There are more than 150 thumbnailed pictures and full descriptions.

"Hey, me too! I took my factory face apart and made a 'fake' cover..." Nope! That was kind of cool about four or five years ago. The factory CD player was modified so that it has a Toslink digital output (Fig. 12-16). This has kept the system stealth while allowing for optimum sound quality by utilizing an outboard D/A converter (Fig. 12-17).

The digital signal is massaged and converted to analog by an Orion

Fig. 12-17 *The Orion DEQ-30 equalizer.* SoundDomain

INSTALLATION

DEQ-30 . The four presets make this EQ an excellent choice for any IASCA competitor. The EQ is housed in a custom fiberglass piece and can be covered with a protective grille.

Because digital signals offer no volume control, an AudioControl MVC was called upon (Fig. 12-18). As you can see, it's mounted on the

Fig. 12-18 *An AudioControl MVC mounted in the other side of the trunk.* SoundDomain

opposite side of the trunk, as compared to the EQ. It also has a custom fiberglass mounting.

Taking care of sub duties is a Focal 27S, a 10-in. dual 6-ohm driver. It's housed in custom fiberglass enclosure in the wheel well (Fig. 12-19). You can see the smooth fiberglass work around the sub. The back of the sub grille (and all other grilles in the car) are finished with white plexiglass.

Just ahead of the sub, you can see the two PPI amplifiers, a 225 and a 425 (Fig. 12-20). They are joined with a heatsink spacer. The amp rack was built slightly larger than needed, just in case we want to move up to a bigger power class later. If we wanted, we could fit a 4100 or a Pro650. You can also see the grille, which is finished with grille cloth, holed steel, and white plexiglass. This allows the amplifiers to breathe. They run quite cool, though.

Fig. 12-19 *The Focal 10-in. subwoofer mounted in the wheel well.* SoundDomain

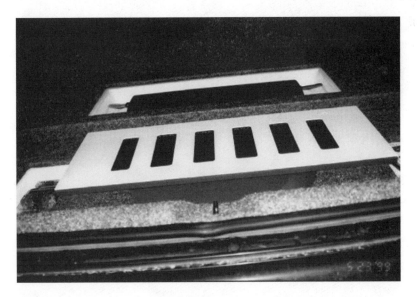

Fig. 12-20 *The PPI amplifers mounted in the rack in the trunk.* SoundDomain

Up close and personal with some Lighting Audio fuse and distribution blocks (Fig. 12-21). It's an older picture, before my RCA ends came in.

We finally got the kickpanels done (Fig. 12-22). They kind of look like Q-forms (but they're not, as you'll see in the next picture).

Fig. 12-21 *Lightning Audio fuse and distribution blocks.*
SoundDomain

Fig. 12-22 *The speaker pod in the kick panel is homemade from fiberglass. Notice how the tweeter is angled toward the heads of the listeners, but the midrange is pointed out.* SoundDomain

With the grille removed (Fig. 12-23), you can see the fiberglass piece around the mid. The grilles are reversible, depending on how much I want to show off.

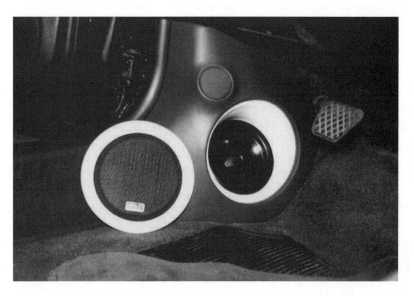

Fig. 12-23 *The grille pulled off of the midrange, showing the reversible grille and the fiberglass edge around the inside of the midrange mounting hole.* SoundDomain

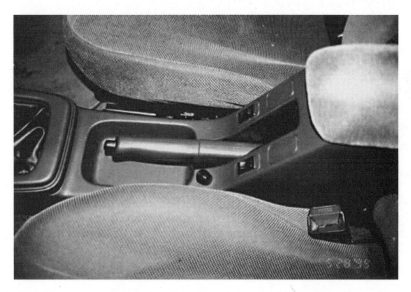

Fig. 12-24 *The center console, showing the control buttons.* SoundDomain

Mounted in the center console is the volume knob from the MVC and a couple of switches (Fig. 12-24). One is a master power and the other is a three-way switch, allowing us to select the system mode: Sound Q, RTA, or SPL.

We maintain an open door policy. If you want to look, listen, take pictures, or just chat, then come look us up at the Finals! Remember, if you didn't install it yourself, you ain't got nothing!

1987 HONDA ACCORD

STEVE , EDMONTON, AB CANADA

http://www.sounddesign.com/installation/
search_details.cgi?id=3625
stevkrla@oanet.com

My car is an 1987 Honda Accord LX, four-door. that I have designed and installed. It's a simple yet effective system that sounds great and pounds (when I want it to). The objectives I had when putting together this system were to keep everything as unobtrusive as possible, and to make sure that any changes that were made could be returned to stock if I ever sold the car and took out the stereo. With that in mind, I started what you see in this section.

The system starts up front with an Alpine CDA-7840 head unit installed in the factory location (Fig. 12-25). The unit was chosen for its 4-V output capabilities along with changer control, remote, disk titling, and

Fig. 12-25 *A view from the back seat of the Alpine head unit mounted in the stock location.* SoundDomain

simply because it is an Alpine.

The front stage consists of Rockford Fosgate RFA-54, 5 1/4-in. midrange and Phoenix Gold Sapphire 1-in. tweeters mounted in custom kick panels (Fig. 12-26).

Fig. 12-26 *A view of the speakers in the kick panel at the driver's side.* SoundDomain

The kick panels were constructed using 3/4-in. MDF baffles and a fiberglass/Bondo enclosures (Fig. 12-27). First, the baffle was made to fit the car in the spot that took up the least room and gave the best imaging. The midrange speakers have a pretty deep mounting depth so care was taken to make sure there was proper clearance. After the

Fig. 12-27 *A view of the kick-panel speaker pods from the front passenger's seat.* SoundDomain

baffles were complete, they were placed in the car, and the floor was lined with aluminum foil. This made an enclosure that shaped the floor/kick of the car. Next, the inside of this enclosure was sprayed with expanding insulating foam and allowed to harden over 24 hours.

Once the foam had hardened, there was an exact copy of the shape that I wanted over which I could mold Bondo and fiberglass. The foam mold was covered in Bondo and fiberglass, then removed, and then the Bondo/fiberglass shell was attached to the baffle. Viola, a kick panel enclosure.

Once the enclosures were made, they needed to be sanded and shaped a little more to mold exactly to the shape of the vehicle. The holes for the mid and tweet were cut earlier. Once again, the clearance for the midrange was checked, and everything was okay. Both the mid and tweet were flush mounted and the factory grilles were covered in brown grille cloth. The entire enclosure was wrapped in brown carpet and attached to the car from inside with screws into the metal on the footwell and kick panel. The final step was to drop the mid and tweet into place, wire them up, and put on the grilles.

In the pictures, the browns do not appear to match that well. While they are not exactly the same, they are far closer in shade than the pictures indicate. If they are ever to be removed, they only need to be unscrewed and taken out, nothing else has been changed.

To help combat theft, a mock faceplate was made using the factory cassette deck. The front of the deck was taken off and all of the buttons/knobs were hot glued on (Fig. 12-28). The entire thing fits over the Alpine unit (once the Alpine faceplate has been removed), and it looks as though the factory deck is still there. If anybody has ever heard the factory deck on a 1987 vintage Honda, they know that it is not worth stealing.

The crossover (a Coustic XM5-e) has a remote bass level controller. It was mounted in the pop-out-panel that resides in the center counsel just behind the shifter location. It cannot be seen in this picture but can just be made out in the first picture on the right side of the counsel. The pop-out panel was the perfect location because it is within easy reach of my hand (I usually rest it on the shifter knob anyway) and also because if I ever decide to get rid of the knob, I can buy a new pop-out panel for $5.00 at the parts store. A larger knob was taken off of an old equalizer, painted brown to match the interior, and then put over the existing knob from the Coustic controller (the stock Coustic knob is very small).

Fig. 12-28 *A view of the interior, showing the fake Honda faceplate placed over the Alpine head unit* SoundDomain

In the trunk, the goal was to take up as little room as possible, and cover all of the components so that a factory look could be achieved. All that can be seen, upon opening the trunk lid, is a wall covered in matching gray carpet (Fig. 12-29). All of the components reside protected inside.

Fig. 12-29 *The trunk of the 1987 Honda, which has been designed to look like a stock trunk, with no visible components.* SoundDomain

Fig. 12-30 *The side "pocket" in the trunk, which currently houses the jumper cables.* SoundDomain

Figure 12-30 is intended to show the location of my next upgrade to the system. I plan to purchase a Phoenix Gold EQ-215. It will fit right into this side pocket (the current home of my jumper cables) and can be covered for protection from thieves as well as objects in the trunk.

Once the cover in the trunk is removed, the remaining components of the system can be seen (Fig. 12-31). The Coustic XM5-e crossover is mounted on top of the sub-box in the middle and is flanked on each side by a Kenwood KAC-644 amplifier. The Coustic was chosen because it has bandpass capabilities for the midrange and it has a remote bass level

Fig. 12-31 *The back of the box, showing the Phoenix Gold amplifier in the front, the Kenwood amplifiers on the top of each side, and the Coustic crossover in the middle.*

controller. The Kenwoods were simply from a previous system. They worked well and made good clean sound. They are both four-channel amps but each is bridged for two channels. One runs the mids and the other runs the tweets.

Mounted vertically (and upside down) on the back of the box is a Phoenix Gold M-50. It is recessed 3 in. in the box and is covered on all sides. Foam sealing tape was placed around the outside of the recess; once the back cover is put on, the recess becomes completely sealed. On the top and the bottom are two 1-in. cooling fans (two push and two pull) that are turned on using a relay connected to the remote turn on lead from the deck. I have gone on a five-hour road trip with the system cranked up, and the M-50 remained cool the whole time.

The M-50 is bridged mono to provide plenty of power to two Kicker F-12a 12-in. subs. The subs are around five-year-old technology but still pound hard and sound great (I am hitting around 132 dB). The only drawback is that they require a large enclosure (they are a free-air design). The box is a single chamber that provides about 1.7 ft.^{3} per sub. It was internally braced and coated on the outside with fiberglass. It is very strong and very stiff, even when the system is pounding hard. Finally the inside was stuffed with about four pounds of fiberfill and the entire thing was installed in the car. The subs face the rear seat and the area around the box was sealed off from the trunk (as was the rest of the interior including the rear deck). With this, all of the sound enters into the interior cabin and none of it is wasted in the trunk.

In addition to the separates up front, the factory rear speakers are used for slight rear fill. They are powered by the deck and faded quite low.

The electrical system starts under the hood where all of the wiring (battery ground, and alternator-to-battery) was upgraded to 2 gauge. There is a fuse right off of the battery and then 2-gauge wire carries the power all the way to the trunk. There, a 1-F Phoenix Gold capacitor is mounted to the right side of the sub-box. Directly above the cap are the distribution/fuse blocks that send the power to the appropriate components. The Kenwoods get 8 gauge power and ground and everything else is 2 gauge.

To protect everything, an Alpine SEC-8027a alarm was installed in the Honda. It has door, trunk, and hood switches as well as dual zone shock sensor and a glass break sensor. In addition, remote locking actuators were installed in the two front doors. They run off of the internal relays in the alarm and allow for silent entry and exit (the chirps from the sirens have been turned off). There are two sirens mounted, each with a different tone, so that the alarm is loud and distinctive. In the future I plan to install a remote trunk release to be operated from the alarm as well. The alarm was chosen because of the features, the price, and because we installed the same alarm in my wife's car and each of us only needs one remote for both cars (the 8027a remotes can be programed for two cars)

There you have it: a clean, simple, stealth install in an 1987 Honda Accord. I have enough room in the trunk for a couple of sets of golf clubs and can still get at the spare tire (very important). This is the third system to go into this car and about the eighth system that I have in-stalled. It is a great hobby and I know that I will continue with it far into the future. (I do at least one major upgrade every year). If you have any questions/comments, send me an e-mail. I would like to hear from you.

CONCLUSION

Even though these systems are all relatively basic, they are all extremely different and show the different approaches that can be taken (and often *must* be taken when trying to assemble a system. Even if you take the brute-force approach and modify your car extensively, you will find that your installation will be heavily influenced by the physical characteristics of your car. Just be prepared to be flexible, creative, and open minded so that you can install a system that will suit your needs.

13
REPAIRS & MORE

Nothing is worse than hopping into your car, ready for a trip, only to find that your car stereo doesn't work. Screaming, pounding the dashboard, and cursing won't help your system a bit. (Although if you do it with enough rhythm, you could eventually land yourself a recording contract).

If you're lucky, the damage will be minor and you can take it to a local car audio shop to have it repaired for a low price. Chances are that even if the problem is minor, the repair will still be costly. Either that or the shop will just suggest that you buy new replacement equipment. Don't even bother with the screaming, pounding, and cursing bit in this case. The repair technician won't be interested; he or she can't sign you to a major label anyway.

In many cases, repairing a problem with an audio system involves nothing more than replacing a fuse, checking wiring connections, or checking the wiring itself. Unless you are friends with an installer or are a regular customer at an installation shop, you will pay plenty of money to have someone else make the minor repairs. Aside from saving money, troubleshooting your system is a great way to learn about its arrangement and connections, and how it works, and it will enable you to do more work on a system in the future.

From an electronics repair point of view, it is both good and bad that the 1950s have passed. In those days, huge, well-built components were screwed and bolted into large steel cabinets (Fig. 13-1). The parts were built well enough that they were expensive, but didn't break down frequently. And they were large enough that they could be replaced without difficulty. Today's advantages are much less expensive components and

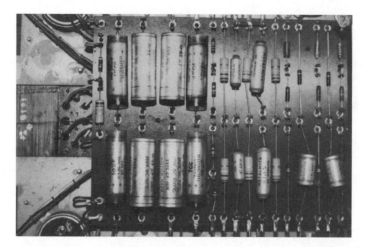

Fig. 13-1 *Compare this nicely layed out block of large components in a 1950s hi-fi amplifier to the insides of a modern head unit or amplifier.*

miniaturization—tiny components are crammed so tight that it seems that only a malnourished seven-year old with tweezers could have assembled the circuit boards. The disadvantage is, in turn, that only that same seven-year-old could disassemble the board without destroying everything else in the process. As a result, in almost all levels of modern electronics, actual repairs are no longer made; instead, the malfunctioning circuit board is pulled out and replaced with another board.

There is very little that you can do to repair failures on these boards, except purchase a few junker units that are the exact same model number as the unit that you own, isolate the problem, and interchange the failed board with one that will work. This is a great possibility, but chances are that you will not find a number of broken-down units that are exactly the same as yours. If you do find a number of these units in an unworking condition, chances are that you picked a poor model and you might be better off dumping yours than trying to repair a cheaply designed piece of electronics. Another problem is that typically there are a few weak points in any piece of electronics; thus chances are fairly good that if you find a broken-down unit to match yours that it will have the same problem that yours has.

Most auto audio components are built using the slide-in board method, except for dedicated power amplifiers. Dedicated power amplifiers, especially the high-quality American-made models, usually use large, heavy components soldered onto thick circuit boards. These amplifiers could be repaired, but they usually don't break down unless they have been mistreated. Even then, it is usually the power transistors (usually field-effect transistors) that go through meltdown.

If you can con the manufacturer out of a repair manual, then you will have a much better opportunity to repair your equipment. However, you probably will not be so lucky. Unfortunately, most companies only distribute this information to their authorized dealers, which forces nearly everyone to go to these dealers for repairs...or buy a new unit. In the 1950s and 1960s, a number of American electronics companies provided extensive support for their products with descriptive lists of components, test point information, troubleshooting information and tips, etc. These days, everything has changed and you are lucky if you can get any free information about any electronic gear.

This book is primarily intended for people who have anywhere from no experience to intermediate experience with car stereo systems. It is not a technician-level book; i.e., it's for consumers, not electronics enthusiasts or repair technicians. So, don't expect to be able to just flip to this chapter and use it to discover that voltage regulator Q86 is blown in your particular head unit and that you should replace it. Information of this nature would easily fill a very large book on its own, and, someday, I'm sure that it will. Instead, this chapter covers a few of the troubleshooting and repairing basics that are relatively easy for the beginner to perform and that don't require the use of expensive test equipment.

TRACKING DOWN THE PROBLEM

Even if you have no intention of repairing your own equipment, it is important to search out the problem and tell the repair tech where the problem is and what is occurring. This will help the technician find the problem in less time and it could save you some money.

I saw one episode of *60 Minutes* several years ago with a segment that dealt with the honesty of various electronics repair shops. They had a woman take a VCR with a simple problem (I believe that the drive belt might have been off) into different electronics repair shops in one city. And, several of the parts were marked with an ultraviolet pen. The end result of the report was that most of the shops were not honest. Some claimed that parts were replaced that weren't; others claimed that they had performed repairs that hadn't been done, etc.

Hopefully, the car audio shops in your area are much more reputable than those that were in the *60 Minutes* report. I would like to think that most people who make a career of car audio would be above scamming their customers, but this is not a perfect world. Even if car stereo installation and repair would be the most honest business in the face of the Earth, there would still be a few dishonest people out there. With this in mind, don't torture your repair technician with accusations; there's no need to ruin their day. But, you should always be as informed and knowledgable as possible on the subject. Nothing will deter getting ripped off on a repair like knowing what has failed where and being able to talk about it with a repair technician.

Determining faults in a system is a matter of taking educated guesses and almost randomly substituting other components for testing purposes. The rationale is that if one part isn't working, you will be able find that problem by substituting different components one at a time until the system works. From this point, if the problem is in a complicated component, such as a head unit or an amplifier, you might not be able to narrow it down further without using a multimeter, a signal generator, and an oscilloscope, so you might be stuck at this point if you don't have this equipment.

But, you should always first check the wiring around where you think the problem is (and possibly over the whole system, if you fail to locate the trouble). Faulty wiring or connections will void the entire trouble-shooting process if you don't immediately check these possibilities. Also, car audio wiring problems normally consist of "is it connected or isn't it?" By finding the faulty connection or wire, you have just saved yourself a trip to the repair shop.

Check the wires by jiggling them and disconnecting or reconnecting them to the power distribution blocks. Beware of disconnecting the wires to the speakers while running the system at a high power level; you can cause severe damage to an amplifier if you run it in a no-load condition. The high power levels would just "sit" at the high-power outputs, then they would overheat and fry the output FETs (field-effect transistors). If you have an amplified head unit, this can be especially dangerous because you would lose your amplifier and head unit in one shot.

NO SOUND

If, for example, your system does not work and no sound is reaching your speakers, check your wiring. Have you ever had any problems with it? Have you recently added any components that could have created problems with your system? If you did, check out the wiring around this component. Next, check for commonsense things that you might have missed. Are the units turned on? Did you forget to plug in any audio cables when installing or rearranging the system?

If these problems aren't applicable, check the displays and power-on indicators on the various components. If you aren't getting any sound, does the head unit even turn on? If not, you should check the connections to the head unit and also check the fuses.

A good way to test the rest of the system and determine whether the problem is with the head unit is to feed another signal through the system. The best method is to use a good portable stereo that has line-level outputs (don't use the speaker-level outputs if you have any amplifiers in your system!) and run the RCA cables into the line-level output jacks (Fig. 13-2). If you only used a "high-power output" head unit and

Fig. 13-2 *An older portable AM/FM/CD/cassette stereo (a.k.a. boom box) with line-level CD outputs. A unit like this is great for feeding a signal to the rest of a system that has amplifiers to test for a faulty head unit.*

don't have any amplifiers in your system, then you must use an amplified output to run the tests. When making these tests, you must be careful not to feed a signal that could overdrive the amplifier or speakers. Overdriving the amplifier into clipping can damage the amplifier and the speakers. If you already have a bad head unit, the last thing you want to do is blow out the rest of the system!

If everything else checks out and the other components in the car work, but the head unit doesn't, then it is probably safe to pull out the head unit and either check it in another car or have it checked at a car stereo repair shop.

WEAK, TINNY AUDIO

Another symptom is if almost no audio can be heard from the speakers, and what you can hear is very tinny. There should be very little speaker "hiss." In this case, the amplifier is not working, it is being bypassed, or some how, the line-level outputs of the head unit were connected to the speakers. Check to see if your amplifier is turned on or is working. After that, check that the audio cables are properly connected.

MUSIC SUDDENLY QUIETS

If you are blasting some tuneage and suddenly the sound virtually disappears, but the head unit is still running, the amplifier has probably shut down. Amplifiers typically only shut down on their own when they overheat (thermal protection). Turn off the head unit for a while and try it again later. If this happens regularly, there's a system problem or several problems. One possibility is that the amplifier fan has stopped. Some more likely problems are that the speakers have been connected at too low of an impedance or the amp is drawing more current than it can safely handle. Other possibilities are strictly physical: the amplifier might be in a tight location without enough ventilation or it might be mounted in direct sunlight.

HOT AMPLIFIERS

Heat and vibration are the two the greatest enemies of any type of electronics. One of the symptoms of overheating is amplifier shutdown, addressed in the previous section. Another symptom might simply be that the amplifier case (heatsink) is very hot to the touch. If this is the case, do your best to keep it cool. Put it in a well-ventilated location (not sealed in a tight, carpeted box, for example). Keep it out of the sun. If you are running it at a lower voltage/higher current, check the amp specs to be sure that it is capable of regular operation at that impedance; if not, return it to an impedance that it can handle. And if the amplifier case is still very hot, but it runs properly, chances are that it does a good job of conducting heat to the heatsinks (i.e., it "runs hot").

TRACKING CONCLUSION

Of course, these tracking examples could be drawn out for a hundred and one different minor problems. Rather than delve into all of these problems, which you probably won't ever encounter, and bore you to tears in the process, this book covers some of the more common problems.

ORGANIZING YOUR WORK

The procedures to disassemble car audio electronic equipment are very complicated, and you must be very careful or you might wind up with a few "extra parts." As you disassemble the electronic components, don't just dump out parts in a pile. Write down the parts that you have removed and put them in labeled sandwich bags or in small containers. Many times, I have torn apart different components and I felt that I would know for sure how to put the parts back together. Before long, it seemed that I had the entire project into hundreds of little pieces and I only remembered how to fix half of the parts in the proper location. As a result, you should even draw a diagram of the assembly and disassembly procedures so that you can repair your equipment and prevent your projects from remaining hopelessly disassembled.

SAFETY PROCEDURES

Safety procedures are never fun because they slow down your progress. I guess I'm just too impatient for safety rules, but it seems as though I have to screw up several times severely before I get the hint that I should be more careful. Then, after a few traumatic experiences, my techniques improve. Fortunately, I've never come close to electrocuting myself, but I have grabbed the soldering iron by the wrong end a few times! Believe me, you're better off avoiding stupid mistakes by reading about them than by doing them yourself!

If you are not a technician or if you have very little or no experience with repairing electronic equipment, stay out of it! If you want to learn about repairing equipment, read some books that are dedicated to the topic of repairs and buy some inexpensive nonfunctioning equipment to experiment with. One of the worst things that you could do is try to repair an expensive piece of equipment (such as a $600 head unit) with minor problems, cause more damage to it, and not have enough money to replace it.

If you have had some experience working on electronics gear and feel comfortable in it, be careful and connect the power only when taking measurements at the manufacturer's listed test points. When testing and taking measurements on the unit, it is much better to pull the unit out of the car, take it to your work area inside, and connect it to a regulated 12-V power supply. This way, you have space and light to work, rather than trying to solder upside down on the floor of the car with a flashlight in your teeth. It is best if you have an open work area, such as an electronics workbench that is clean, stocked with parts, and well lit.

Be sure to check for any manufacturer's warranties that you might void by removing the case and digging around inside. For the most part, if you remove the case of an electronic component, you will void the warranty. Considering that you probably will not be digging around in your new $300 amplifier unless it has malfunctioned, voiding the warranty is bad news.

ELECTROCUTION AND ELECTRICAL SHOCKS

The following section is primarily only a concern when working with amplifiers, amplified head units, and possibly when working with batteries and alternators; no other auto audio components (equalizers, CD changers, unamplified head units, etc.) contain high-powered components. Always be careful when working with electronics; there is always the possibility that you could make the big mistake. Several times I have heard people say that they didn't have to worry about car electronics because it was only 12 volts and 12 V, which isn't dangerous. This simply isn't true. Any voltage can be dangerous, depending on the amount of current that is flowing. Remember the equation for power:

$$P = IE$$

Where:

P is the power in watts
I is the current in amperes
E is the voltage in volts

If the car is putting out 12 V (usually, it varies between 11.8 and 14 V, depending on whether the car is running, etc.) and the amplifier is outputting 250 W in bridged mono mode, then:

$$250 = I \times 12$$

$$I = \frac{250}{12}$$

$$I = 20.83 \text{ amperes}$$

However, this equation only applies if the amplifier is operating at 100% efficiency, which is not possible. Chances are that the amplifier is closer to 50% operating efficiency, for example. With this being the case:

$$I = 20.83 \times 2$$
$$I = 41.66 \text{ amperes}$$

Although 12 V is a relatively low voltage, 41.66 A is a huge amperage. You might also have heard the old electronics adage, "it's not the voltage, it's the amperage that will get you." That's not entirely the case, it's the total power that will weld your feet to the floor. Still, the adage is a good way to remember not to neglect the amperage. Part of the reason for ignoring the dangers of 12-Vdc electricity is because direct current is less likely to stop a heart than a 60-Hz alternating current waveform. So, your heart is much more touchy when dealing with standard house electricity than with that which is available from your car's power system.

It is still possible to be electrocuted with 12 V, particularly if you are well grounded and if you are making a strong contact with the electricity (such as if your skin is wet, if it is entering through a cut, etc.). To prevent being grounded, don't stand in water, wear rubber-soled athletic shoes, and stand on a rubber mat, if possible. Electricity always takes the shortest path with the least resistance to ground. So, if you get shocked, you are actually a giant resistor, but if you are grounded through a puddle on the floor, you are a giant conductor. From a safety standpoint, you are much safer being a giant resistor (however, you are much safer, and happier, not being an electrical component at all!).

Because of the shortest-path-to-ground rule, it is best to avoid having electricity grounding in a path that leads through the heart. For this reason, one commonly used rule in electronics is to work with the left hand in a pants pocket. Thus, if you get shocked with a great amount of power, the electricity will not pass through your heart and you won't get killed. It's a simple and effective theory, except for one drawback; it's really tough to work with one hand in your pants pocket. After years of working with your hand in your pants pocket, you probably won't get electrocuted, but your scarred hands and mangled projects will testify as to the clumsiness of the arrangement.

As stated previously, be sure to unplug the unit that you are checking (unless you are taking measurements at various test points) so that you don't cause yourself bodily harm. And remember, from the operational theory of stiffening capacitors, that capacitors store electricity until that charge is dissipated. This charge doesn't quickly dissipate while it sits in a circuit; you could easily dig into an amplifier weeks or months later and find out that the heavy-duty capacitors still pack a wallop. Usually, for smaller discharging operations, the standard method is to cross the leads of the capacitor with a large plastic-handle screwdriver (Fig. 13-3).

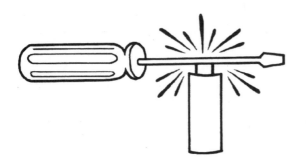

Fig. 13-3 *The typical method of shorting out capacitors, although it's safer to also run a grounding wire from the screwdriver blade.*

However, to prevent the possibility of having a charge jump over the shaft of the screwdriver and jolt you, it is best to attach the screwdriver shaft to ground via an alligator clip. Be sure to discharge each large capacitor several times because most capacitors will still store some electricity even after you have discharged them the first time. For a more scientific discharge method, cross the leads with a resistor of a value that has been recommended by the manufacturer.

SAFETY WITH ELECTROSTATICS

To protect electronic equipment from electrostatic discharges (also known as *static electricity*), you must take almost the opposite mindset and approach than you did with protecting yourself against dangerous voltages. That doesn't mean that you should stand naked in a puddle of water while groping the insides of a plugged-in cassette head unit, but it is somewhat different.

Many of today's microelectronic components are intended to handle only minuscule amounts of power. Because of the need for miniaturization in mobile electronics, it is better for the parts to be used closer to the damage tolerances than to be forced to build the piece of audio equipment into a much larger enclosure. As a result, it is very easy to damage equipment with levels of electricity that we would have never considered to be harmful to anything just one or two decades ago.

However, with modern integrated circuits, even a small blast of static electricity can melt a tiny hole through the package and destroy one of the microscopic components or interconnecting wires. These blasts of static electricity will either destroy or impair the performance of the integrated circuit. It might not seem like much, but this destructive static electricity is the very same as that which is discharged from your body. Just wearing tennis shoes and walking across carpeting on a dry day will cause an electrostatic that is easily powerful enough to destroy a typical integrated circuit. According to an article in *Electronic Servicing and Technology*, one person (depending on the clothing and other environmental conditions) can build up a charge of static electricity that exceeds 35,000 V!

As you can see, it is very difficult to handle integrated circuits without damaging or destroying them. To prevent damage, it is important to wear a grounded wrist strap (Fig. 13-4). The grounded wrist strap is a conductive strap that is connected to ground via a wire. This method is effective because the ground bleeds off the electricity (rather than allowing it to suddenly build up), then releases it through the integrated circuit that you are handling.

So, if you are working on complicated integrated circuit-laden units, such as head units, be sure to use grounded wrist straps. Otherwise, even getting too close to the unit (without touching it) could cause your body to discharge electricity through it and damage components.

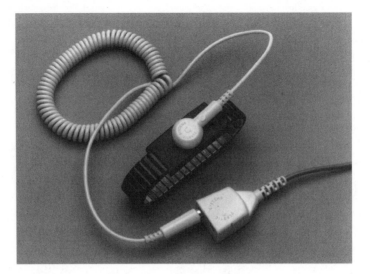

Fig. 13-4 *A grounded wrist strap, which is essential whenworking in close proximity to modern electronics circuitry.* Plastic Systems

REPAIRING SPEAKERS

Over the years, I have heard stories about how the Kinks' guitarist Dave Davies slashed the speakers in his guitar amplifier with a razor blade, then taped the shreds back together with cellophane tape. And that's the rumor behind the pre-fuzz box guitar distortion that helped make "You Really Got Me" a classic. The Kinks have never dropped by my house for a pizza and a chat, so I've never been able to validate the truth in this story. But the fact remains that a torn speaker cone will significantly alter the speaker's sound. And although that tinny guitar sound rocked a generation in 1964, running an entire song through a torn speaker will ruin the sound of your system.

According to the fundamentals of electronic audio, the speaker cone must rapidly push in and out, like a piston in an engine. Obviously, a hole in that audio piston destroy its efficiency, alter its resonant frequency, and will thus make the speaker reproduce some frequencies less effectively.

Never continue to use a speaker with a torn speaker cone, if it has any value to you. That piston-like action will only cause the speaker to tear even further if you continue to use it. Pull the speaker out immediately and replace it, stop using your system until you replace it, or disconnect the speaker wires that you would have left hanging.

The options that you are left with are either to buy a new replacement speaker or to repair the torn speaker. By this point, you already know how to buy a speaker, so it's time to repair one instead.

First, it's typically not recommended by most resources that anyone repair their speaker cones. One reason is that it's not in the best interest of the manufacturers to have you repairing your speakers instead of buying them. But, it's also going to be very difficult to make your patch flex exactly the way the cone did before it was ripped. This difference means that the speaker will respond at least somewhat differently than it did. Also, chances are that the cone will be weaker and more apt to tear again in the area where it has been repaired. So, you might consider repairing a sub that's torn if you need to spend that $100 on snowtires, not new speakers. And if it sounds good, you can let it there until you feel like replacing it. If you don't like the way it sounds, you haven't lost anything.

PUNCTURES, TEARS, AND HOLES

Speaker cones can be ripped in a variety of ways, but any way you slice 'em, they still require somewhat similar repairs. Small punctures in the speaker cone are the easiest type of cone problem to repair. Simple, clean tears can be repaired easier than holes and "rough" tears, which branch out from the main tear line (Fig. 13-5). Large holes and rough

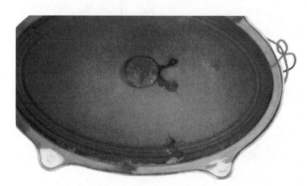

Fig. 13-5 *A cheap speaker with a torn speaker cone.*

tears all require special treatment, and even after a good repair job, you still might notice somewhat of a difference in the sound quality between it and the other undamaged speakers. You will probably notice less of a difference if you make the major repairs on woofers or subwoofers, where the cone is much larger and thicker and where the resonant frequency is low.

If you are repairing a small puncture in a paper or paper-composition speaker, try pushing the displaced paper from the back side. If you can pull this paper back together, try dabbing some clear fingernail polish on both sides of the puncture to hold the tiny fragments of cone material back together. If the punctured speaker cone is clear poly or something similar, try creasing the displaced material back toward the center of the hole, and dab either clear fingernail polish or model airplane glue on both sides of and over the puncture.

If you have a midrange or tweeter with a light tear in the cone, cut out a small piece of clean, unwrinkled tissue paper. Then, lightly cover one side of the paper with either clear fingernail polish or a thin, heavy-duty, general-purpose adhesive. Be sure to cover all of the edges with the adhesive. After the adhesive has dried thoroughly, apply a thin coat of clear nail polish over the edges or else they will be much more likely to peel and potentially resonate. Another good method to avoid peeling edges is to round the corners of the tissue paper patch (Fig. 13-6).

Fig. 13-6 *Repairing a torn speaker cone with tissue paper and glue.*

Repairing a large speaker tear or hole will probably require more ingenuity and skill on your part. One of the best methods to repair paper speaker cones with large tears is to pull a few old speakers out of your junk box. Unfortunately, most people don't have an electronics junk box so that they can pull out parts for important repairs or fun projects. If you have an old, dead, or cheapo speaker laying around the house somewhere, this the time to sacrifice it for the good of your audio system. In this case, the arrangement would be the same as in the last case: cut out a piece of the sacrificial speaker cone that is large enough to patch over the tear in the good speaker. When you cut the patch out, make sure that it will perfectly adhere to the surface of the cone that you are repairing (for example, you wouldn't use a ribbed cone patch over a tear on a smooth speaker cone). Then, apply and cover the patch, as was discussed in the previous paragraph.

In this case, where the speaker has a large tear or a hole, and if the tear in the speaker cone is in an area that is not smooth, such as a ribbed section, use a tissue-paper patch instead of one from a cannibalized speaker. Be sure to use another tissue paper patch on the other side from the one that you made or cover the torn area with a light coat of clear nail polish to seal and protect the speaker cone patch.

If you have a large tear or hole in a clear poly speaker, you must have really abused it! Regardless, try to seal it up with a seam of model airplane glue, if possible. If you can't make both sides reach, then get a sheet of the thin plastic that is used to make transparencies for college lectures, group singing, etc. Just cut a patch out of this material using the methods described in the previous paragraphs. Then, use model airplane glue or another type of plastic adhesive to hold the patched speaker cone together. As in the other cases, be sure to seal up the rough edges with a hard, clear adhesive.

Repair techniques change slightly for woofers and subwoofers, which generally must have much larger and heavier speaker cones. Because woofers and subwoofers are intended only to reproduce low frequencies, you can get away with using a relatively heavy patch without causing much of a difference in sound quality. Because of the woofer movement, you should always use a patch to prevent further damage, whether or not the tear is clean or not. The cannibalized speaker patch that was mentioned several paragraphs ago is a good method, whether this paper or paper-compound speaker material is heavy or not. Another possibility is a patch made from a paper grocery bag! It's ugly, but it works.

UGLY, PATCHED SPEAKERS IN YOUR CAR?

Because I have little concern for the beauty and styling of anything technical or electronic, I don't really care how ugly it looks as long as it works well and is solid. As a result, ugly, repaired speakers don't really bother me, as long as they sound okay. I do, however, understand that some people might not want to have subwoofers that have been patched with paper grocery bags in the rear deck of their hot new car. One way around this is to tightly cover the top of the speaker with grille cloth or metal grilles so that the speakers will not be visible. Grille cloth is relatively *acoustically transparent*, which means that it won't "soak up" the sound or "deaden" certain frequencies. Parts Express currently sells three different colors of grille cloth and Scosche offers 11 different colors to match the interior of your car. With a bit of a creativity, you can do a custom installation that looks as if it was performed at the factory.

DETERIORATING SURROUNDS

Aside from dampness, one of the most damaging conditions encountered in the car stereo environment is that of ultraviolet rays from the Sun. Speaker cones have to pound in and out as your audio system is in use. However, the cones remains generally solid, and it is the speaker's surround that must continuously flex in and out. Surrounds are typically made of paper, cloth, and poly foam. Some of the synthetic materials that were used to make surrounds over five years ago have been gradually breaking down in the sunlight. One of my friends has a car with speakers like these, and the surrounds have developed cracks and thin tears in the foam material (Fig. 13-7). The speakers will eventually need to be replaced.

Rather than pitch out your once-prized speakers with the dry-rotting surrounds, you might consider repairing them. No, this time, I don't mean pulling out the grocery bags, blown speakers, tissue paper, and clear finger nail polish. Parts Express currently offers speaker surround repair kits to save your speakers. You must remove the old surrounds from the speaker, and install the new surrounds with a high-strength adhesive that is included with the kit. Unfortunately, the kits are only available for round speakers that are 8 in. (20.32 cm) (or larger) in diameter. So, you can save your woofers and subwoofers, which are generally much more expensive than tweeters and midranges, but kiss the other speakers goodbye.

Fig. 13-7 *Surrounds that have almost totally disintegrated after too many years of ultraviolet light exposure.*

EQUALIZERS

Most equalizers consist primarily of variable potentiometers that are used to vary the strength of the various frequency ranges. Many equalizers also have built-in amplifiers or preamplifiers to boost the levels.

The three basic types of separate equalizers are dash-mounted units that also contain amplifiers, active dash-mounted units (they contain preamplifiers), and active floor- or trunk-mounted units. The dash-mounted units are all generally those that contain some combination of slider potentiometers—usually anywhere from 3 to 12, either per channel or for both channels (mono). The floor- or trunk-mounted models are nearly always have dial-type knob potentiometers instead of the sliding faders. The difference is that the dash-mounted units are intended to be adjusted frequently to compensate for or alter the sound of the source. The floor- or trunk-mounted units, on the other hand, are intended only to be occasionally adjusted to compensate for or alter the sound of the system.

As far as repairs are concerned, the only weak areas in a good-quality equalizer are the potentiometers. After several years of dust, dirt, grease, and use, the slider and standard knob-type potentiometers will sometimes become scratchy-sounding or intermittent. Spray a cleaner chemical, such as Jet-Lube Terminal contact cleaner, into the potentiometers and slide them back and forth to work the chemicals into the contacts. Once you have worked the fluid into the contacts, check to see if it works any better. If the equalizer is more than 10 years old, some of the potentiometers might be wearing out and need to be replaced, particularly if they were of a lesser-quality manufacture.

Replacing slider potentiometers can be tough because they must match the original one in value and must perfectly match the size of the others. For best results, consult the manufacturer or the manual for part numbers (if available) or page through electronics parts catalogs and check the values and sizes until you find an exact replacement.

HEAD UNITS

CASSETTE DECKS

Cassette head units often require more maintenance and repair than any other piece of car audio equipment because they have more moving parts and have to make contact with dirty materials. As a result, it is common for a cassette deck to croak: begin sounding bassy, slow down, or eat tapes after a few years of use. Then you question why you ever thought that deck sounded great and start looking for a new model. And then the forlorn deck is sold off cheap or is simply thrown away. Most problems with cassette decks are relatively minor and inexpensive to remedy, so it's a real shame when one of these head units gets pitched. Because of limitations in the scope and size of this book, it is somewhat limited in its troubleshooting and repairing information. For over 400 pages worth of information on the subject, read *Troubleshooting & Repairing Audio & Video Cassette Players & Recorders* by Homer L. Davidson.

MUFFLED AUDIO/TAPES ARE EATEN

The most common problems with cassette head units are that the audio is muffled or that the tapes get eaten by the playback mechanism. There's nothing worse than having your brand new $10.99 cassette by the Paul Johnson Trio eaten—especially when these problems have been occurring with increasing regularity over the past few months. You could even make a fist and scream "When will this lust for ferric oxide coated tape ever end?!" But the wanton cassette violence won't end until you stop using the deck—unless you choose a route of maintenance.

Although muffled audio and problems with the playback mechanism seem thoroughly unrelated, both can be different symptoms of the same problem. Of course, all standard cassettes consist of some mixture of a magnetic substance (usually ferric oxide, chromium oxide, or metal oxide) that has been very thinly coated onto a synthetic tape. After some wear, these oxides will eventually build up a light coating of residue across the parts that rub against the tape. The residue resembles dirt, and it is exactly that: foreign matter that must be removed in order to preserve the most accurate sound reproduction possible.

The best way to take care of these problems is to clean everything that is in the path of the tape with rubbing alcohol. With a standard home audio cassette deck, this is an easy task. Just open the cassette door, dip a cotton swab or a cleaning stick into rubbing alcohol, and carefully clean the erase head, the tape head, the pinch roller, and the capstan. Even though the auto cassette head unit doesn't have an erase head, it is still much more difficult to dig your way in through the tiny slot to clean the tape head, capstan, and especially the pinch roller. To reach back to these parts, you will need to use long cleaning sticks instead of cotton swabs. Because of the small slot, you will probably need to have sunlight directly behind you or a flashlight shining into the hole. If you don't know what the tape head, capstan, and pinch roller look like, see Fig. 13-8. All of these parts look quite similar between head units that have been made by various manufacturers.

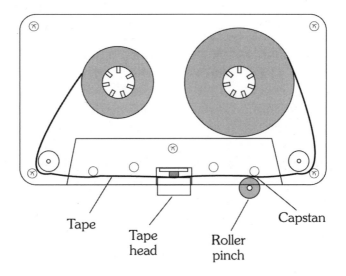

Fig. 13-8 *The head, capstan, and take-up reel of a standard cassette head unit.*

The capstan and tape head should be easy to clean; just rub it with the dipped cleaning sticks a few times. The pinch roller is more difficult because it is rubber and you must rub it hard to remove the tape residue. After the tape deck has been used for some time without being cleaned, you will notice that there is a stripe of tape residue running through the middle of the pinch roller. When you clean the pinch roller, you must turn it as you rub it clean. Otherwise, only one spot of the pinch roller will be clean. By the time you are finished, you should barely be able to see any of the residue stripe. Cleaning the heads are a common part of audio maintenance, and it is recommended that you clean your cassette heads for every 40 hours of use, although few people adhere to this advice. A clean playback mechanism is essential for the head unit to perform up to its capabilities. When I worked at a radio station, we were required to clean the heads on the cassette decks and open reel decks at every use. I have to admit that I have slacked off considerably since that time, but a clean playback mechanism is still essential to achieve good cassette performance.

I talked to one of my friends about the wonders and difficulties of cleaning the playback mechanism. He said "Why don't you just use a head cleaner cassette?" Some head cleaner cassettes use abrasive tape to clean the heads. These abrasives can wear out the heads if you played them constantly. Frankly, after paying several hundred dollars for a new cassette unit, I would much rather pull out the rubbing alcohol and the cotton swabs than risk the life of that precious magnetic head. Also, some head cleaner cassettes only clean the heads, not the capstan or the pinch roller, both of which really should be cleaned regularly. If you are looking for a cleaner cassette, make sure that it is nonabrasive and that it cleans the heads, capstan, and pinch roller (Fig. 13-9).

If the head unit has been sounding muffled, it was probably a dirty tape head. If you clean it, but a few stubborn dirt spots remain, try rubbing it very gently with a soft, clean pencil eraser. Don't use older or dirty erasers because they can leave difficult-to-remove smudges. Don't use pen erasers because they can scratch the fragile tape head.

If you mostly just had problems with tapes being eaten, also look around the capstan for any remaining pieces of tape. These pieces can cause further problems with head units getting the munchies. Little pieces of tape are easy to remove from the capstans of home cassette decks because you can easily reach inside. With auto decks, however, all you can do is take apart the case to reach inside or reach the capstan from the outside with a pair of tweezers.

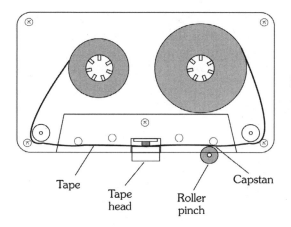

Fig. 13-9 *Compact disc laser lens cleaner (left) and cassette.head cleaner (right).*

Tape

Tape head

Roller pinch

Capstan

If the sound is still too muffled, try cleaning the heads again. If you still don't have any luck, try using a head demagnetizer. They usually cost about $5 to $10, or you might know someone who you can borrow one of these units from. Most of the time that the tape heads become magnetized, it's because the heads are too close to a powerful speaker or some other magnetic field. I doubt that you'll be sitting any 18-in. subwoofers on the dashboard, but demagnetizing the heads is worth a shot anyway. To demagnetize the heads with one of the handheld units, plug in the head demagnetizer and turn it on. While it is running, put the end of it in the cassette slot and put it near the heads, then pull it out and draw it away while it is still running. If you turn off the demagnetizer while it is running, it will magnetize your heads—possibly even worse than they were originally. Because of the difficulty in accessing the insides of any auto head unit, cassette-shaped demagnetizers are available that you can just plug into the cassette slot and demagnetize the heads—much more convenient than the handheld units.

If you have tried everything and the sound is still too muffled, check the speakers. It is possible that you have overdriven and blown the tweeters in your system. Try listening to the tweeters where they are. If you are sure that they are working (i.e., they are producing sound), leave them alone and move on to the other speakers. If you aren't sure, try disconnecting any other speakers (such as subwoofers) in the system. If you still aren't sure if the problem lies with the head unit or the speakers, try the speakers on your home stereo. Then, you should have some reference concerning the sound of your speakers—although they will sound different in the much larger setting. (Note that if they don't have enclosures, they will sound entirely different than they would installed in your car).

If after all of this the speakers check out, chances are that the heads are wearing out. At this point, it is best to take the deck to a reputable auto audio repair shop to have it inspected. Heads and the labor for head replacement can be quite expensive, so if this is indeed the problem, make sure that you get a quote so that you can either get an estimate from another shop or you can decide whether the replacement is worth the money.

WRONG OR VARIABLE TAPE SPEED

The most common cause of problems with the tape speed involves the drive belts. The drive belts are fine black rubber belts that look much like thin rubber bands. They drive the various moving parts in the cassette deck, such as the capstan.

If the head unit is running slow, chances are that the belt is too loose. If the head unit is playing back at faster-than-normal speeds, the belt might have slipped around the flange of one of the pulleys. If the head unit is playing back at variable speeds, the belt might be slipping—either because it is loose or because the pulleys have gotten in contact with some light oil or grease.

In all of the conditions, the only recourse is to pull out the head unit, open up the case, and replace the belts. It is bad enough to pull the head units out of most cars, but tearing apart the unit to find the drive assembly *and* replace the old belts is a real annoyance.

First, you have to try to find the appropriate belt for your head unit. Check the owner's manual to see if a part number is listed for the problematic belt. Chances are that it won't be listed, so you will have to look elsewhere. Call a few auto audio installation/repair shops in the area to see if they can provide the part or at least give you the part number. Otherwise, check with some of the electronics mail-order companies that handle parts for various audio equipment. Even if the exact part number is not available for your particular model, the salespeople might be able to provide a replacement belt that has the same dimensions. If you have looked everywhere, but you still can't find a belt with the right dimensions, try buying a smaller belt and stretching it enough that it will fit and run properly. It's not the best solution, but it beats buying a new head unit.

But how much tension is appropriate for the belts? You can skip this question if you have a strain gauge (by which you can measure the amount of tension on a belt) and if you have pried the privy information on belt tension from the manufacturer. Of course, few people have strain gauges, and they would be impractical unless you had a small electronics repair business.

Unfortunately, you might have some problems just accessing the drive belts, let alone being able to test their tension at your leisure. With the cassette deck in Fig. 13-10, the drive belts are buried under the motor and the cassette playback assembly. To perform this common, simple

Fig. 13-10 *The belts are buried under several layers of electronics and mechanical parts in this head unit.*

maintenance task, you must pull the deck out of the car, open up the top panel of the cabinet, unscrew the cabling, unscrew all of the screws on the underside, disconnect the front panel, and pull everything out of the box. If you were intent on replacing the belts on this model, chances are that you would break something else while you were just trying to reach the drive belts.

Other problems can result in fitting those thin belts through tiny little nooks and around a few pulleys until they fit properly. I have never read about anyone who seemed to think that this task was difficult. Usually, the troubleshooting and repair books just say something like "replace the belts and move on to...." I think that replacing the belts on an auto cassette deck is often more akin to sitting on a chair, putting your hands underneath, and trying to thread a needle. With some patience and perhaps an instrument to help move the belt into place (such as a ballpoint pen), you can replace the belts. You are just better off not doing it while you are in a bad mood or feeling impatient!

COMPACT DISC PLAYERS

Like all head units, compact disc players are very complicated units that are packed with tiny components, some of which are sensitive to static electricity. Thus, these units are very difficult to repair, but it is fairly easy to perform some easy maintenance tasks that will keep your discs running properly. The compact disc head unit troubleshooting informa-tion included in this book is limited. For much more information (nearly 500 pages worth), read *Troubleshooting & Repairing Compact Disc Players (3rd Edition)* by Homer L. Davidson.

SAFETY

Compact disc players of all sorts can be very dangerous to work on, both because of your own safety and the safety of the player itself. The com-pact disc player operates somewhat like a record player, but rather than using a needle to pick up vibrations from the disc, a laser beam is used to read the disc. You can disable the mechanism that turns off the laser and put your hand in front of the beam for a long time. You won't suddenly cut through your hand and you won't feel any pain. For that matter, you won't even feel anything. And you thought it was going to be like the scene in *Goldfinger*. Bummer, man. But instead of being totally harmless, this laser can cause damage to your eyes if you look at it. So, don't look at it! And to keep your eyes safe when working on a powered disc player, place a CD in the machine if you need to poke around inside. The CD will cover the beam. Obviously, your eyes are very important, so be careful when working inside of compact disc players.

In addition to the hidden potential for physical bodily harm with work-ing on compact disc players, they also present a potential for self de-struction. As was mentioned in the safety section at the beginning of this chapter, compact disc players are more prone to destruction from static discharges from your body. When working on compact disc players, you should be sure to use a grounded wrist strap and ground your soldering iron to prevent dangerous levels of static electricity from damaging the fragile integrated circuits. Some references also state that you should use grounded electrically conductive mats under yourself and the com-pact disc player that you are working on.

THE SKIPPING HEAD UNIT

The most common gripe among auto audio enthusiasts who own compact disc players is that they skip too much. Some units skip constantly, some only skip when it is cold, or hot, or rainy; others were fine initially, but gradually began to skip more and more until they were virtually unusable. Although I have had a blast making Neil Diamond discs skip so that he sounds like a rapper, skipping isn't much fun otherwise.

The fact is that many compact disc players are more prone to skipping than others. Over the years, better anti-skipping mechanisms have been built into these players. So, if you buy an older, used model, you will probably have more problems with skipping than if you purchase one that has been made within the past few years. Although I have heard a number of good and bad comments about models from different companies, the two companies that have been consistently praised for the quality of their compact disc players are Alpine and Clarion. Owners of players from these two companies consistently speak of how they rarely skip.

Other than the skipping problems that are inherent in the designs of compact disc players, the most common skipping problems are caused by poor installations. The problem is that most of these head units are installed well, but not vibration proof. The small vibrations from the car at the head unit will cause the compact discs to skip. One of few ways to correct this problem is to tighten up the mounting brackets in the dashboard and mount the unit more solidly. Make sure that the unit will not wiggle or vibrate within the mounting when the vehicle is moving. It won't look pretty, but if you have small cracks, you can even try jamming shims around the edges of the mounting to tighten in up further.

If your car has a tight suspension and rides rough, you might have problems with the compact disc player skipping, even if the mounting is tight. The bounces are just too rough for the machine. If this is the case, you should consider mounting the head unit on a layer of rubber when you mount it in the dash board. You might have success with the rubber absorbing the shock from the bumps in the road. Like in any other arrangement, you must mount the head unit solidly into the dashboard; the rubber is not a viable replacement for a solid mounting.

The only other vibration-related alteration that you can make to prevent your compact disc player from skipping is to alter the suspension in the vehicle so that everything has a smoother ride. On the other hand, the skipping could be caused by other problems (see the next section).

CLEANING THE LASER OPTICS ASSEMBLY

Aside from a loose head unit or tight suspension, one of the worst causes of skipping is a dirty or dusty laser optics assembly. Little effort is required to clean the laser optics assembly; it is very similar to cleaning the heads in a cassette deck. Just get some cotton swabs and a bottle of rubbing alcohol dip one of the swabs in alcohol and rub it over the glass laser optics assembly. If you see other wads of dust inside, clean those up, too, or use a compact disc player cleaning kit. Otherwise, they might work themselves over toward the laser optics assembly and cause even more skipping later on.

If you are using an in-dash head unit, as opposed to portable player that has been wired to a cassette head unit, you might have a few more problems cleaning the laser optics. If your head unit is older and you think that the laser optics might be dirty, then you will probably have to pull out the unit, remove the top cover, and clean the laser optics. If you don't think that this assembly is causing the problem, don't bother tearing everything apart for no reason. Because the disc entry slot is so small, dirty optics are much more of a problem with portable disc players than with auto units.

CHECK THE SOURCE

Although chances are that any skipping that your head unit is experiencing is caused by the installation itself, it's worth checking the CDs themselves. If your reference compact disc or discs have been scratched or are smudged or dirty, they might be the reason why your head unit is skipping. I have heard some people claim that if the discs are scratched, they rub nail polish remover over the scratches. I haven't scratched any of my discs, so I have not been forced to try this method and verify it. However, if you feel uncomfortable using varnish remover on your precious audio, you might want to check out the CD Finishing System from Allsop, which is a disc scratch repair kit. This is the only kit of this type that I have seen on the market, so if you can't find it in a store, you can try writing for information directly from Allsop, which is listed in the Sources appendix.

If the discs are dirty, clean them with a plastic-safe, nonabrasive cleaner, such as a common glass cleaner. Or try one of the compact disc optics cleaners that are available from a number of different companies.

TECHNICAL ADJUSTMENTS

As stated earlier, technical adjustments are well beyond the scope of this book, especially for compact disc players. For most work on compact disc players, an oscilloscope and other electronic test equipment are required. As a result, there is very little that a beginner is able to maintain or repair on a compact disc player.

DEDICATED AMPLIFIERS

Dedicated amplifiers are a difficult fix for the nontechnician. There are no moving parts and no belts or motors to maintain. Everything is entirely electrical, not mechanical. Because of the lack of moving parts, amplifiers rarely fail (unless they have been driven too hard), and as a result, the better manufacturers have warranties of several years on each amplifier. Normally, when something goes wrong, the amplifier fails entirely. Then, chances are that you're stuck. You must take the amp to a factory service center because if you open up the amplifier to see what failed, the warranty will be voided.

If your amplifier no longer operates and the LED on indicator doesn't even light, first check the fuse to make sure that it hasn't blown. If it has, replace it only with a fuse of the same value and type. If you use any other type or rating of fuse, you won't be able to get the amplifier running. If the fuse value is too low, it will blow. If the fuse value is too high, the electricity will be below the cutoff values of the fuse and yet above the ratings of the parts inside. The "on" indicator will probably stay on for a few seconds, and in the mean time, the components inside will be getting fried.

If the amplifier won't turn on, but yet the fuse is fine, check all of the power connections between the amplifier and the battery. Possibly one of those came loose. An easier way to make sure that the amplifier is receiving power is to check the power leads with a voltohmmeter. If you don't have a voltohmmeter, then it's back under the seat with you, Mr. Amplifier! While you are checking out the connections and the integrity of the wiring, also check under the dashboard to make sure that the car's fuses are all in working order. If not, replace any that have blown. If the wiring is in working order and is connected up to the amplifier, yet you still can't get it working, chances are that the amplifier has some internal problems.

If the on indicator is lit, but there is no audio, check the audio lines and connections from the head unit through any other processing boxes to the amplifier. Then, make sure that any of these boxes are turned on and working properly. Check the volume controls on the processing boxes and check the gain control on the amplifier to make sure that they are all turned up to an appropriate level. See Chapter 5 for more information on amplifier tuning.

If your amplifier appears to be dead or not working properly and you plan to take it in for repairs soon, wait a few days first. Check everything over a few times and give it a few days so that you can think of any simple means that you could use to correct the problem.

When an amplifier is overdriven, overheats, and finally melts down, usually the power amplifier blows out its transistors in the final amplification stage. Although sometimes a fair number of components are destroyed along with these transistors, at other times this output stage overheats, then fails. As a result, a blown amplifier is usually either severely damaged (many destroyed parts) or minorly damaged (the final output transistors are destroyed), but usually not in between. Unfortunately, many power transistors are expensive, so it is a somewhat rare case when you can pick up a few replacement transistors for 50 cents apiece, pop them in place of the burned out parts, and have your amplifier working properly.

In general, other than checking out everything out with your system, you are better off taking a nonfunctioning amplifier to a professional repair shop or sending it back to the factory for repairs. The exception is if you are an electronics technician or a hobbyist who has spent an extended amount of time using test equipment and making simple electronics repairs.

PREVENTING AMPLIFIER DESTRUCTION

Unlike compact disc, MiniDisc, and cassette head units, which have moving parts and are subject to dirt and wear, dedicated amplifiers generally will not break down unless they have been abused. Three of the most common ways to destroy an amplifier are to connect the power leads to the wrong battery terminal polarity, to overdrive the amplifier by running it into speakers with too low of an impedance, or by running speaker-level outputs from a head unit or preamplifier into line-level inputs. If you avoid these unsafe practices, chances are that you will have few problems with an amplifier—especially if you choose a model that is known for being built solidly.

CONCLUSION

Although the electronics layperson is severely limited by what he or she can do to repair an auto audio system, it is possible to perform some simple maintenance and repair procedures that can save quite a bit of money and prolong the life of your system.

SOURCES

This chapter contains a long list of contact information for car stereo manufacturers and dealers. It is not meant to be an all-inclusive resource because almost every town has a car stereo shop or shadetree installer. Also, the car stereo field is very competitive, for both dealers and manufacturers. By the time you read this, several of these companies are sure to have moved, been sold to another company, or gone out of business. Finally, inclusion within this list is not an endorsement of either products or services from a company.

INTERNET RESOURCES

Usenet
rec.audio.car

Audio Market
http://www.audiomarket.com

Auto Audio Central
http://www.autoaudio.com

Crutchfield Comparison Lists
http://www.crutchfield.com

Sound Domain Forums and Chat
http://www.sounddomain.com

MANUFACTURERS

a/d/s
One Progress Way
Wilmington, MA 01887
(617) 729-1140
(508) 658-8498 (fax)

Adcom
10 Timber Lane
Marlboro, NJ 07746
(732) 683-2356
(732) 683-9792
http://www.adcom.com
info@adcom.com

Advent Mobile
25 Tri-State Office Ctr. #400
Lincolnshire, IL 60069
(800) 284-7234
(708) 317-3826 (fax)

AI Research
P.O. Box 159
Stillwater, OK 74074
(405) 624-7622
(405) 372-5489 (fax)
http://www.airesearch.com

Aiwa
35 Oxford Dr.
Moonachie, NJ 07074
(800) 289-2492
(212) 512-3710 (fax)
http://www.aiwa.com

Alphasonik
701 Heinz Ave.
Berkeley, CA 94710
(510) 548-4005
(510) 548-1478 (fax)

Alpine
19145 Gramercy Pl.
Torrance, CA 90501
(310) 326-8000
(310) 782-0726 (fax)
http://www.alpine1.com

Altec Lansing
P.O. Box 277
Milford, PA 18337
(800) 258-3288
(717) 296-2213 (fax)

Alumapro
100 Inustrial Rd.
Addison, IL 60101
(630) 543-9112
(630) 543-0287 (fax)
http://www.alumapro.com

American Bass
5242 Warrensville Center Rd.
Maple Heights, OH 44137
(216) 475-9311
(717) 296-2213 (fax)

American Terminal Supply Co.
48925 West Rd.
Wixom, MI 48393
(800) 999-1610
(313) 380-8890 (fax)
http://www.american-terminal.com

Amptech
2305 Montgomery St.
Ft. Worth, TX 76107
(800) 364-9966
(800) 324-4405 (fax)
http://www.amptech.com

Anamir Electronics (Crystal-Line)
2075 Byberry Rd., Suite 104
Bensalem, PA 19020
(215) 638-1600
(215) 638-4515 (fax)
http://www.anamir.com
http://www.crystal-line.com

Apogee Electronics
3145 Donald Douglas Loop S.
Santa Monica, CA 90405
(310) 915-1000
(310) 391-6262 (fax)
http://www.apogeedigital.com
info@apogeedigital.com

Audio Art
152 S. Brent Circle
City Of Industry, CA 91789
(909) 598-0515
(909) 595-4694 (fax)
http://www.audioart.net
sales@audioart.net

Audio Connection
7950 E. Redfield Rd., Suite 130
Scottdale, AZ 85260
(800) 825-7311
(717) 296-2213 (fax)

AudioControl
22410 70th Ave. W.
Mountlake Terrace, WA 98043
(425) 775-8461
(425) 778-3166 (fax)
http://www.audiocontrol.com
info@audiocontrol.com

Audio Gods
5101 Lankershim Blvd.
North Hollywood, CA 91601
(818) 509-8879
(818) 760-8484 (fax)

AudioLink
23241 La Palma Ave.
Yorba Linda, CA 92687
(800) 327-5905
(714) 692-0068 (fax)
http://www.linkmeup.com

Audio Products, Inc.
2510 Commonwealth Avenue
North Chicago, IL 60064
(800) 635-4380
(847) 578-0001 (fax)
http://www.hifonics-audio.com

Audioquest
P.O. Box 3060
San Clemente, CA 92674
(949) 498-2770
(949) 498-5112 (fax)
http://www.audioquest.com
customerservice@audioquest.com

Audiovox
150 Marcus Blvd.
Hauppauge, NY 11788
(800) 645-4994
(516)273-5939 (fax)
http://www.audiovox.com
ae_customerservice@audiovox.com

Audison
S.S. Regina 571 Km.
6.250 - 62018 Potenza Picena (MC)
Italy
+39-0733-870800
+39-0733-870880 (fax)
http://www.audison.com
com@audison.com

Authorized Parts Company
420 Industrial Dr.
S. Elgin, IL 60177
(800) 654-6464
(847) 608-6982 (fax)

Autosound 2000
2563 Eric Lane, Suite D
Burlington, NC 27215
(910) 570-0341
(910) 570-1268 (fax)

Autotek
855 Cowan Rd.
Burlingame, CA 94010
(650) 692-2444
(650) 692-2448 (fax)
http://www.autotek.net
sales@autotek.net

Avalanche
4117 Lindberg Dr.
Addison, TX 75001
(972) 233-3337
(972) 661-8882 (fax)

BBE Sound Inc.
5381 Production Dr.
Huntington Beach, CA 92649
(714) 897-6766
(714) 896-0736 (fax)
http://www.bbesound.com

B&G Mobile Concepts
P.O. Box 202902
Austin, TX 78720
(800) 874-8803

Blaupunkt
2800 South 25th Ave.
Broadview, IL 60153
(800) 323-1943
(708) 865-5209 (fax)
http://www.blaupunkt.com

Boss Audio
20450 Plummer St.
Chatsworth, CA 91311
(818) 700-9944
(818) 700-8999 (fax)
http://www.bossaudio.com
boss@bossaudio.com

Boston Acoustics
300 Jubilee Drive
Peabody, MA 01960
(978) 538-5000
(978) 538-5199 (fax)
http://www.bostonacoustics.com

Bostwick
125 Old Monroe Rd.
Suite 200
Bogart, GA 30622
(706) 543-9494
(706) 369-9519 (fax)
http://www.bostwick.com

Cadence
6519 Hwy. 9 N.
Howell, NJ 07731
(908) 370-5400
(908) 370-5553 (fax)
http://www.cadencesound.com
cadence@cadencesound.com

Calcell
17980 S. Savarona Way
Carson CA 90746
(310) 217-0100
(310) 523-1557 (fax)
http://www.calcell.com
calcellusa@calcell.com

Canton
1723 Adams St. NE
Minneapolis, MN 55413
(612) 706-9250
(612) 706-9255 (fax)

Carin
188 Brooke Rd.
Winchester, VA 22603
(888) 535-3500
(800) 663-0913 (fax)
http://www.carin.com

CarPlayer.com
http://www.carplayer.com
hubsite@xoommail.com

Cascade
19135 Kiowa Rd.
Bend, Oregon 97702
(541) 389-6821
(541) 389-5273 (fax)
http://www.cascadeaudio.com

Case Logic
6303 Dry Creek Parkway
Longmont, CO 80503
(800) 447-4848
(303) 530-3822 (fax)
http://www.caselogic.com

CDT Audio
290 E. Hwy 246
Buellton, CA 93427
(805) 693-1980
(805) 693-1898 (fax)
http://www.cdtaudio.com
info@cdtaudio.com

Cerwin-Vega
555 E. Easy St.
Simi Valley, CA 93065
(805) 584-9332
(805) 583-0865 (fax)
http://www.cerwin-vega.com

Clarion
661 W. Redondo Beach Blvd.
Gardena, CA 90247
(310) 327-9100
(310) 327-1999 (fax)
http://www.clarionmultimedia.com

Clark Synthesis
8122 Southpark Ln., Suite 110
Littleton, CO 80120
(800) 898-1945
(303) 797-7501 (fax)
http://www.clarksyn.com

Coustic
7676 S. 46 St., Ste. 2020
Phoenix, AZ 85040
(602) 438-2020
(602) 438-7313 (fax)
http://www.coustic.com

Craig Consumer Electronics
13845 Artesia Blvd.
Cerritos, CA 90701
(310) 926-9944
(310) 926-9269 (fax)
(416) 673-3307 (Canada)

Crystal-Line *(See Anamir Electronics)*

Crystal Mobile Sound
9855 Joe Vargas Way
S. El Monte, CA 91733
(626) 579-2095
(626) 579-9985 (fax)
http://
www.crystalmobilesound.com
techsupport@crystalmobilesound.com

Custom Autosound
808 W. Vermont Ave.
Anaheim, CA 92805
(714) 535-1091
(714) 533-0361 (fax)
http://www.custom-autosound.com
info@custom-autosound.com

Dakota Digital
3421 W. Hovland Ave.
Sioux Falls, SD 57107
(800) 852-3228
(605) 339-4106 (fax)
http://www.dakotadigital.com

dB Speakerworks
1430 Dalzell
Shreveport, LA 71103
(318) 425-2525
(318) 227-8058 (fax)

DEI Audio *(See Directed Electronics)*

Denon Electronics
222 New Road
Parsippany, NJ 07054
973-396-0810
973-396-7459 (fax)
http://www.dei.denon.com

Diamond Audio Technology
3030 Pennsylvania Ave.
Santa Monica, CA 90404
(310) 582-1121
310 582-1502 (fax)
http://www.diamondaudio.com
12vsales@diamondaudio.com

Digital Designs Audio
912 N. Classen Blvd.
Oklahoma City, OK 73106
(888) 563-4448
(405) 239-7100 (fax)
http://www.ddaudio.com

Directed Electronics
2560 Progress St.
Vista, CA 92083
(800) 274-0200
(760) 599-1389 (fax)
http://www.directed.com

Dynamat *(See Dynamic Control)*

Dynamic Control
3042 Symmes Rd.
Hamilton, Ohio 45015
(513) 860-5094
(513) 860-5095 (fax)
http://www.dynamat.com
info@dynamat.com

Dynaudio
1144 Tower Ln.
Bensenville, IL 60106
(630) 238-4200
(630) 238-0112 (fax)
http://www.dynaudiona.com

Earthquake Sound
1215 O'Brien Dr.
Menlo Park, CA 94025
(650) 327-3003
(650) 327-0179 (fax)
http://www.earthquakesound.com

Eclipse
19600 S. Vermont Ave.
Torrance, CA 90502
(800) 233-2216
(310) 767-4375 (fax)
http://www.eclipse-web.com

Eminent Technology
225 E. Palmer St.
Tallahasse, FL 32301
(904) 575-5655
(904) 224-5999 (fax)

Esoteric Audio
44 Pearl Pentecost Rd.
Winder, GA 30680
(770) 867-6300
(770) 867-2713 (fax)
http://www.eau.com
sales@eau.com

ESX
Rt. 1 Box 598A
Slocomb, AL 36375

(334) 886-3025
(334) 886-3892 (fax)
http://www.esx.net
info@esx.net

Fultron *(See Memphis Car Audio)*

Graffiti Sound *(See Helix Electronics)*

H45 Technologies
620-B Clyde Ave.
Mountain View, CA 94043
(650) 961-9114
(650) 964-2426 (fax)
http://www.h45.com
sales@h45.com

Harrison Labs
P.O. Box 1349
Parker, CO 80134
(303) 841-5360
(303) 841-2927 (fax)
http://www.hlabs.com

Helix Electronics
13723 Harvard Pl.
Gardena, CA 90249
(310) 532-1770
(310) 532-4145 (fax)
http://www.graffitisound.com

HiFonics *(See Audio Products)*

Hitron
933 E. 11th St.
Los Angeles, CA 90021
(213) 623-1071
(21) 623-2340 (fax)

Hollywood Sound Labs
4327 Temple City Blvd.
Temple City, CA 91780
(626) 301-7828
(626) 301-7833 (fax)
http://
www.hollywoodsoundlabs.com

Illusion Audio
422 S. Madison Dr., Ste. #4
Tempe, AZ 85281
(602) 966-3455
(602) 966-3499 (fax)

Image Dynamics
22123 S. Vermont Ave.
Torrance, CA 90502
(310) 787-2399
(310) 787-7699 (fax)
http://
www.imagedynamicsusa.com

JBC
4100-B Ardmore
South Gate, CA 90280
(323) 249-1444
(323) 249-1454 (fax)
http://www.jbc-usa.com
info@jbc-usa.com

JBL
80 Crossways Park W.
Woodbury, NY 11797
(800) 645-7484
(516) 682-3527 (fax)
http://www.jbl.com

Jensen
2950 Lake Emma Rd.
Lake Mary, FL 32746
(800) 323-0221
(407) 333-1628 (fax)
http://www.jensenaudio.com

Jensen Transformers
7135 Hayvenhurst Ave.
Van Nuys, CA 91406
(818) 374-5857
(818) 763-4574 (fax)
http://www.jensen-
transformers.com

JL Audio
10369 N. Commerce Pkwy.

Miramar, FL 33025
(954) 443-1100
(954) 443-1111 (fax)
http://www.jlaudio.com

JVC Company of America
41 Slater Dr.
Elmwood Park, NJ 07407
(800) 252-5722
http://www.jvc.com

KEF Audio
Eccleston Rd.
Tovil, Maidstone
Kent, ME15 6QP
UK
+44-0-1622-672261
+44-0-1622-750653 (fax)
http://www.kef.com
enquiries@kef.com

Kenwood
2201 E. Dominguez St.
Long Beach, CA 90801
(800) 536-9663
(310) 631-3913 (fax)
http://www.kenwoodusa.com

Kicker *(See Stillwater Designs)*

Kimber Kable
2752 South 1900 W.
Ogden, UT 84401
(801) 621-5530
(801) 627-6980 (fax)
http://www.kimberkable.com
info@kimber.com

Lanzar Car Audio
1600 63rd St.
Brooklyn, NY 11204
(718) 236-8000
(718) 236-2400 (fax)
http://www.lanzar.com

L.A. Sound
2919 E. Philadelphia St.
Ontario, CA 91761
(909)-673-0188
(909)-673-0660 (fax)
http://www.lasound.com

Lightning Audio
1835 E. 6th St., Ste. 6
Tempe, AZ 85281
(602) 966-8278
(602) 966-0393 (fax)
http://www.lightningaudio.com

Linear Power
381 Nevada St.
Auburn, CA 95603
(800) 538-8911
(530) 823-5649 (fax)
http://www.linearpower.com

LinearX Systems
9500 Tualatin-Sherwood Rd.
Tualatin, OR 97062
(503) 612-9565
(503) 612-9344 (fax)
http://www.linearx.com
sales@linearx.com

Madisound Speaker Components
8608 University Green
Box 44283
Madison, WI 53744
http://www.madisound.com

Magnadyne
1111 W. Victoria St.
Compton, CA 90220
(800) 638-3600
(310) 637-9542 (fax)
http://www.magnadyne.com

Majestic Electronics
16745 Saticoy St., Ste. 101
Van Nuys, CA 91406
(818) 781-8200
(818) 989-3154 (fax)

http://www.majestic-electronics.com

Matsushita Electronic Corp. of America (Panasonic)
50 Meadowland Parkway
Seacaucus, NJ 07094
(201) 348-7000

Maxxima Marine
125 Cabot Ct.
Hauppauge, NY 11788
(516) 434-1200
(516) 434-1457 (fax)

MB Quart
15 Walpole Park S.
Walpole, MA 02081
(508) 668-8973
(508) 668-8979 (fax)
http://www.mbquart.com

McIntosh
661 W. Redondo Beach Blvd.
Gardena, CA 90247
(310) 327-9107
(310) 217-9288 (fax)

Memphis Car Audio
122 Gayoso
Memphis, TN 38103
(901) 525-5711
(901) 525-7993 (fax)
http://www.memcaraudio.com

Milbert Amplifiers
P.O. Box 1027
Germantown, MD 20875
(301) 963-9355
(301) 840-0511 (fax)
http://www.milbert.com

MMATS Professional Audio
863 W. 13th Ct.
Riviera Beach, FL 33404
(561) 848-7578
(561) 848-1518 (fax)

Monolithic
515 Sandydale Rd.
Rancho Nipomo, CA 9344
(805) 929-3251
(805) 929-2222 (fax)

Monster Cable
455 Valley Dr.
Brisbane, CA 94005
(415) 840-2000
(415) 468-0311 (fax)
http://www.monstercable.com

Morel Acoustics USA
414 Harvard St.
Brookline, MA 02446
(617) 277-6663
(617) 277-2415 (fax)
http://www.morelusa.com
sales@morelusa.com

MTX
The Pointe at South Mountain
4545 E. Baseline Rd.
Phoenix, AZ 85044
(602) 225-5689
(602) 438-8692 (fax)
http://www.mtxaudio.com

Nakamichi America
955 Francisco St.
Torrance, CA 90502
(310) 538-8150
(310) 324-7614 (fax)
http://www.nakamichiusa.com

NoiseKiller
2440 W. 10th PL, Suite B
Tempe, AZ 85281
(480) 804-1124
(480) 804-1153 (fax)
http://www.noisekiller.com
info@noisekiller.com

Orion
9235 S. McKemy St.
Tempe, AZ 85284
(480) 705-5600
(480) 705-5788 (fax)
http://www.orion-audio.com

Oz Audio
1300 SW 10th St. #2
Delray Beach, FL 33444
(561) 279-0072
(561) 279-0051 (fax)
http://www.ozaudio.com

Panasonic
One Panasonic Way
Secaucus, NJ 07094
(800) 211-7262
(201) 348-7209 (fax)
http://www.panasonic.com

Paramount Audio
12737 Moore St.
Cerritos, CA 90703
(562) 483-8111
(562) 483-8106 (fax)
http://www.crossfirecaraudio.com

Peripheral *(See Stinger)*

Phase Linear *(See Recoton)*

Phoenix Gold
P.O. Box 83189
Portland, OR 97283
(503) 288-2008
(503) 978-3380 (fax)
http://www.phoenixgold.com

Pioneer Electronics
2265 E. 220th St.
P.O. Box 1720
Long Beach, CA 90801
(800) 421-1404
(310) 952-2402 (fax)
http://www.pioneerelectronics.com

Sources

Polk Audio
5601 Metro Dr.
Baltimore, MD 21215
(800) 377-7655
(416) 847-8888 (Canada)
http://www.polkaudio.com
polkcs@polkaudio.com

Polydax Speaker Corp.
10 Upton Dr.
Wilmington, MA 01887
(508) 658-0700
(508) 658-0703 (fax)

Power Acoustik
5920 E. Slauson Ave.
Commerce, CA 90040
(800) 832-4672
(323) 722-1122 (fax)
http://www.poweracoustik.com

PowerAmper
4962 N. Palm Ave.
Winter Park, FL 32792
800-324-1426
407-678-3577 (fax)
http://www.poweramper.com
power@gdi.net

Precision Interface Electronics
9601 Mason Ave.
Chatsworth, CA 91311
(818) 678-3690
(818) 678-3697 (fax)
http://www.pie.net

Precision Power
4829 S. 38th St.
Phoenix, AZ 85040
(800) 627-6937
(602) 414-3502 (fax)
http://www.precisionpower.com

Profile
17625 Fabrica Way
Cerritos, CA 90703

(714) 690-4949
(714) 690-4957 (fax)
http://www.profileusa.com

PTS
461 DuPont St.
Ontario, CA 91761
(909) 390-6661
(909) 390-6217
http://www.ptswoofers.com
info@ptswoofers.com

Pyle
1600 63rd St.
Brooklyn, NY 11204
(718) 236-8000
(718) 236-2400 (fax)
http://www.pyleaudio.com
service@pyleaudio.com

Pyramid *(See Sound Around)*

Q Forms *(See AI Research)*

Radio Shack
100 Throckmorton St.
Ft. Worth, TX 76102
(800) 843-1840
(817) 415-6508 (fax)
http://www.radioshack.com

Recoton
2950 Lake Emma Rd.
Lake Mary, FL 32746
(800) 732-6866 Customer Service
(407) 333-1628 Fax
http://www.recoton.com

Rockford Fosgate
546 South Rockford Drive
Tempe, AZ 85281
(480) 967-3565
(480) 967-8132 (fax)
http://www.rockfordfosgate.com

Rockwood
4480 Pacific Blvd.
Vernon, CA 90058
(323) 588-2999
(323) 588-4999 (fax)
http://www.rockwoodhifi.com
rockwood@rockwoodhifi.com

R&T Enterprises
P.O. Box 1215
Kelso, WA 98626
(360) 423-1840
(360) 423-3396 (fax)
http://www.rtboxes.com

Sanyo Fisher USA
21605 Plummer St.
P.O. Box 2329
Chatsworth, CA 91313
(818) 998-7322
(818) 701-4149 (fax)
http://www.sanyo.com

SAS/Bazooka
15049 Florida Blvd.
Baton Rouge, LA 70819
(504) 272-7135
(888) 329-2727 (fax)
http://www.bazooka.com

Scosche
P.O. Box 2901
Oxnard, CA 93033
(800) 363-4490
(805) 486-9996 (fax)
http://www.scosche.com

Sea Speakers
204 N. Elm Ave.
Sanford, FL 32771
(407) 322-2239
(407) 322-1964 (fax)
http://www.sea-speakers.com
sales@sea-speakers.com

Select Products
2320 S.W. 60th Way
Miramar, FL 33023
(954) 985-2698
(954) 985-2661 (fax)
http://www.selectproducts.com
sales@selectproducts.com

Sherwood
14830 Alondra Blvd.
La Mirada, CA 90638
(800) 962-3203
(714) 521-4900 (fax)
http://www.sherwoodusa.com

Sony
One Sony Dr.
Park Ridge, NJ 07656
(800) 222-7669
(201) 930-7909 (fax)
http://www.sony.com

Sound Around
1600 63rd St.
Brooklyn, NY 11204
(718) 236-8000
(718) 236-2400 (fax)
http://www.pyramidcaraudio.com
pyramidsnd@aol.com

Sound Barrier
6971 NW 51 St.
Miami, FL 33166
(800) 859-7027
(305) 594-0969 (fax)
http://www.soundbarrier.com

Sound Cube
P.O. Box 237
Flushing, MI 48433
(810) 789-6062
(810) 659-5614 (fax)
http://www.soundcube.com
info@soundcube.com

Soundgate
152 S. Jefferson St.
Sheridan, WY 82801
(888) 760-4707
(307) 674-4819 (fax)
http://www.soundgate.com

Soundstream Technologies
11365 Sunrise Park Dr.
Rancho Cordova, CA 95742
(916) 351-1288
(916) 351-0414 (fax)
http://www.soundstream.com

Southern Audio Services (SAS)
15049 Florida Blvd.
Baton Rouge, LA 70819

Stillwater Designs
P.O. Box 459
Stillwater, OK 74076
(405) 624-8510
(405) 377-3272 (fax)
http://www.kicker.com

Stinger
13160 56th Ct.
Clearwater, FL 33760
(727) 572-9255
(727) 573-9326
http://www.stinger-aamp.com

Straight Wire
2032 Scott St.
Hollywood, FL 33020
(954) 925-2470
(954) 925-7253 (fax)
http://www.straightwire.com

Streetwires *(See Esoteric Audio)*

Subzero
6210 NE 92nd Dr. #109
Portland, OR 97220
(503) 261-1028

(503) 261-1034 (fax)
http://www.subzeromfg.com

Targa *(See Sherwood)*

Toby
2060 Montgomery St.
Ft. Worth, TX 76107
(800) 214-4957
(817) 377-3947 (fax)
http://www.toby.com

U.S. Amps Inc.
7325-100 NW 13th Blvd.
Gainesville, FL 32653
(352) 338-1926
(352) 371-4122 (fax)
http://www.usamps.com
sales@usamps.com

Ultimate Sound
138 University Parkway
Pomona, CA 91768
(909) 594-2604
(909) 594-0191
http://www.ultimate-sound.com
info@ultimate-sound.com

Universal Electronics
4917 W. Oakton
Skokie, IL 60077
(847) 673-4488
(847) 673-8239 (fax)
http://www.uespeakers.com

Urban *(See Sherwood)*

US Acoustics
2424 Blanding Avenue
Alameda, CA 94501
(510) 864-7005
(510) 864-1478 (fax)
http://www.usacoustics.com

CAR AUDIO DEALERS

A & S Speakers
3170 23rd St.
San Francisco, CA 94110

ABC
116 Craig Rd.
Englishtown, NJ 07726
(800) 354-1324

AC Components
P.O. Box 212
LaCrosse, WI 54602
(608) 784-4579

Ace Distributing
956 E. 11th St.
Los Angeles, CA 90021
(213) 688-7878
(213) 688-7664 (fax)
http://www.impulseusa.com
ace@impulseusa.com

Advanced Audio
4425 E. Main St.
Columbus, OH 43213
(614) 239-6764
(614) 239-6938
http://www.advanced-audio.qpg.com

All Star Sound and Security and Window Tinting
4138 Boston Rd.
Bronx, NY 10475
(718) 325-7388
(718) 325-0702
http://www.allstarsound.qpg.com

AMS Car Stereo
40 W. El Camino Real
Mountain View, CA 94040
(650) 967-2267
(650) 967-3836 (fax)
http://www.amscarstereo.com
info@amscarstereo.com

Audio Excellence
143 West 26th St.
New York, NY 10001
(212) 229-1622

Audio Headquarters.com
http://www.audioheadquarters.com
info@audioheadquarters.com

Audio Images
7141-A N. 9th Ave.
Pensacola, FL 32504
(850) 475-9577
(850) 475-9578 (fax)
http://www.audio-images.com
info@audio-images.com

Audio Warehouse Express
(800) 831-5622
(732) 926-8464 (fax)
http://www.audio-warehouse.com

Autotoys.com
177 Main St.
Ft. Lee, NJ 07024
(888) 570-5696
http://www.autotoys.com
info@autotoys.com

Audio'N'More
33 Catalina Dr.
Brick, NJ 08723
(732) 920-5917
(732) 477-4281 (fax)
http://www.audio-n-more.com
sales@audio-n-more.com

Audio Video
2898 N. University Dr. #35
Coral Springs, FL 33065
(800) 348-7799

SOURCES

Bay Car Stereo and Accessories
3829 Geary Blvd.
San Francisco, CA 94118
(415) 221-9600
http://www.sfprestige.com/
baycar/index.html

Beach Sales
80 VFW Parkway
Revere, MA 02151
(800) 562-9020

BJ Audio Inc.
991 Beachmeadow Ln.
Cincinnati, OH 45238
(513) 451-0112

Car Audio Excellence
9 Loftus St.
Leederville
Western Australia
+ (08) 9381 3055
+ (08) 9381 4988 (fax)
http://www.crystal.com.au/
~caraudio
caraudio@crystal.com.au

Car Audio Concepts
306 Rt. 46 E.
Rockaway, NJ 07866
(800) 906-1222
(732) 356-3250 (fax)
http://www.caraudioconcepts.com
custserv@caraudioconcepts.com

Car Audio Works
6284 Fair Oaks
Boise, ID 83703
(208) 440-6694
http://www.caraudioworks.com
sales@caraudioworks.com

Car Stereo Masters
16511 Whittier Blvd.
Whittier, CA 90603
(562) 947-2424

(562) 947-1105 (fax)
http://www.carstereomasters.com
sales@carstereomasters.com

Car Stereo Wholesale Warehouse
(800) 814-2496
http://www.carstereoww.com
csww@iglou.com

Crutchfield
1 Crutchfield Park
Charlottesville, VA 22911
(800) 955-3000
(800) 388-9756 (fax)
http://www.crutchfield.com

Damark
7101 Winnetka Ave. N.
P.O. Box 29900
Minneapolis, MN 55429
(800) 827-6767
http://www.damark.com

DB Systems
P.O. Box 460
Rindge, NH 03461
(603) 899-5121

ElectroWorks Inc.
100 Highway 34
Mattawan, NJ 07747
(800) 662-8559

Ever-Li
908 Upper Thomson Rd.
Singapore 787111
+4544933
+4599176 (fax)
http://www.ever-li.com.sg
everli@pacific.net.sg

Global Electronics
(800) 842-9915
http://www.globalelectronics.com
support@globalelectronics.com

Gold Sound
4285 S. Broadway
Englewood, CO 80110

H & R Auto Radio Service
157 York Rd.
Warminster, PA 18974
(800) 523-6605
http://www.hrautoradio.com
bobatown@voicenet.com

Illinois Audio
1284 E. Dundee Rd.
Palatine, IL 60067
(800) 621-8042

J.C. Whitney
1917-19 Archer Ave.
P.O. Box 8410
Chicago, IL 60680

JD's Car Stereo
10925 Cote De Liesse
Montreal, PQ H9P 1A7
Canada
(514) 631-2102
(514) 631-3137 (fax)
http://www.jdcarstereo.com

J&R Music World
59-50 Queens-Midtown Expressway,
Maspeth
Queens, NY 11378
(800) 221-8180

Kief's Audio/Video
24th & Iowa
Lawrence, KS 66046
(913) 842-1811

Landes Audio
73 W. Main St.
Chester Mall
Chester, NJ 07930

(908) 879-6999
(908) 879-6889 (fax)
http://www.landesaudio.com
mail@landesaudio.com

LAT International
317 Provincetown Rd.
Cherry Hill, NJ 08034

Leary Enterprises
130 Quigley Blvd., Suite A
New Castle, DE 19720

Madisound Speaker Components
8608 University Green
Madison, WI 53744
(608) 831-3433
http://www.madisound.com

Meniscus
2575 28th St. Unit 2
Wyoming, MI 49509
(616) 534-9121

Mobile Authority
3116 Via Mondo
Rancho Dominguez, CA 90221
(800) 848-6748
(310) 223-0412 (fax)
http://www.mobileauthority.com

Mobile Electronic Service
408 S. Cliff Ave.
Sioux Falls, SD 57103
(888) 535-6291
(605) 334-6481 (fax)
http://www.mobile-e-service.com
repair@mobile-e-service.com

New York Wholesale
2 Park Ave.
New York, NY 10016
(212) 684-6363
(212) 684-8046 (fax)

O&R Car Audio
519 E Merritt Island Causeway
Suite #4
Merritt Island, FL 32952
(407) 454-7408
(407) 454-7408 (fax)
http://
www.orcaraudio.nv.switchboard.com
macblastr@aol.com

Parts Express
340 E. First St.
Dayton, OH 45402
(800) 338-0531
http://www.partsexpress.com

Q Audio
95 Vassar St.
Cambridge, MA 02139
(617) 547-2727

Rapid Audio Warehouse
800-870-1933
256-586-8072 (fax)
http://www.rapidaudiow.com
raw@rapidaudiow.com

Reference AudioVideo
18214 Dalton Ave.
Gardena, CA 90248
(301) 517-1700
(301) 517-1732 (fax)

Rexstores.com
5540 Webster St.
Dayton, OH 45414
(937) 276-3931 ext. 293
(937) 276-8643 (fax)
http://www.rexstore.com

Richmond Sound
6381 Amboy Rd.
Staten Island, NY 10309
(718) 967-2000
(718) 948-7902 (fax)
http://www.richmondsound.com
info@richmondsound.com

River Oaks Car Stereo
4129 Richmond Ave.
Houston, TX 77027
713-626-7627
http://installer.com/rocs.html
rocs@installer.com

RTRD
3021 Sangamon Ave.
Springfield, IL 62702
(800) 283-4644

Salesco
800-407-8665
909-394-3096 (fax)
http://www.salesco.com

Samman's Electronics
1166 Hamburg Turnpike
Wayne, NJ
(800) 937-3537

SBH Enterprises
1678 53rd St.
Brooklyn, NY 11204
(800) 451-5851

6th Avenue Electronics
1030 6th Ave
New York, NY 10018
(800) 394-6283

Sound Conceptions *(See Autotoys.com)*

Sounds Fine
171 E. State St.
Ithaca, NY 14850
(607) 277-4766
http://www.soundsfine.com

Sounds Incredible
2012 North Union
Ponca City, OK 74601
http://www.carstereos.com
blaster@carstereo.com

Speaker World
535 Tabor Rd.
Morris Plains, NJ 07950
(201) 984-5200
(201) 538-2578 (fax)

Stereo World
P.O. Box 596
Monroe, NY 10950
(914) 782-6044

Steward's Car Stereo
3126 Summer Ave.
Memphis, TN 38112
(901) 458-2333
(901) 458-2668 (fax)
http://
www.stewardscarstereo.qpg.com

The Sound Approach
6067 Jerico Turnpike
Commack, NY 11725
(800) 368-2344

The Sound Seller
2808 Cahill Rd.
P.O. Box 224
Marinette, WI 54143
(800) 826-0520

Ultimate Sound & Security
58 Rt. 35 N.
Keyport, NJ 07735
(732) 888-0050
(732) 888-5958 (fax)
http://www.ultimatesound.com
info@ultimatesound.com

USA Media Junction
9 Whippany Rd.
Whippany, NJ 07981
(800) 872-1002

West End Electronics
3 Blackmarsh Rd.
St. John's, NF
Canada
(800) 563-0050
(709) 739-8911 (fax)
http://westendelectronics.com
westend@westendelectronics.com

Wholesale Products
400 West Cummings Park
Suite 1725-122
Woburn, MA 01801
(978) 524-0023
(978) 524-0290 (fax)
http://
www.wholesaleproducts.com
shopping@wholesaleproducts.com

World Wide Audio Warehouse
(888) 435-0101
(817) 656-7202 (fax)
http://www.worldwideaudio.com
sales@worldwideaudio.com

World Wide Stereo
754 Rt. 309
Montgomeryville, PA 18936
(215)368-8343
(215)855-9306 (fax)
http://www.wwstereo.com

INDEX

About the Author

One of the "brightest stars" in hobby electronics writing, according to *Monitoring Times*, Andrew Yoder is the author or coauthor of a dozen books about radio, audio, and video, including *Home Audio, Home Video*, and *The Complete Shortwave Listener's Handbook (5th Edition)*, also published by McGraw-Hill. He has contributed articles to *Electronics Now, Popular Electronics, Radio!, Radio World, New Jersey Monthly, Popular Communications*, and other magazines.